Modelling Infrastructure Investments, Growth and Poverty Impact

T0326475

DEVELOPMENT ECONOMICS AND POLICY

Series edited by Franz Heidhues and Joachim von Braun

Vol. 56

PETER LANG

Frankfurt am Main · Berlin · Bern · Bruxelles · New York · Oxford · Wien

Modelling Infrastructure Investments, Growth and Poverty Impact

A Two-Region Computable General Equilibrium Perspective on Vietnam

Clemens Breisinger

PETER LANG
Europäischer Verlag der Wissenschaften

Bibliographic Information published by Die Deutsche Bibliothek
Die Deutsche Bibliothek lists this publication in the Deutsche Nationalbibliografie; detailed bibliographic data is available in the internet at <http://dnb.ddb.de>.

Zugl.: Hohenheim, Univ., Diss., 2006

D 100
ISSN 0948-1338
ISBN 3-631-55557-1
US-ISBN 0-8204-8724-4

© Peter Lang GmbH
Europäischer Verlag der Wissenschaften
Frankfurt am Main 2006
All rights reserved.

Printed in Germany 1 2 4 5 6 7

www.peterlang.de

Preface

The book addresses three highly important issues for development economics and policy: pro-poor growth, the role of infrastructure investments and the challenge of promoting development in lagging regions. The author combines these issues by building a macro-micro economic model with a regional dimension. This approach contributes to the opening up of a promising research field and produces policy relevant results.

Since the governments of 189 countries committed themselves to achieving the Millennium Development Goals (MDG), policy makers are increasingly keen on identifying development interventions that yield high returns to capital in terms of poverty reduction. Major questions in this context are, how policy measures can be designed to reduce poverty and how economic growth processes can be shaped to achieve the MDGs by 2015. To effectively support pro-poor growth processes and to efficiently allocate private and public capital across space and sectors, analytical tools are needed to analyse patterns of growth, structural change and poverty impacts of investments.

Empirical studies suggest that reducing poverty requires investments in rural sectors and disadvantaged regions. A partial perspective is criticised on the ground that it may overestimate the impacts of region- or sector-specific investments as economy-wide effects are not considered. The model presented in this book incorporates sectoral and spatial dimensions and includes them into an economy-wide framework. This approach thus overcomes the limitations of partial models and can contribute to a more comprehensive understanding of underlying mechanisms and more substantiated investment decisions.

Results of the study underline the importance of taking a combined macro-micro perspective to comprehensively assess the impacts of investments on poverty. It further confirms the existing empirical evidence that particularly investments in rural areas and the agricultural sector can contribute to poverty reduction in the short- and medium term. It thus supports a stronger emphasis on rural development and the agricultural sector in national poverty reduction strategies and international investments in achieving the MDGs.

Prof. Dr. Franz Heidhues   Prof. Dr. Joachim von Braun
University of Hohenheim   International Food Policy Research Institute
Stuttgart   Washington, D.C.

Acknowledgements

During the three years of this dissertation research, I have received multifaceted support from numerous people. First and foremost, I would like to express my special gratitude to Prof. Dr. Franz Heidhues. Far more than being the supervisor of this dissertation, he encouraged me for the cause of developing countries and provided me with invaluable opportunities that boosted my personal and professional experiences. I am also indebted to my second supervisor, Prof. Dr. Ansgar Belke for his very kind and useful support and the insights I gained into the functioning of financial markets and central banks. Furthermore, I would like to thank Prof. Dr. Jürgen Zeddies and Prof. Dr. Valle-Zarate for serving on the examination board.

Despite several months of data collection and travelling, the major part of this dissertation was accomplished at the Institute for Agricultural Economics and Social Sciences in the Tropics and Subtropics at the University of Hohenheim. I thank all my colleagues for a very productive and enjoyable working environment. I especially appreciate the help of Ira Matuschke and Nils Teufel for their detailed comments, technical support and review of English on several versions of this dissertation. Thanks also go to Olivier Ecker for his contributions in the course of his master thesis and Gudrun Contag, Anne Schempp and Coni Schumacher for their administrative support. Life during this time was a lot about work and all the more important were the stimulating discussions with all the other colleagues, including Martina Bergen, Gertrud Buchenrieder, Pamela Marinda, Marcus Mergenthaler, Beyene Tadesse, Stephan Piotrowski and Jia Xiangping, to name some of them.

Effective field research in Vietnam was made possible by the Thai-Vietnamese-German collaborative Special Research Programme (SFB) "Sustainable Land Use and Rural Development in Mountainous Regions of Southeast Asia" that provided the facilities and the network needed for productive work on-site. I especially thank Harald Leisch and Ngyuen Hong for great organisational support and Nguyen Manh Hai and Javier Delgado for their assistance in data hunting. Also, the financial support of the Eiselen Foundation and the SFB is kindly acknowledged.

For support in the methodological parts of this dissertation, I thank Peter Wobst for getting me started with CGE modelling and Xinshen Diao and James Thurlow from IFPRI for their valuable technical and intellectual assistance and their encouragement. Furthermore, I thank Rajul Panja-Lorch and Joachim von Braun for an interesting time at DGO and Soledad Bos, Marianne Haug, Dorothee Heidhues, Divya Nair and Rüdiger Süß and for having a really fruitful and good time in DC.

A class of her own, always encouraging, optimistic and ready for possible and impossible missions is my girlfriend Milena Winklbauer. Thank you very much! Last but not least will ich diese Dissertation meinen Eltern Maria und

Ralph Breisinger widmen, die durch Ihren großen Rückhalt und Ihre stets uneingeschränkte Unterstützung die Grundlage für diese Arbeit gelegt haben. Herzlichen Dank!

Clemens Breisinger   Hohenheim, May 14, 2006

Table of Contents

List of Tables

List of Figures

List of Abbreviations

ADB	Asian Development Bank
APEC	Asian-Pacific Economic Cooperation
ASEAN	Association of South East Asian Nations
BMZ	Bundesministerium für wirtschaftliche Zusammenarbeit und Entwicklung
CBA	Cost Benefit Analyses
CES	Constant Elasticity of Substitution
CET	Constant Elasticity of Transformation
CGE	Computable General Equilibrium
CIEM	Central Institute for Economic Management
CPI	Consumer Price Index
CPRGS	Comprehensive Poverty Reduction and Growth Strategy
CU	Currency Unit
DFID	Department for International Development, United Kingdom
EIU	Economist Intelligence Unit
EU	European Union
EVN	Electricity of Vietnam
FCU	Foreign Currency Unit
FDI	Foreign Direct Investment
FP	Factor Productivity
GDP	Gross Domestic Product
GIC	Growth Incidence Curve
GO	Gross Output
GSO	General Statistics Office
GSO SL	General Statistics Office Son La
GTAP	Global Trade Analysis Project
ha	Hectare
HDI	Human Development Index
HV	Housing Value
I/O	Input/Output
IC	Intermediate Consumption
ICOLD	International Commission of Large Dams
ICOR	Incremental Capital to Output Ratio
IFPRI	International Food Policy Research Institute
IRR	Internal Rate of Return
JBIC	Japan Bank for International Co-operation
LCU	Local Currency Unit
LES	Linear Expenditure System
LSD	Large-Scale Dam

LSI	Large-Scale Infrastructure
MDG	Millennium Development Goal
MOLISA	Ministry of Labour, Invalids and Social Affairs
MU	Monetary Unit
NCSSH	National Center for Social Sciences
NPV	Net Present Value
ODA	Official Development Aid
OECD	Organisation for Economic Co-operation and Development
PIP	Public Investment Program
PPA	Participatory Poverty Assessments
PPG	Pro-Poor Growth
PPP	Purchasing Power Parity
PRSP	Poverty Reduction Strategy Paper
REG	Regional Economy
REGSAM	Regional Social Accounting Matrix
RHA	Representative Household Approach
ROC	Rest Of the Country
ROV	Rest Of Vietnam
ROW	Rest Of the World
SAM	Social Accounting Matrix
SAP	Structural Adjustment Program
S&I	Savings & Investment'
SNA	System of National Accounts
SOE	State Owned Enterprise
SRV	Socialist Republic of Vietnam
TFP	Total Factor Productivity
UN	United Nations
USD	US Dollar
VA	Value Added
VDG	Vietnam Development Goals
VDR	Vietnam Development Report
VHLSS	Vietnam Household Living Standard Survey
VLSS	Vietnam Living Standard Survey
VIETSAM	National SAM for Vietnam
VND	Vietnamese Dong
WCD	World Commission of Dams
WHO	World Health Organisation
WTO	World Trade Organisation

Currency unit: Vietnamese Dong (VND).
Exchange rate: 1USD=15250 VND in 2002 (EIU, 2004)

Executive Summary

Infrastructure investments play a most important role in the development process of countries. There are several good reasons to emphasise infrastructure investments in developing countries. Infrastructures are directly or indirectly related to all eight Millennium Development Goals (MDG). Furthermore, the effective protection caused by the lack of infrastructure is for many countries considerably higher than those caused by tariffs, hampering the empowerment of people to benefit from trade liberalisation and economic growth. Finally, earlier problems of infrastructure projects have been identified and a stronger emphasis on accountability, capacity building and decentralisation can be expected to contribute to more effective and efficient capital allocation.

Infrastructure investments in general and pro-poor growth enhancing investments in particular, require comprehensive appraisal methods. Traditional methods, so far, have taken a project or sector perspective that did not capture economy-wide effects. This limits the evaluation of infrastructure investments to sectoral effects on growth and poverty reduction. If negative effects from the same investment occur in other sectors, economy-wide impacts are certainly lower and might even be negative. In addition to these inter-sectoral effects, investments in infrastructure can have long-term impacts on national capital formation, the government budget and foreign trade patterns. To address this research gap, this dissertation uses the computable general equilibrium (CGE) model approach. CGE models can incorporate intersectoral, nonlinear relations and behavioural parameters to define the relations between all sectors and agents in an economic system. Poverty impacts are addressed by adding a micro-accounting module for post-simulation analysis. The application of such a type of macro-micro model to infrastructure investments is a new approach to gain insights into the usefulness of economy-wide models; it also produces specific results for the case study country - Vietnam.

Vietnam is an emerging economy with high growth rates. Over the past two decades, the country reduced poverty rates rapidly. Vietnam's status as a WTO accession candidate confirms its increasing integration into the world economy and marks another milestone in the transition from an inward-looking agriculture-based economy to an outward-oriented economy. However, high growth came at the cost of widening regional disparities and stagnating economic development in disadvantaged regions of the country. The virtuous circle created in the export-oriented growth centres find their antonyms in the mountainous regions of Vietnam, which are trapped in vicious circles of poverty. Rising spatial disparities are characteristic for many transition countries and are incorporated in the CGE model by building a two-region model. One of the model regions is the north-western mountainous province of Son La, which is a typical example of a poor region and one of the key regions for national poverty reduction strategies; the other region represents the rest of Vietnam.

A major component of this study is the setup of a social accounting matrix (SAM) for this province - the first SAM for Vietnam that has been build at the provincial level. It represents a snapshot of the economy in the year 2002, allows for a qualitative analysis of structural features and serves as the basis of the CGE model. Major data to construct this comprehensive database include the Son La Statistical Yearbook, the tableau of provincial intermediate consumption and value added data, the national input-output table, and the representative household survey for Vietnam.

As the basis for modelling, I use the International Food Policy Research Institute's (IFPRI) Standard CGE model and calibrate it to the provincial Son La SAM and a national SAM for Vietnam. Activities, factors and households are region-specific, while commodities are traded in a single national market. The CGE model comprises 60 production activities, 30 commodities, 8 factors, 4 household classes and 6 enterprise types. The model further includes the central government. The capital market is represented by a savings and investment account. Imperfect substitutability of region-specific production activities reflects spatial differences in timing, quality and location of production. Furthermore, the model includes transaction costs for nationally and internationally marketed goods, which is particularly relevant for the analysis of transportation infrastructure. Non-tradable goods are incorporated by accounting for home consumption of self-produced goods. To incorporate the persisting un- and underemployment in the unskilled labour market in Vietnam, the model allows each activity to employ labour at its fixed and activity specific wage.

Three scenarios are defined to assess the impacts of infrastructure on growth and poverty. Scenario 1 quantifies the impact of rural and urban road investments. The implementation of the scenario follows the empirical evidence, which identifies quantity and quality of roads as major determinants of transaction costs and factor productivity (FP). Scenario 2 analyses the impacts of a large-scale hydropower dam. Major local and national impacts are simulated, including the construction boom, the loss of land, better availability of electricity and flood mitigation. Finally, Scenario 3 addresses the question, how much growth in the agricultural sector is needed to achieve MDG 1 in Son La province.

Four major results and conclusions emerge from this analysis. First, CGE models have the ability to incorporate several dimensions of infrastructure investments and can thus analytically support the integration of investment patterns into poverty and distribution-oriented development strategies. Their major strength lies in their ability to capture intersectoral and interregional multiplier effects. Second, especially rural road investments can contribute to economic growth and poverty reduction in Vietnam. In Son La province, rural roads induce additional growth between 4 and 13 percentage points translating in rural poverty reduction between 11 and 14 percentage points. Despite these positive impacts, the poverty gap in Son La remains above 500,000 VND per capita in all road investment simulations, as compared to the poverty line of around 2 million VND. Third, the Son La hydropower dam poses a threat and an opportunity for regional development. Without complementary measures, the rural poverty rate in Son La province can increase from 63 to 74 percent, which would effectively add 100,000 people to the poor. Fourth, high multipliers indicate that pro-poor growth enhancing investments should focus on the agricultural sector. A poverty elasticity of agricultural FP growth in Son La province of about -1 indicates that achieving MDG 1 in Son La province roughly requires a doubling of its agricultural GDP.

Several policy recommendations emerge from this study. The set-up and maintenance of SAMs in national statistics offices for major regions of a country should be promoted. They can serve as the basis for qualitative and quantitative analyses of poverty reduction strategies and MDGs and thus contribute to effective and efficient policy planning. Additionally, investments in rural roads are crucial to prevent further increases in regional disparities in Vietnam and to create opportunities for the rural poor to gain from national growth. To foster pro-poor growth through sector-specific investments, public resources should be used to design and implement agricultural productivity enhancing policies. Finally, the international donor community that has largely retreated from supporting large-scale infrastructures should re-engage in this sector. Infrastructures such as roads and power plants are directly or indirectly related to all MDGs and can therefore play an important role in reducing hunger and poverty and promoting equal opportunities for all.

Zusammenfassung

Infrastrukturinvestitionen in Entwicklungsländern haben oft zum Bau überdimensionierter Prestigeprojekte und Korruption geführt und hatten kaum positive Wirkungen auf arme Bevölkerungsschichten. Es gibt jedoch Gründe, Infrastrukturmaßnahmen wieder stärkere Beachtung im Entwicklungsprozess zukommen zu lassen. Infrastruktur ist direkt oder indirekt mit allen Millenniums-Entwicklungszielen (MDG) verbunden. Darüber hinaus haben Handelsliberalisierungen zu einer substantiellen Reduktion von Zöllen geführt. Der durch mangelnde Infrastruktur verursachte Anteil an der effektiven Protektionsrate ist in vielen Ländern dadurch höher als der auf tarifäre Handelshemmnisse zurückzuführende Anteil, was die Partizipation von Ländern und Regionen an durch Handel generierten Wohlfahrtsgewinnen verhindert. Schließlich wurden die Probleme von Infrastrukturinvestitionen und Instandhaltung weitgehend identifiziert. Eine stärkere Beachtung von Rechenschaftslegung, Ausbildung und Dezentralisierung kann zu einer effizienteren und effektiveren Kapitalallokation beitragen.

Infrastrukturinvestitionen im Allgemeinen und breitenwirksames Wachstum fördernde Investitionen im Speziellen, erfordern umfassende Bewertungsmethoden. Traditionelle Methoden beruhen auf projekt- oder sektorbasierten Ansätzen und können volkswirtschaftliche Effekte nur bedingt einbeziehen. Dies limitiert die Evaluation von Infrastrukturinvestitionen auf sektorale Effekte von Wachstum und Armutswirkungen. Wenn negative Effekte dieser Investitionen in anderen Sektoren oder Gegenden auftreten, ist der volkswirtschaftliche Nutzen geringer und kann sogar negativ werden. Zusätzlich zu diesen intersektoralen Effekten können Infrastrukturinvestitionen Langzeitwirkungen auf die nationale Kapitalbildung, den Staatshaushalt und die Handelbilanz haben. Um diese Forschungslücke anzugehen, benutzt die vorliegende Dissertation ein Computable General Equilibrium Modell (CGE). CGE Modelle können nichtlineare Beziehungen und Verhaltensparameter zur Abbildung der Relationen aller Sektoren und Agenten einer Volkswirtschaft berücksichtigen. Armutswirkungen werden in die Analyse einbezogen durch ein der Simulation nachgelagertes Mikromodell. Die Anwendung eines solchen Modells zur Bewertung von Infrastrukturinvestitionen ist ein neuer Ansatz. Es können damit sowohl Erkenntnisse zum Mehrwert der Anwendung solcher gesamtwirtschaftlicher Modelle als auch spezifische Aussagen über die volkswirtschaftlichen Effekte des für die Fallstudie betrachteten Landes – Vietnam – gewonnen werden.

Vietnam ist ein aufstrebendes Land mit hohem Wirtschaftswachstum und hat über die letzten beiden Jahrzehnte den Anteil der in Armut lebenden Bevölkerung stark reduziert. Vietnams Status als WTO Beitrittskandidat unterstreicht seine zunehmende Integration in die Weltwirtschaft und markiert einen weiteren

Meilenstein im Übergang von einem agrarisch geprägten und nach innen gerichteten zu einem der Weltwirtschaft geöffneten Land. Diese erfolgreiche Entwicklung wird überschattet von wachsenden regionalen Einkommensdisparitäten und stagnierender Wirtschaftsentwicklung in benachteiligten Gebieten Vietnams. Während die Wachstumszentren beträchtliche Wohlfahrtssteigerungen erzielen konnten, sind gerade die Bergregionen gekennzeichnet von Stagnation und anhaltender Armut. Solche Disparitäten sind charakteristisch für viele Transformationsländer und werden im CGE Modell durch die Einarbeitung zweier vietnamesischer Regionen berücksichtigt. Eine dieser Regionen ist die nordwestliche Bergprovinz Son La, die ein typisches Beispiel für eine von Armut gekennzeichnete Region und damit ein Schlüsselgebiet für nationale Armutsreduzierungsstrategien darstellt. Die zweite Region repräsentiert den Rest Vietnams.

Einen wichtigen Teil dieser Studie stellt die Entwicklung einer Social Accounting Matrix (SAM) für Son La dar, die erste ihrer Art für Vietnam. Die SAM bildet die regionale Wirtschaftsstruktur für das Jahr 2002 ab und dient sowohl qualitativen Analysen als auch als Basis für das CGE Modell. Hauptdatenquellen, die bei der Erstellung Verwendung fanden sind das Statistische Jahrbuch von Son La, die Statistik zu sektoralen Vorleistungen und Wertschöpfung auf Provinzebene, die nationale Input/Output Tabelle und eine repräsentative Haushaltsbefragung.

Als Basis für die Modellierung wird das Standard CGE Modell des International Food Policy Research Institutes verwendet und für die Son La SAM und eine nationale SAM für Vietnam kalibriert. Produktionsaktivitäten, Faktoren und Haushalte sind regionsspezifisch, während Güter und Dienstleistungen auf einem gemeinsamen nationalen Markt gehandelt werden. Das CGE Modell beinhaltet 60 Aktivitäten, 30 Güter und Dienstleistungen, 8 Produktionsfaktoren, 4 Haushaltstypen und 6 Unternehmenstypen, sowie die Zentralregierung. Der Kapitalmarkt wird durch Spar- und Investitionswerte abgebildet. Unvollständige Substituierbarkeit von regionsspezifischer Produktion reflektiert die bestehenden Unterschiede in Zeit, Qualität und Ort der Produktion. Zusätzlich enthält das Modell Transaktionskosten für national und international gehandelte Güter. Nichthandelbare Güter werden durch den Heimkonsum privat hergestellter Güter berücksichtigt. Um der persistenten Unterbeschäftigung und Arbeitslosigkeit im Niedriglohnsektor Vietnams Rechnung zu tragen, erlaubt das Modell jeder Aktivität Arbeitskräfte zu einem aktivitätsspezifischen und fixen Preis einzustellen.

Drei Szenarien werden definiert, um die Auswirkungen von Infrastrukturmaßnahmen auf Wachstum und Armut zu analysieren. Szenario 1 bewertet den Einfluss von ruralen und urbanen Straßeninvestitionen. Die Implementierung dieses Szenarios folgt der empirischen Evidenz, welche Qualität und Quantität des Straßennetzes als Hauptdeterminanten von Transaktionskosten und Faktorproduktivität (FP) identifizieren. Szenario 2 analysiert die Auswirkungen eines Staudammbaus. Hauptauswirkungen des Baus auf lokaler und nationaler Ebene werden simuliert, welche die Bauphase, den Landverlust durch das Staubecken, die bessere Elektrizitätsverfügbarkeit und den Hochwasserschutz beinhalten. Schließlich geht Szenario 3 der Frage nach, wie viel Wachstum im Agrarsektor zu einer Erreichung des MDG 1 in der Provinz Son La führt. Vier Hauptergebnisse folgen aus dieser Analyse. Erstens erlauben CGE Modelle verschiedene Dimensionen von Infrastrukturinvestitionen einzubeziehen und können deshalb die Integration von Investitionen in Armuts- und verteilungsorientierte Entwicklungsstrategien analytisch unterstützen. Eine Hauptstärke liegt in der Erfassung von intersektoralen und interregionalen Multiplikatoreffekten. Zweitens können besonders Straßen in ländlichen Gebieten einen Beitrag zu Wirtschaftswachstum und Armutsreduzierung in Vietnam leisten. In Son La führen Investitionen ins rurale Straßennetz zu gesamtwirtschaftlichen Wachstumsraten von 4-13 Prozentpunkten. Ungeachtet dieser positiven Effekte können die Armen in allen Straßenbausimulationen nur ca. 75 Prozent des zur Überwindung der Armutsgrenze notwendigen Einkommens erzielen. Drittens bietet der Son La Staudamm Chancen und zugleich eine Gefahr für die Regionalentwicklung. Ohne komplementäre Maßnahmen wird die ländliche Armut von 63 Prozent auf 74 Prozent steigen, was eine Zunahme der Armen um ca. 100.000 Personen zur Folge hätte. Viertens deuten hohe Multiplikatoreffekte darauf hin, dass breitenwirksames Wachstum am besten durch Investitionen in den Agrarsektor erreicht werden kann. Eine Armutselastizität landwirtschaftlichen Wachstums von -1 bedeutet, dass das Erreichen des MDG 1 in Son La etwa einer Verdoppelung des landwirtschaftlichen BIPs bedarf.

Verschiedene Politikempfehlungen ergeben sich aus dieser Studie. Die Erstellung von SAMs in nationalen Statistikbüros für Hauptregionen eines Landes sollten gefördert werden. Sie können als eine Basis für qualitative und quantitative Analysen von Armutsreduzierung- und Wachstumsstrategien dienen und somit einen wichtigen Beitrag zu effektiver und effizienter Politikplanung leisten. Investitionen in den ländlichen Straßenbau sind nötig, um ein Ansteigen regionaler Disparitäten zu verhindern und um der ländlichen Armutsbevölkerung die Möglichkeit zu geben, an nationalen Wachstumsprozessen zu partizipieren. Um breitenwirksames Wachstum auf Sektorebene zu fördern, sollten öffentliche Ressourcen dazu genutzt werden, produktivitätssteigernde Strategien im Agrarsektor zu fördern und zu implementieren. Schließlich sollte die internationale Gebergemeinschaft sich wieder verstärkt im Infrastrukturbereich engagieren. Aufgrund der engen Verknüpfung von Infrastrukturinvestitionen und MDGs spielen diese eine wichtige Rolle in der Reduzierung von Hunger und Armut und in der Schaffung von fairen Chancen für alle.

1 Introduction

1.1 Setting the Stage

Disparities within and among countries are rising and elasticities of poverty reduction to economic growth are declining in many countries. Resulting inequalities in opportunities sustain extreme deprivation, result in wasted human potential and often weaken prospects for overall prosperity and economic growth (WORLD BANK, 2005). This development creates vicious circles and pockets of poverty, where certain regions cannot benefit from national growth and improved global trade. Such disparities do not only undermine the objective of freeing the world from absolute poverty, but also bear the risk of social instability and threaten future growth within countries (VAN DE WALLE AND GUNEWARDENA, 2001; KANBUR AND VENABLES, 2005; KANBUR ET AL., 2005; WORLD BANK, 2005).

To address this growing divergence and to promote growth in disadvantaged regions within countries, poverty reduction strategy papers (PRSP) and Millennium Development Goals (MDG) increasingly include regional development objectives (WORLD BANK et al., 2003; UN, 2002). Within these plans, renewed focus is on the importance of physical infrastructure in the development process. Empirical evidence supports the importance of infrastructure. It has the potential to contribute to growth and poverty reduction by kick-starting regional economies, attracting private investments and increasing productivity (WORLD BANK, 1994; DFID, 2002; JBIC, 2003). However, large-scale infrastructures investments in roads, water systems or power plants have often not benefited the poor due to bad governance, the neglect of environmental and maintenance issues and the bias towards large-scale capital projects ("white elephants") (DFID, 2002; OECD, 2005).

Increasing attention on infrastructure investments can be expected for three reasons. First, infrastructure is directly or indirectly related to all MDGs. Second, bilateral and multilateral trade liberalisation led to a substantial decrease in tariffs over the last two decades. As a result, the effective protection caused by transport costs is for many countries considerably higher than those caused by tariffs. Third, earlier problems have been identified and a stronger emphasis towards accountability, capacity building and decentralisation in infrastructure can contribute to a more effective and efficient capital investments in this sector (WORLD BANK, 1999B; LIMAO AND VENABLES, 2001; DFID, 2002; JBIC, 2003).

A strong emphasis on assessing impacts of investments and a pro-poor orientation of infrastructure also requires sound feasibility and appraisal tools. Ideally, these take financial, economic, social and environmental impacts into account. However, socio-economic impacts alone have multiple dimensions, which make comprehensive assessments a difficult task. Traditional tools for socio-economic assessment of the impacts of public investments take a project or sector perspective and do not capture economy-wide effects (WCD, 2000). This might lead to a situation, where infrastructure investments are evaluated to be poverty reducing and growth enhancing from a sector perspective. However, if negative effects from the same investment occur in other sectors, economy-wide impacts are certainly lower and might even be negative. To prevent such misleading results and to capture indirect effects, a macro-economic model is required. Such type of model can incorporate indirect effects between economic sectors and can account for linkages between infrastructure investments and macroeconomic variables such as the government budget and the trade balance. Due to rising regional disparities and spatially diverging impacts of investment projects, such a macro model should ideally also incorporate region-specific features. In addition, such a multi-region macro-economic model should be complemented by a micro model that can capture distributional and poverty impacts. The resulting combined macro-micro model can be expected to contribute to a better understanding of underlying mechanisms and economy-wide effects of public investments. It can thus also contribute to a more effective and efficient allocation of infrastructure investments.

The first objective of this dissertation is to build such a multi-region macro-micro model to evaluate its potential contribution to the assessment of infrastructure investments. The following three major hypotheses will be of guidance to tackle this objective:

(I)   An economy-wide model can contribute to the comprehensive assessment of infrastructure investments.
(II)   Infrastructure investments have important indirect effects, which are left out in traditional sector-focused analysis.
(III) Infrastructure investments may have considerable interregional impacts.

These hypotheses are investigated by using Vietnam as a case study. Due to the scope of this dissertation, I restrict the application of the model to road and large-scale dam investments. However, this methodology can be applied to any other type of public or private investment.

Vietnam is an emerging economy and one of the fastest growing countries in the world (THE ECONOMIST, 2006B). At the same time, the country has shown a rapid reduction in poverty rates over the last two decades. Its status as a World Trade Organisation (WTO) accession candidate confirms Vietnam's increasing integration into the world economy and marks another milestone in the transition from an inward-looking agriculture-based economy to an outward-looking economy, which is increasingly dominated by the industry and services sector. This rapid development makes the country not only a success story among developing countries but also an interesting case study. On the one hand, it can provide insights into the drivers of growth and poverty reduction. On the other hand, it features many challenges and problems that are characteristic for transition economies. High growth came at the price of widening regional disparities and stagnating economic development in disadvantaged regions. The virtuous circle created in the export oriented growth centres find their counterparts in the mountainous regions of Vietnam, which are trapped in vicious circles of poverty. The north-western mountainous province of Son La is a typical example for a disadvantaged and poor region. This province will constitute one of the regions of the model, which is analysed in this dissertation.

The second objective of the dissertation is to analyse the economic impacts of different infrastructure investments in Vietnam in general, and their poverty reducing potential in a northern mountainous province in specific. The following three hypotheses specify this objective further:

(IV) Infrastructure investments have the potential to contribute to poverty reduction in Vietnam.

(V) Investments in roads are vital elements for sustainable economic growth and poverty reduction, especially in the disadvantaged regions of Vietnam.

(VI) The agricultural sector is a main driver of pro-poor growth in rural Vietnam and thus a prime target of investments that aim at reducing poverty.

1.2 Structure of the Study

The dissertation is structured as follows: Chapter 2 introduces the concept of pro-poor growth and relates it to infrastructure investments. It starts with the general analysis of relationships between growth, income distribution and poverty. Section 2.2 puts forward a general framework, which shows linkages between public investments, economic sectors, regions and institutions. Special emphasis is on roads and large-scale dams investments. The final section reviews different analytical tools used to assess the impacts of investments on poverty. As an economy-wide tool for infrastructure assessments, background information on computable general equilibrium models (CGE) are introduced and major fields of their application presented.

Chapter 3 provides country-specific information on Vietnam. It takes an international, national and a regional perspective and sums up major socio-economic developments over the past two decades. The chapter starts by reviewing the growth and poverty reduction process. Besides analysing factors behind Vietnam's success, it also attempts to point out potential weaknesses for the country's future development. Section 3.2 assesses Vietnam's regional disparities, which are one of the major future development challenges. The final section of this chapter examines current public spending patterns in Vietnam and its public investment program (PIP), in order to identify distributional characteristics of public investments.

Chapter 4 puts forward the CGE model by presenting the compilation of the core model database. Special emphasis is on the Son La Social Accounting Matrix (SAM), which was developed in the course of the dissertation research. Section 4.2 introduces the specification of the CGE model, including technical details of the simulation parameters. Section 4.3 discusses general concepts of poverty and defines a region-specific poverty line for Northern Vietnam. Furthermore, it describes the structure of the micro-accounting module for poverty analysis.

Chapter 5 presents the model results. The baseline solution introduces key characteristics and structural features of the Vietnamese economy and discusses the inter-linkages between the two regional economies (section 5.1). Based on that, chapter 5.2 assesses the impacts of three scenarios: road investments, large-scale dam investments and the impacts of agricultural growth. Section 5.3 takes on the task of testing the sensitivity of the model parameters and assumptions.

Chapter 6 concludes with major findings, policy recommendations and further research needs.

2 Reviewing Growth, Poverty and Infrastructure: Theory and Empirical Evidence

A vital issue in the analysis of economic growth is the fact that even marginal differences in growth rates can lead to huge disparities in economic and human development between countries (AHLFELD et al., 2005).[1] From this aggregate perspective, one can therefore conclude that attempts to reduce income gaps between countries and reduce poverty on a global scale have to focus on efforts increasing per capita incomes at national level. KRAAY (2004) supports this view by stating that in the medium- to long run most of the variation in changes of poverty is attributable to growth in average incomes. There is, however also growing evidence that growth is a necessary but not a sufficient condition to eliminate poverty (RAVALLION AND CHEN, 1997; DEININGER AND SQUIRE, 1998; BOURGUIGNON, 2002). Income disparities are increasing in developing countries, which bears the risk of social instability (VAN DE WALLE AND GUNEWARDENA, 2001). In this regard, redistribution of income is one option for governments to address growing income disparities and public investments are a powerful tool to influence economic developments and ultimately to reduce poverty.

Against this background, the following chapter reviews empirical evidence on the linkages between growth and poverty. It presents the concept of pro-poor growth, which allows for a comprehensive analysis of the relationship between growth, income distribution and poverty (section 2.1). The second part of the chapter assesses public investments and their role in growth and poverty reduction. Special emphasis is put on infrastructure investments (section 2.2). Finally, different analytical tools used to assess the impacts of investments on poverty are reviewed and discussed in the context of CGE (section 2.3).

---

[1] AHLFELD et al. (2005) use an example of PRITCHETT (2000) to exemplify the point in case: Japan's per capita income over the period of 1870 to 1980 grew at an average rate of 2.64 percent per annum. The cumulative impact of a 0.8 percent lead over the United States contributed to its rise to the second biggest economy in the world. This can be underlined for developing countries by the fact that in the 1960's several African and Asian countries had comparable development indicators and preconditions: Nigeria had more favourable development indicators than Indonesia, the Congo's indicators looked better than South Korea's and the initial position of the Ivory Coast was comparable with Indonesia's (BMZ, 2006).

2.1 Revisiting Pro-Poor Growth

Poverty reduction is a top priority of international and national development agendas. The first MDG explicitly sets the target of reducing global poverty levels by half by 2015.[2] PRSPs and more recently country-specific MDG goals set targets and define plans to achieve these national *targets for reducing poverty*.[3] One of the contributions of development economists to formulating and achieving these goals is to explore the factors that determine successful economic and social development. In this regard, pro-poor growth (PPG) has become a new favourite topic in the development discussion. It provides a framework that relates economic growth to income distribution and poverty and thus offers a comprehensive basis for analysing the linkages. However, PPG and its implicit emphasis on income distribution as a concept are not new. CHENERY et al. (1974, p.209) pointed out that "distributional objectives should be treated as an integral part of development strategy. They should be expressed in terms of growth of income and consumption of different socioeconomic groups, with special weight being given to growth in low-income target groups".

The renewed focus on *distributional aspects* is not at least due the recognition that growth does not automatically trickle down and large-scale redistribution among income groups in developing countries does not automatically occur (WORLD BANK, 2000). Furthermore, income disparities in many countries such as China, Russia, Mexico, and Vietnam are on the rise, and it remains yet to be seen on how economically and socially sustainable such unequal developments can be. Empirical evidence on how far economic growth, income distribution and the incidence of poverty are causally linked and how growth affects poverty is subject to ongoing research and political discussion. The concept of PPG provides a useful framework for such analysis, however there is no single definition of PPG. In the following, I present two definitions of PPG and discuss four major questions surrounding PPG by reviewing cross-

---

[2] Eight Millennium Development Goals have been declared: 1. eradicate extreme poverty and hunger 2. achieve universal primary education 3. promote gender equality and empower women 4. reduce child mortality 5. improve maternal health 6. combat HIV/AIDS, malaria and other diseases 7. ensure environmental sustainability 8. develop a global partnership for development.

[3] Vietnam for instance has launched the Vietnam Development Goals (VDG). The VDGs are directly based on the MDGs, adding four points: reducing vulnerability, improving governance for poverty reduction, reducing ethnic inequality, ensuring pro-poor infrastructure development (UN, 2002).

country empirical studies and other secondary literature on this issue. [4] These four questions are:

- What is PPG, how can it be defined and measured?
- Is economic growth a sufficient condition to achieve poverty reduction?
- How does growth influence income distribution?
- What are the major factors making growth pro-poor?

- What is PPG? How can it be defined and measured?

According to a *"strong" definition* of PPG, growth is only pro-poor, if the poor benefit relatively more from growth than the average population; i.e. if the average real income of the poor segment of the population increases disproportionally more than the average real income of the population (RAVALLION, 2004A; KLASEN, 2005). A major criticism of this definition is that a strong, but inequality increasing growth does not qualify as PPG (RAVALLION, 2004; KLASEN, 2005). This may be the case even if growth leads to large absolute gains for the poor. The point in case is e.g. China, which has a high elasticity of poverty reduction to economic growth, but by the same time rapidly increasing income disparities and higher absolute benefits for the non-poor. Is Chinas growth not pro-poor?

The *"weak" definition* accounts for this criticism by stating that any growth that reduces poverty is pro-poor (RAVALLION, 2004). With this definition, however, the question on "to what extend was growth pro-poor" arises. Since the poverty impact of growth depends strongly on the level of average income growth, measurements of the development of income distribution and change in poverty are needed to quantify the distributional impacts of growth. A direct approach to measure PPG is to calculate growth rates for different income percentiles with special regard to the poor. To assess, whether and how growth was pro-poor, one can compare the income growth rate of the poor percentiles of the population with the average income growth rate. Extending this concept, RAVALLION AND CHEN (2001) suggested in their seminal paper on measuring pro-poor growth the use of growth incidence curves (GIC), which is widely applied in PPG analysis.[5] The GIC has the advantage that it graphically

---

[4] By doing this, I will concentrate on the results of the presented studies rather than analytical strengths and weaknesses of the methodologies used. For a critical review of some of the mentioned studies and cross-country comparisons in general see e.g. EASTWOOD AND LIPTON (2001).

[5] Chapter 3.1 presents and discusses a GIC for Vietnam.

illustrates the variability of the growth rate across income percentiles that are ranked by income and thus allows for tracking changes across the whole income distribution spectrum. Even though this concept is mostly used for the income dimension of poverty, it can easily be adopted to illustrate distributional effects of non-income dimensions such as education, health and nutrition (KLASEN, 2005).

•   Is economic growth a sufficient condition to achieve poverty reduction?

There is broad consensus that *growth is a necessary condition* for poverty reduction. The only theoretical cases, where poverty could be reduced without growth, involve either transfers from the rich to the poor or a distribution of existing wealth among an exogenously reduced number of people. However, case one is neither politically feasible on a wider scale nor a promising approach to sustainable development.[6] Case two is only imaginable in the context of war, large-scale natural disasters or pandemics. In other words, economic growth is clearly required for sustainable poverty reduction.[7] This view is supported by several studies that find that "growth is good for the poor" (RAVALLION AND CHEN, 1997; DOLLAR AND KRAAY, 2002; KRAAY 2004). However, empirical evidence suggests that there is considerable variance between countries as well as the poverty-reducing effect of different growth rates (RAVALLION AND CHEN, 1997). Economic growth might therefore be a necessary, but not a sufficient condition for poverty reduction. Furthermore, even though growth seems to promote poverty reduction from the macro perspective and in the long run, growth can certainly be harmful to the poor from a micro perspective. Especially due to short-term effects the poor may be negatively affected by unfavourable relative price effects on the demand and supply side (EASTWOOD AND LIPTON, 2001).

---

[6] The land redistribution in Zimbabwe is an example for such kind of redistribution.

[7] Redistribution is an important and evolving issue in development research. The basic concern is that transfers financed by taxes might reduce savings and investments and thus hamper growth, let alone the weak tax and collection systems. For further discussion see e.g. CHENERY et al. (1974).

• How does growth influence income distribution?

The classical view on the relation between income distribution and growth in the development process as defined by the Kuznets curve states that inequality increases in early stages of development and then subsequently decreases at later stages of development (KUZNETS, 1968). This hypothesis has been questioned by empirical evidence indicating that growth does not necessarily worsen the income distribution (WORLD BANK, 1990). RAVALLION AND CHEN (1997) find that income changes and changes in inequality are largely uncorrelated, implying that inequality has remained relatively stable across most countries. These findings are surprising and partly counterintuitive, since experiences from countries such as China and Vietnam, for example, show strongly rising inequalities. However, the results of the studies can be explained by their aggregate and long term perspective. Medium-term and country-specific analysis has to look into intra-country distribution of growth. An interesting branch of literature looks at the sectoral distribution of income. SHARMA AND POLEMAN (1993) find that Gini coefficients in the crop sector of India have a much larger value compared to the dairy sector. RAVALLION AND DATT (1999) show that poverty reduction in India is a result of intra-sector growth rather than inter-sector growth and that almost all poverty reduction that occurred during the study period was due to agricultural growth.

• What are the major factors making growth pro-poor?

To analyse this question, a further examination of the role of *income distribution* provides some relevant insights. Several studies find that the impact of economic growth on poverty reduction is lower in cases where inequality is high (DEININGER AND SQUIRE, 1997; BOURGUIGNON, 2002). This finding follows an intuition, which can be described by a little example: take a country A, where 99 percent of the population earns 50 cents per day and 1 percent earns 10 dollar a day. In country B, all people earn 99 cents a day. Assuming a poverty threshold of one dollar a day, it is clear that an average income growth is more likely to reduce poverty (i.e. lift people above the poverty threshold) in country B than it is in country A. Accordingly, RAVALLION AND CHEN (1997) find in their cross-country analysis that a country with a Gini index of 0.25 can be expected to have an elasticity of poverty to growth of about -3.3, whereas the respective elasticity for a country with a Gini index of 0.6 is only -1.8. In addition to this finding, RODRIGUEZ AND RODRIK (1999) find that countries with low levels of initial inequality are likely to grow faster. For different states in India, for example, it was demonstrated that the higher the initial poverty rate, the more effective is agricultural growth and the less effective is growth in non-agricultural activities

(RAVALLION AND DATT, 1999). These last findings imply that a more equal initial income distribution is not only more likely to produce better poverty reduction results but also a faster pace of economic growth. However, KRAAY (2004) puts the importance of the distribution of income into perspective by the finding that in the medium- to long run, most of the variation in changes in poverty is attributable to growth in average incomes.

To push the discussion beyond the relevance of initial distribution, some studies attempted to identify the *factors causing this inequality*. A spatially disaggregated study on India identifies sectoral and spatial composition of growth, initial conditions related to rural development and human resource endowments as the factors that matter most for poverty reduction (RAVALLION AND DATT, 1999). Furthermore, human capital appears to be the most important factor through which inequality hampers growth (DEININGER AND SQUIRE, 1998). LOPEZ (2004) identifies education, infrastructure and macroeconomic stability as win-win policies in the sense that they can be associated with growth and progressive distributional change.

In an attempt to bring the discussion on a more policy-relevant level, RAVALLION (2004) suggests in his primer on pro-poor growth that making growth more pro-poor entails a combination of higher growth and a more *pro-poor distribution of the gains from growth*. Additionally, inequality has to be seen as a multidimensional problem, including access to private and public assets and goods (physical and human). In this context, access to infrastructure, health, and schooling credit are thus important ingredients for the empowerment of people to participate in the growth process (RAVALLION, 2004). Sharing the view on the importance of more concrete information, BOURGUIGNON (2004) emphasises the importance of country-specific combinations of growth and distribution policies. However, inequalities of all sorts (spatial, sectoral, ethnic etc.) cannot be separated from each other; they are often interlinked, influence each other and might even reinforce each other. Such a situation might lead to pockets of deep poverty in particularly backward regions (KLASEN, 2003). Such poverty-trapped regions require strong involvement of the government, including the stimulation of relevant economic activities, private sector engagement and adequate migration policies (KLASEN, 2003).

In order to operationalise PPG, CHENERY et al. (1974) and KLASEN (2003) distinguish between direct and indirect ways, on how growth can be pro-poor. *Direct ways* are defined as growth that benefits sectors and regions where the poor are or going to be and use factors of production that they possess. *Indirect ways* work via redistribution, including transfers and other government spending. This approach is used as a starting point for the framework presented in the following chapter and further elaborated in the course of this study.

Some general conclusions can be drawn from the empirical evidence presented in this chapter on PPG. First, the most effective strategy to reduce poverty would be to achieve *high growth* combined with an *increase in equality*. Second, additionally to the size of growth, *initial income distribution* determines the poverty reduction effect. Third, growth that is accompanied by increasing inequalities will reduce the elasticity of poverty reduction and is likely to increase *spatial disparities*. Fourth, the findings suggest that however important the cross-country perspective of aggregate correlation between growth, inequality and poverty is, spatial, sectoral and functional growth patterns have to be looked at the *country level*.

2.2 Infrastructure Investments from an Economy-wide Perspective

The importance of infrastructure for economic development is described as "vital components in the engine of growth", the "wheels of economic activity" or as "as fuel for the engine of growth" (DEMETRIADES AND MAMUNEAS, 2000, p.687; WORLD BANK, 1994, p.1990; LARSEN et al., 2004, p.1, respectively). In addition, its importance for human development is reflected by the statement that access to minimal infrastructure is one of the essential criteria for defining welfare (WORLD BANK, 1990). In fact, all of the eight MDGs are directly or indirectly linked to infrastructure provision. The following chapter thus defines infrastructure and reviews the role of infrastructure investments in development and the role of governments in the provision of infrastructure (section 2.2.1). Furthermore, I put forward a framework that incorporates the relevant linkages and channels between infrastructure provision, economic growth and poverty (section 2.2.2.). Sections 2.2.3 and 2.2.4 explicitly concentrate on two types of infrastructure that are of special interest for the present study: roads and large-scale dams.

2.2.1 Infrastructure and Development

Following World War II until the 1960's, the development paradigm favoured an active role of the state in providing public goods and services. This *Keynesian consensus* comprised the extensive use of public investments in infrastructure to achieve economic growth by stimulating economic growth in designated centres ("growth poles").[8] This approach was inter alia inspired by the successful implementation of the Marshall Plan in Europe. The expected trickle down effects, however, did not materialise in most of the developing world (WORLD BANK, 2000). Regarding infrastructure investments, the Organisation for Economic Co-operation and Development (OECD) states that "infrastructure developments have often not benefited the poor, or have only led

---

[8] see SINGER (1997) for a further discussion on Keynes influence on development theory and policy.

to short-lived improvements in productivity or access to services" (OECD, 2005, p.8). Furthermore, there was a bias towards large-scale capital projects ("white elephants") and a neglect of institutional, environmental and maintenance issues (DFID, 2002). These problems further undermined the belief that government and public investments in infrastructure can efficiently support economic development. This development let to the *Washington Consensus*, dominating the 1980's and 1990's. The belief in the functioning of markets led to the reduction of the role of the state, privatisation and a general decrease in public spending. However, FAN AND RAO (2003) find that structural adjustment programs (SAP) not generally decreased the size of government spending and find differences between sectors and continents. As a share of total government spending, however, expenditures on infrastructure declined in Africa and Latin America. These selective cutbacks in government spending and the privatisation of services led to mixed results and largely failed to reduce global poverty.

With the extension of SAPs to PRSPs and the introduction of the MDGs, renewed focus was placed on the role of the state in development at the beginning of the third Millennium. Under this *new consensus*, major policy fields with direct poverty impacts range from monetary and trade policies to structural reforms, the quality of governance and the quality and targeting of public investments. (UN, 2002; WORLD BANK et al, 2003; WORLD BANK et al., 2004). However, despite these volatile development paradigms, the state remains to play an important and in many cases almost exclusive role in infrastructure investments and the provision of related services. Estimates indicate that 70 percent of worldwide infrastructure investment in developing countries is financed by governments, 5 percent by official development aid (ODA) and the rest by the private sector (DFID, 2002). This dominance of the public sector in infrastructure can be explained by its production characteristics and the public interest involved.

There are several *definitions of infrastructure*: infrastructure is an umbrella term for activities referred to as "social overhead capital" and is an important part of production, consumption and economic life as a whole (WORLD BANK, 1994). It can be classified into two types: first, public utilities such as power, telecommunications, piped water supply, sanitation and sewerage, solid waste collection and disposal and piped gas; second, transportation infrastructure such as roads, railways, airports, harbours etc. (WORLD BANK, 1994). Furthermore, infrastructure can also be differentiated by "economic infrastructure" and "social infrastructure". Economic infrastructure includes transportation, power etc.; social infrastructure includes schools, health centres, cultural centres (DFID, 2002). Attributes of such infrastructures are: (i) they are capital goods that are usually fixed over long time periods and not consumed directly but in combination with other inputs; (ii) they provide services infrastructure is often long lasting and thus requires long term planning; (iii) maintenance and financing infrastructure is often space-specific and thus immobile (PRUD'HOMME, 2004) (iv) Investment in infrastructure has supply-side effects of increasing the capital stock and demand-side effects of generating additional effective demand. These characteristics make clear that infrastructure investments need sound planning and can determine the economic geography for a long time. Large-scale infrastructure (LSI) projects can be defined as "major important construction projects and investments serving production, business activities and social life, which can create strong and long lasting socio-economic development on a large scale" (SRV 2003, p. 67).

Combining infrastructure with poverty, *pro-poor infrastructure investments* can be defined as the commitment of public resources to build up a capital stock available to the poor to directly or indirectly empower them to raise their incomes. These characteristics underline the priority role of infrastructure. The adequacy of infrastructure plays a key role in the diversification of the economy, the expansion of trade, coping with population growth and enhancing productivity growth (WORLD BANK, 1994). However, international donors remain reluctant in engaging in infrastructure projects. This critical view of the development donor community is reflected by the fact that infrastructure lending has been steadily declining, from 15 percent of ODA in the 1970's to around 3 percent today (OECD, 2005). However, more recently the role of infrastructure resurfaces again and there is increasing understanding among policy-makers that infrastructure is an important component of comprehensive development planning (OECD, 2005). A revival of infrastructure is supported by the fact that while interventions are not feasible or reasonable in all policy areas, public spending and public interventions are an established redistribution mechanism. Public investments are thus increasingly again recognised as important tools to fight poverty and public investment programs (PIP) are considered to have big potentials to contribute to this objective (FAN, 2003; SRV, 2003; WORLD BANK et al, 2003). Infrastructure development, which channels resources towards the poor is explicitly announced in many PRSPs. In the case of Vietnam, a separate chapter on large-scale infrastructure has been added to the CPRGS (SRV, 2003)[9].

Despite this generally important role, the more specific role of infrastructure in the poverty reduction process remains controversial. *Causalities* between infrastructure, growth and poverty are unclear, especially whether infrastructure triggers growth or vice versa. What seems to be clear is that appropriate levels of infrastructure are necessary but not sufficient conditions for growth and poverty reduction (WORLD BANK, 1994). One of the core problems of infrastructure investment remains its difficult targeting. While the World Bank comes to the conclusion that "infrastructure is a blunt instrument for intervening directly on behalf of the poor" (WORLD BANK, 1994, p.80), a study of JACOBY (2000, p.735) finds that infrastructure is "certainly not the magic bullet for poverty reduction". In addition, PIPs face a number of problems and have scope for improvements. Major areas critical for public investments in the

---

[9] In Vietnam the PRSP is called Comprehensive Poverty Reduction and Growth Strategy (CPRGS).

context of poverty reduction are: balancing economic and social investments between richer and poorer areas and provinces, improving access, prioritising financial resources (WORLD BANK, 2005).

The provision of such infrastructure has direct and indirect impacts on an economy and pro-poor growth and depends upon the complementary conditions of many different factors. The following chapter introduces a model of linkages between infrastructure and poverty. These theoretical linkages are substantiated and described by presenting the results of selected studies that analyse the impact of infrastructure. According to the focus of the model simulations presented in chapter 5, the discussion concentrates on large-scale infrastructure.

2.2.2 Infrastructure and Poverty: A General Framework

The importance and role of infrastructure for economic development is confirmed by a number of studies. The main line of empirical research in the field of infrastructure and its impacts on economic growth extends the conventional production function and makes use of cross-country and cross-regional data. According to this model, output is not only a function of labour, capital and land, but also of infrastructure. The following chapter integrates the results of these empirical studies to support the development of an economy-wide model for public infrastructure investments. One of the causes why infrastructure investments remain controversial is the fact that such investments without complementary policies are not likely to lead to economic growth and poverty reduction (WORLD BANK, 1994; VAN DE WALLE, 2002). Investments in infrastructure can take various forms ranging from investments in physical infrastructure to human capital. Furthermore, poverty can be affected by both the infrastructure investment and by the use of services that are provided because of this infrastructure. For example, access to affordable transportation service increases mobility and expands the opportunities for employment or self-employed activities that require commuting (TACOLI, 2003). In fact, service provision seems at least as important as the underlying physical infrastructure. This becomes clear when imagining a new school building without a teacher or a coach company without a road.

To account for the diversity of impacts, Figure 1 puts infrastructure investments into an economy-wide context. It includes macroeconomic conditions, governance, production activities, factors, households, commodity markets and the rest of the world. The challenge in drawing such a graph, and generally in analysing the impacts of public investments on poverty, is the large amount of linkages and channels that affect each other in diverse ways. Even though the following model can easily be adopted to all types of infrastructures, I explicitly focus on large-scale economic infrastructure in the following description. This has two major causes. First, the use of an economy-wide model seems only reasonable for infrastructure investments that have a certain size. Second, poverty impacts of large-scale infrastructure are highly topical in Vietnam. In addition, due to the poverty focus of this study, special emphasis is laid on geographically disadvantaged regions. This theoretical framework for economy-wide impacts of infrastructure investments is subsequently discussed. The discussion proceeds from the top to the base of Figure 2.1, starting from the government budget and macroeconomic policies (I) to the household level (IV).

(I) Government Budget, Macroeconomic Policies, Governance and Institutions

Sound and stable *macroeconomic conditions*, institutions and market policies as prerequisites for successful development have led to sustainable economic growth (WORLD BANK, 2000).The size of the budget per se is a major determinant of public investment opportunities in various kinds of physical infrastructure and service provision. The size of the budget is determined by fiscal policies, interest rates, performance of state owned enterprises etc. and thus ultimately by the performance of the economy as a whole. Sound macroeconomic policies and stability are essential prerequisites for PPG, including low inflation, limited budget deficits and openness to trade (WORLD BANK, 1990; WORLD BANK, 2000; KRAAY, 2004). Fewer consensus exists on more specific tasks such as the level of state intervention in the exchange rate regime, the mix between tax increases and expenditure cuts and sustainable levels of imbalances and deficits (KLASEN, 2005). Regarding financial markets, it seems favourable for developing countries to take a gradual approach towards liberalisation. Such a gradual approach allows for the development of a domestic banking and financial market system prior to full liberalisation (BMZ, 2005A). [10]

---

[10] The negative effect of the liberalisation of the capital account is caused by the increase in volatility. Since the poor tend to be relatively less capable to insure against risk, they might tend to disfavour fierce liberalisation. Furthermore, structural effects tend to weaken the poor, which necessitates state action to antagonise undesirable effects (BMZ, 2005A).

Figure 2.1 Theoretical Framework for Economy-wide Impacts of Infrastructure Investments

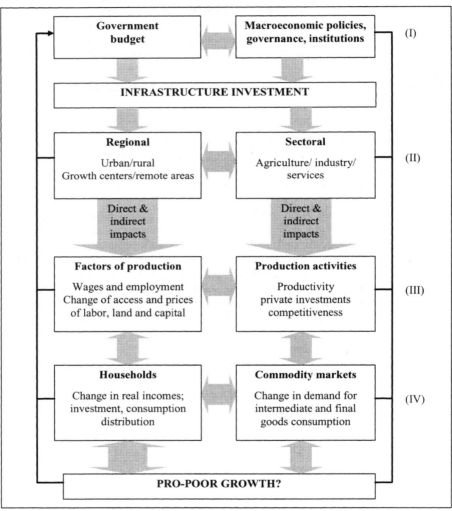

Source: Own illustration

Regarding *trade liberalisation*, it is increasingly acknowledged that in the short- and medium run losers from liberalisation do exist and that they should be compensated (WINTERS, 2000; BMZ, 2005B). To give the poor the opportunity to share the benefits of trade liberalisation, intra-country-trade barriers, such as high transaction cost, have to be reduced, human capital investments have to be made and the negative bias against agriculture in developing countries as well as in the trade policies of industrialised countries have to be reduced (BMZ, 2005B).[11]

Good governance at the national and local level is crucial for successful infrastructure investments. Accordingly, the 2005 Vietnam Development Report (VDR) documents the importance of decentralisation, the participation of local governments and authorities and the fight against corruption in the context of infrastructure (WORLD BANK et al., 2004). The quality and responsibility of decision-making at the different hierarchical level and the collaboration between them are important determinants of good governance (TACOLI, 2003). Good governance is not only crucial during the construction phase of infrastructure but also in the medium to long-term maintenance and service provision. Accountable and decentralised governments can support the local population in taking advantage of newly created opportunities, make investments in the region attractive and help to retain added value from local production (TACOLI, 2003). According to the same source, regulating the remaining natural monopoly elements of an infrastructure sector is the main engine of the distributional effects of infrastructure reform. The specific design of regulation and the competence, independence, and skills of its implementation agency determines the extent to which the efficiency gains achieved by reform can be passed on to users. Good governance can thus be identified as a key to successful development. Given this macroeconomic and institutional setting as a precondition for successful contribution of infrastructure investments, such investment can have spatial and sectoral dimensions.

(II) Regional and Sectoral Dimensions

Given the financial limitations of government budgets and the goal of poverty reduction, spending and investment have to be carefully targeted in order to achieve optimal poverty reduction. An increase in the spending towards one region or sector equals the decrease of the spending towards another. Such *government intervention* in the regional and sectoral balance of the economy, can have direct and indirect impacts on income distribution and poverty

---

[11] Anti poor bias exists in many developing countries through anti-agricultural price bias. This is often caused by exchange rate manipulation or domestic measures to artificially reduce food prices for urban consumers (see e.g. EASTWOOD AND LIPTON, 2001).

reduction. LARSEN et al. (2004) assess the impacts of the 1996-2000 Vietnam PIP by province and sector. They find a substantial contribution of public investments to poverty reduction in Vietnam, but suggest that the quality rather than the by international standards already relatively high quantity has to be increased. The estimation of the actual contribution of the overall PIP from a regional and sectoral perspective indicates that the poverty impact at the provincial level in transport and water and sanitation is much higher than the average impact of PIP. Furthermore, the impacts are progressive in a sense that the poverty reduction impact in poorer provinces is higher (LARSEN et al., 2004). This finding suggests that investments in transport and water and sanitation can be an effective tool in poor provinces. Government spending in production related infrastructure such as power and transportation can compensate for market imperfections, which are a main cause for regional disparities (GAILE, 1992). Similarly supporting public investments in lower potential areas are the findings of FAN AND HAZELL (1999). Results suggest higher marginal impact on agricultural production and poverty alleviation occurs in less favoured (rain fed versus irrigated areas) in China and India.

From a *sector perspective*, several studies find that agricultural growth has been more pro-poor than industrial growth. This can be largely explained by the fact that a large share of the poor depend on agriculture. Therefore, making improvements to agricultural productivity and farm incomes are central to poverty reduction (TIMMER, 1997; EASTWOOD AND LIPTON, 2001). Intuition thus clearly suggests that if poverty reduction is the prime target of development policy, the agricultural sector has to play an important role. However, as MELLOR (1999, p.11) notes "nowadays we have departed so far from the agricultural emphasis that a more sophisticated approach to the data" and "this (substantial reduction in ODA towards agriculture) is of course a radical turn away from pro-poor growth". Investments in the agricultural sector, including irrigation infrastructure, rural roads, extension and research can lead to improved productivity and thus enhance economic growth in rural areas. By comparing for example poverty reduction processes in India and China, it becomes clear that slower growth in the agricultural sector in China was one of the major reasons behind slower poverty reduction (VON BRAUN et al., 2005). Furthermore, evidence from India suggests that growth in non-farm sectors might be hampered by poor initial conditions in terms of farm productivity, rural living standards and education levels (RAVALLION AND DATT, 1999). Furthermore, output and employment multiplier effects of agriculture are important determinants since they tend to be oriented towards locally produced goods and services and thus stimulate a sector largely unaffected by international markets (MELLOR, 1999). For an agricultural production function estimated for Vietnam, FAN et al. (2004) find high significant levels for variables related to public spending including education, irrigation, roads and access to telephone and electricity. The same applies for these variables if tested on rural non-farm employment.[12] Furthermore, investment in agricultural production enhancing measures contributed not only to growth of agricultural output, but also to rural poverty reduction and regional inequality (FAN et al., 2002). From a sector perspective it can thus be concluded that the agricultural sector seems to have large poverty-reducing potentials. However, the targeting of specific measures has to be country or even region specific.

The *regional dimension* of infrastructure investments is gaining in importance, since intra-country disparities in many countries such as China, Vietnam, India, Russia, Mexico etc. are on the rise. The following paragraph thus shortly reviews theory explaining geographic disparities by concentrating on infrastructure investments towards less favoured and remote areas.[13] Geographers distinguish between first nature and second nature geography. Regions with advantages in first nature geography are well endowed with or geographically closed to rivers, coasts, borders and ports. Second nature positive geographic effects refer to increasing returns to scale effects caused by agglomeration, higher productivity and self-enforcing virtuous circles (VENABLES, 2005). Along the same line, geographic economists differentiate between "push" and "pull" factors explaining the sorting of economic activity across space. Push factors include urban amenities and economies of scale effects. Pull factors include transportation costs, diseconomies of scale and congestion effects (ROSENSTEIN-RODAN, 1943; HIRSCHMAN, 1958; CITED IN TIMMINS, 2005). These factors lead to agglomeration effects, drawing in more population and creating new employment.[14] Geographic characteristics of a country or region are thus generally regarded to have a direct and significant influence of its developmental state. According to this "geography hypothesis", the availability of geography-related resources and the possibility of their productive use determine development (HEMMER, 2002). Geographically disadvantaged regions in developing countries have some common characteristics: these include geographic remoteness, unsustainable population growth, low quality and quantity of agricultural land, a lack of physical

---

[12] In this paper, FAN et al. (2004) model poverty as a function of growth in agricultural production, changes in rural wages, growth in rural non-farm employment and changes in agricultural prices. The second equation models agricultural production as a function of conventional inputs and public investment variables such high yielding crop varieties, irrigation, roads etc. Finally, rural wages and non-farm employment are modelled as functions of growth in agricultural production as well as public investment variables.

[13] That does, however, not exclude measures for extremely disadvantaged areas unresponsive to such measures to facilitate migration through education etc.

[14] However, important questions regarding the relationship between spatial inequality and development have to be further investigated (i) what are the forces that tend to concentrate growth in a few regions (ii) what are the forces for dispersion (iii) how does the balance between these forces evolve during the development process (iv) what is the role of migration in the progress remain (KANBUR AND VENABLES, 2005).

infrastructure, unfavourable climatic conditions, low human capital endowments and problems with governance. These disadvantaged regions are often rural and tend to have high shares of poor. The majority of these poor depend directly or indirectly on agriculture. Due to the geographic conditions, however, agricultural production and marketing potentials are limited. In addition, population growth can lead to growing pressure and overuse of natural resources further undermining the development potentials of these regions. Moreover, spatial and regional divisions often go hand in hand with political and ethnic tensions and their persistence or increasing might undermine social and political stability (KANBUR et al., 2005). Such regions have also often been neglected by central governments, leading to insufficient institutional and physical infrastructure and market access. In sum, geography thus influences the competitiveness of a region in two main ways: production costs and transportation costs.

However, spatial economic disparities are common not only in developing countries. They are also a common feature of industrialised countries. Nonetheless, contrary to developing countries, extensive redistribution schemes such as structural fund in the European Union (EU) buffer the regional disparities and support disadvantaged areas through various transfer schemes. In both cases, however, public spending constitutes one important tool for governments to reduce poverty by targeting specific regions and groups. Economic growth and prosperity on the national level should therefore directly benefit the central governments budget and thus its ability to redistribute national income to disadvantaged regions or persons.

The role of infrastructure for disadvantaged regions has been examined in several studies. JACOBY (2000) finds in a case study for Nepal that rural infrastructure can contribute much to economic development and bring about substantial benefits for poor households. However, the study also emphasises that this kind of public investment can not be targeted efficiently and thus can not contribute to reducing income inequality. However, CALDERON AND CHONG (2004) show in their empirical investigation of 100 countries that the quality and quantity of infrastructure (roads, railways, telecom and energy) are negatively correlated to income inequality, effectively having a positive impact towards more equal income distribution. FAN and CHANG-KANG (2005) underline the importance of investing in low-quality and rural roads. They find for China that rural roads will generate larger marginal returns, reduce poverty and regional development disparities more per yuan invested than investments in high-quality roads. HEIDHUES and SCHRIEDER (1993) find that access to credit is significantly affected by the permanent accessibility of villages. Adding to these positive impacts of infrastructure, VAN DE WALLE (2002) emphasises the important role of non-monetary benefits for poor people. Qualitative research in the form of participatory poverty assessments (PPA) confirm that the poor value infrastructure as an important factor improving their lives. Perceived benefits include improved mobility, security and health in a PPA in India (DFID, 2002).

The specific role of roads in the context of market opening and price transmission is further examined in section 2.2.3.

From the geographic perspective it becomes clear that strategies that aim at PPG and poverty reduction have to focus on regions, where the poor live. Infrastructure can contribute to reducing spatial disparities by increasing productivity and reducing transaction costs.

(III) Factors of Production and Production Activities

When assessing the impacts of infrastructure from a poverty perspective, the identification of changes in factor markets is clearly important. In general, the poor tend to be less endowed with all factors of production, including human capital (expressed as unskilled labour), land and capital. For the factor dimension of infrastructure it is also useful to differentiate between direct and indirect impacts: access, quality and cost to infrastructure for factors of production activities, where the poor are directly engaged or access, quality and cost to infrastructure for factors of production activities, where the poor are indirectly affected. *Direct or demand-side effects* of infrastructure occur predominantly in the short and medium term and explicitly during the construction period. A crucial determinant of the regional impacts of infrastructure construction is its demand for local labour, goods and services, which can be driving forces of regional development. Empirical evidence on *indirect effects* confirms that physical capital such as roads may enhance labour productivity. AGENOR et al. (2005) identifies two major channels through which public investments can affect economic growth. First, public investments can increase productivity growth and thus have an impact on production output growth. If there is enough complementarities between the additional services provided by the investment in infrastructure it might increase private capital formation and will also make the stock of private capital more productive (AGENOR et al., 2005). Another indirect channel through which improved infrastructure (roads, telecommunication) and therefore communication possibilities can raise productivity works via the expansion of banks lending to farmers and farmers buying fertilizer, increasing yields (WORLD BANK, 1994).

Both the direct and the indirect effects cause at least two *impacts on production*: activating the regional economy and attracting new investors who will set up new businesses. The creation of new economic opportunities and the productivity enhancement of existing economic activities play a significant role in development. In the case of rural economies experiencing investment in large-scale infrastructure, the intensification and specialisation of agricultural production and the expansion of off-farm business activities to remote areas, such as trading, small-scale manufacturing and tourism, can contribute to an economic development (JBIC, 2003). However, the supply-side effects occur generally in the longer term – the earliest when the project is implemented – and often in broader spheres, which makes their benefits less obvious and the evaluation more difficult (WORLD BANK, 1994; DFID, 2002).

In his seminal paper on the role of infrastructure for economic growth, ASCHAUER (1989) finds that the productivity decline in the USA in the seventies was at least partly due to underinvestment in infrastructure. PAU (2003) estimates cost functions incorporating public investments in infrastructure for the private sector using time series data from 1968 to 1996. The study comes to the conclusion that public infrastructure has a significantly positive effect on productivity in private sector industries. This conclusion is supported by a number of other studies including DEMETRIADES AND MAMUNEAS (2000), VON OPPEN AND GABAGAMBI (2003) and DEICHMANN et al., (2000). Transportation infrastructure plays the most direct role in this process, because of the straightforward links between road infrastructure and transportation costs (MINTEN AND KYLE, 1999; LIMAO AND VENABLES, 2001).

(IV) Households and Commodity Markets

The nature and impact of infrastructure investments for poverty reduction depends upon the *characteristics of the poor*. For agricultural households, income is largely determined by the access and availability of production factors, inputs and prices. For non-farm households, labour income is determined by employment opportunities and wages Five channels can be identified through which these households are affected by economic infrastructure such as roads: commodity price changes and the availability of goods, factor prices changes and employment effects, growth effects caused by changes in incentives for investment and innovation, vulnerability and short run risks to negative external shocks and government income and redistribution (WINTERS, 2000).[15] Since households tend to be more specialised in income than in expenditure, factor markets might be the most important linkage between trade and household welfare (REIMER, 2002; HERTEL AND REIMER, 2004). The main channels captured by the general equilibrium models through which households are affected by LSI are commodity price changes and factor income changes. Due to the fact that the poor spend a large part of their income on food and are by the same time often producers of food, lower food prices have a particularly large effect. A decrease in prices leads to higher real incomes of households and lower production costs for local activities. This stimulates

---

[15] Winters formulates these impacts on households for the case of trade liberalisation. However, due to the comparable price effects, they are equally applicable to large-scale infrastructure investments, especially roads.

demand for locally produced goods and services and alters their comparative advantage. The size of these impacts clearly depends upon the nature of the consumption basket and market participation. For poor subsistence farmers for examples, impacts might be small. On the consumption side, this is due to the fact that such households rely to a large extent on home-produced food and that their consumption basket includes few traded items. On the income side, subsistence production activities are extensive and thus use few imported intermediate inputs. That means that without structural changes towards market-orientation and intensification, these groups are not likely to share the benefits of improved infrastructure.

The above outlined linkages between infrastructure investments, production, factors and households lead to *multiplier effects*. The basic mechanism can be described as follows: higher income generated by the infrastructure-induced economic growth leads people to spend more on consumption and investment, which in turn benefits further economic activities. The first round impacts follow multiplier effects in the subsequent rounds due to spending and investing the income generated in the previous round. The repetitive process of accumulation and distribution results in a circular flow of income that eventually trickles down to the poor. The size of the multiplier effect depends on the marginal propensity of outflows, from the economic system. Consequently, it holds that the more the project and the population spend on locally produced goods and services, the greater the multiplier effect. The central coefficient in the context of poverty alleviation is therefore the share allocated to the products and services provided by the poor. Hence, the circular flow of income determines the sustainability of poverty reduction and the success of pro-poor investment.

The CGE model presented in chapter 4 mathematically links these sectors, factors and institutions in order to quantify the impacts of selected infrastructure investments scenarios. In the following sections, the role of transportation in the context of non-tariff barriers, large-scale dams and investments are addressed in detail. These two types of infrastructure have been selected for more detailed analysis due to their importance for the study region.

2.2.3 Investments in Roads

Bilateral and multilateral trade liberalisations led to a substantial decrease in tariffs over the last two decades. As a result, the *effective rate of protection* caused by transport costs is for many countries considerably higher than those caused by tariffs (LIMAO AND VENABLES, 2001). The size of transportation costs depends on factors like the quality and quantity of physical infrastructure, geography, institutional regulations and the structure and functioning of the transport industry. A lack or bad quality of infrastructure accounts for 40 percent of predicted transportation cost for countries with coastal access and to up to 60 percent for landlocked countries (LIMAO AND VENABLES, 2001). In a rather anecdotal contribution, THE ECONOMIST shows that the price for a case of beer transported from the Cameroonian capital Yaoundé to a 300km distant location increases by 30 percent (THE ECONOMIST, 2002). The importance of road quality in determining transportation costs is analysed by MINTEN AND KYLE (1999). They find that the cost of transport doubles for dirt roads as compared to paved roads. Equally interesting is the finding in this study that other transaction costs including traders' wages are significantly higher on bad roads.

In a regional context, new roads to formerly secluded areas are thus in many respects comparable to national trade liberalisation and have similar impacts on markets. In addition, road access is a prerequisite for remote regions to share the benefits of national trade liberalisation. The aim of the following chapter is therefore to link these two topics and to provide some theoretical background on trade liberalisation and market opening in the context of remote regions. Economic theory suggests that open markets are better for growth in the long-run. The more specific discussion, on how far market opening, structural characteristics of economies and growth are causally linked and how growth affects household welfare is less obvious (RODRIGUEZ AND RODRIK, 1999, DOLLAR AND KRAAY, 2004; MILANOVIC, 2002; RAVALLION, 2004;). Even if these studies relate to comparisons between countries, several lessons can be learned for within-country market opening.[16] First, straightforward relations between market opening and household welfare do not exist. In fact, complementary measures in the field of macroeconomic policy, institution building and infrastructure in the context of successful liberalisation might play a similar or even more important role (RODRIGUEZ AND RODRIK, 1999; MCCULLOCH et al., 2001). Second, generalisations are hardly possible. Policy-relevant analysis thus calls for case by case studies that make use of household data (MCCULLOCH ET AL., 2001; REIMER, 2002) and even within countries, impacts of market opening vary significantly. Third, market opening is extremely difficult to measure. It can rarely be observed as a single phenomenon and the complexity of interrelations and causal relationships between different measures is difficult to disentangle (BERG AND KRÜGER, 2003). Finally, market opening might produce losers even in the long-run and developing countries often do not have the means to compensate them. Especially marginal groups such as ethnic minorities are more likely to be among the losers. They are often not the primary target group of government support programs, are less well endowed with capital and skills, their access to information and public services

---

[16] These studies use cross-country data. Results and implications are also applicable to regions within countries, since growth, income distribution and poverty play similar roles in both cases.

is often worse and they tend to live in remote areas (WORLD BANK et al., 2003, BAULCH et al., 2002).

An assessment of tariff and non-tariff barriers at the national boarder would only be of limited use for intra-country market opening scenarios. For remote areas with their generally higher transaction costs, an additional step in the *price transmission* model is particularly useful, because national market liberalisation might not affect isolated regions at all. In Mexico, for example, cuts of agricultural tariffs had no significant impact on remote areas due to high transportation costs (NICITA, 2004). Access to markets on the national level is therefore of increasing importance and growing intra-country disparities are seen as one cause of geographic, infrastructural and institutional disadvantages. These variables are to a certain degree dependent on each other and determine transportation costs to a large degree. In the following chapter discusses these variables in the context of market opening.

Figure 2.2 illustrates price transmission mechanisms of tradable goods and the three major "barriers" that separate remote households from the international market. Imported goods are distributed within the country and consequently face costs for transportation and trade. The world market price of good A is increased by tariffs and non-tariff barriers and affected by the exchange rate to result in the post-tariff boarder price (pb). Within the country, the good eventually faces domestic taxes, fees, regulations, compulsory payment procurements of authorities and transport costs to become the wholesale price (pws) (MCCULLOCH et al., 2001). From the distribution centre the good is moved to regional and local markets facing additional costs for trade and transport that largely depend on road conditions and trade structures.

Lack of physical infrastructure is an important factor in the price transmission model and acts as a barrier to trade. Additionally to insufficient transportation infrastructure, imperfect trade structures and inadequate institutional infrastructure effectively function as trade barriers and exclude particularly disadvantaged areas in developing countries from participation in national and international markets (ADB, 2002; MCCULLOCH et al., 2001; RODRIQUEZ AND RODRIK, 1999). Disentangling effects of infrastructure investments should ideally be done in a sector- and location specific way along the supply chain. Market opening, however, can also be seen as a practical outcome rather than a set of policies. This assumption is supported by the fact that isolated measures in the context of market opening can practically not be observed in real world affairs (WINTERS, 2002).

Figure 2.2 Price Transmission from World Markets to Rural Households

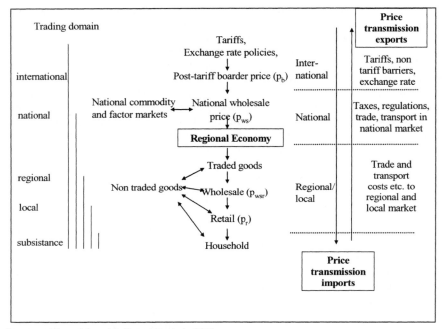

Source: Adapted from MCCULLOCH et al., 2001
Notes:
Pb: Post-tariff boarder price. Pwsr: Regional wholesale price. Pws: National wholesale price.
Pr: Regional retail price

In general, transportation infrastructure facilitates the exchange of goods, services and ideas. Their quantity and quality determines *transaction costs* and thus the prices of traded goods. This is easily confirmed by the examination of input-output tables, where infrastructure such as electricity and telecommunication is involved in most and transportation in virtually all production activities as inputs. Impacts of improved infrastructure can be summarised as reducing transaction costs and facilitating trade flows, enabling economic actors to participate in new markets, lowering the costs of inputs, creating employment including public works, enhancing human capital, improving environmental conditions, lowering the effective rate of protection of exports (JBIC, 2003; DFID, 2002). Roads might contribute to the reduction of inequality, thus leading to pro-poor orientation of growth (JACOBY, 2000). Apparently, these effects are not independent from each other. Multiplier effects of a road project in Vietnam are confirmed by an ex-post evaluation of the Hanoi-Hai Phong Highway. It shows that the upgrading of this major highway linking the capital with a main port has let to significant increases of foreign direct investment (FDI) inflows, a spread of economic growth to neighbouring provinces, an increase in domestic investment accompanied by job creation and a rise in the tourist industry (JBIC, 2003).

However, market opening can also have *negative effects* and the virtuous circle of public investments can also turn out to be a vicious circle. TACOLI (2003) makes the following points: prerequisite for this transmission is that the poor have access and are empowered to participate and make use of the newly emerging opportunities. For example, access to capital, land and labour may be more important than access to commodity markets. The increased availability of goods can also lead to crowding-out effects of domestic/local goods and services. Since imported goods are often cheaper than locally produced goods, local producers can not compete with imports. This is especially the case for small-scale enterprises, where the poor tend to work. On the export side, new opportunities arising from better infrastructure might be limited by the export trade structure, which tends to be controlled by international traders that do not lead to substantial value added at the local level and often stringent quality controls that exclude small-scale producers. In addition, a specialisation in few export products (in the case remote regions often primary products) increases the volatility of regional and household income. The non-economic impacts of market access are hard to classify as good or bad. However, expected impacts of market opening include changes through better access to information which has impacts on value system. Migration can lead to a shake up of hierarchical systems through new employment opportunities and increased individual independence (TACOLI, 2003).

The previous chapter has pointed out that investments in infrastructure in general and in roads specifically alone might be a necessary but not a sufficient condition for poor households to take advantage of improved access to markets. Research has shown that complementary policies are needed to support and enhance the positive impact of roads. A comprehensive approach to market opening work thus has to include a process in which physical barriers to trade are reduced (improvement of transportation infrastructure), imperfect markets (caused by lack of market places, competition between traders, lack of information) become more competitive and institutional obstacles (corruption; lack of appropriate laws, regulation and executive power) are removed. In addition, the poor have to be empowered to be able to take advantage of new opportunities and developments. Especially in cases of extreme poverty, however, low output and the absence of markets, public spending might only be effective in reducing poverty and altering market equilibria by direct transfer payments to the poor (TACOLI, 2003).

2.2.4 Investment in Large-Scale Dams

During the 1950's and 1960's, large dams were almost synonymous with development (WORLD BANK, 2000). More recently, large-scale dams are surrounded by controversies about their economic, social and environmental impacts and THE ECONOMIST (1999) speculated that India's Narmada and China's Three Gorges Dam might be the last of their kind. However, due to increasing *global energy demand*, dams might come back. Vietnam has announced to build a big dam in its Son La province, which will be subject of the analytical part of this dissertation in section 6.2. The large amount of capital associated with investments in large-scale dams raises the question on how far the implementation of such projects can contribute to the economic development of their surrounding environments. Due to the special characteristics and the manifold impacts of such projects, the following chapter aims at summarising the most important characteristics and impacts of such structures.

Dams generate 19 percent of world electricity and provide about 30-40 percent of worldwide irrigation (WCD, 2000). Economic growth and energy demand are highly correlated in emerging economies, which makes electricity generation by large-scale dams a matter a national interest. Dam projects have in many cases significant impacts on the national budget and the trade balance and might contribute to export earnings from energy intensive industries. An increased supply of electricity benefits particularly the industrial and mining sector and urban areas (WCD, 2000). *Advocates of dams* argued that the financial costs of dams are below that of other energy sources (WCD, 2000). Furthermore, construction, additional infrastructure and other follow-up initiatives (increased irrigation, tourism, fisheries etc.) contribute to a boost in local development. National economic growth is assumed to trickle down to the local level affected by large-scale dams. However, empirical evidence of socio-economic benefits for affected regions have been modest and mostly of temporary nature in the past (WCD, 2000). Case studies of successful project implementation underline the importance of participation of the local population, design and implementation of comprehensive follow-up planning, training of local people etc. (SCUDDER, 2005; WCD, 2000).

Opponents of dams argue that the building and operation of dams led to significant cost overruns, below-target performance and the lowering of living standards of millions of people worldwide. Accompanied by multifaceted environmental damage, these negative impacts have raised increasing awareness (SCUDDER, 2005; WCD, 2000). As a consequence, large contributors, such as the World Bank, cut its lending for large dams (LSD) by 90 percent between 1990 and 2002 (THE ECONOMIST, 1999).[17] The key problem and one of the major challenges surrounding large-scale dams is its diametrical impact on people. Particularly in the case of hydropower dams, benefits and costs are distributed unequally. While environmental and social costs have to be carried largely by the local population, benefits are mostly enjoyed by urban centres and industries (WCD, 2000). Moreover, the costs often have to be carried by poor and vulnerable groups such as indigenous people, because the site of those facilities is often located in remote and economically disadvantaged regions (WCD, 2000). These people often rely on common resources, lack legal titles and suffer disproportionally from relocation (WCD, 2000). In addition, relocations to environmentally already fragile areas can lead to a rapid erosion and fertility loss of land, thus threatening the most important factor of production in agriculture.

The framework linking infrastructure investments and poverty presented in section 2.2.2 can also be applied to large-scale dam investment. Of particular importance is the differentiation between impacts that occur on the local level and those that occur on the national level. In addition, it is useful to distinguish between direct and indirect effects of large-scale dams. Table 2.1 summarises the major impacts of large-scale dams. It becomes clear that while the negative effects occur mainly on the local level, positive effects such as improved electricity provision occur in other regions. In addition local impacts such as employment effects tend to be of short-term nature. The WORLD COMMISSION OF DAMS (WCD)[18] (2000) report characterises the direct impacts of construction as follows: (i) construction of dams and associated infrastructure benefits especially employees and shareholders of construction services and the suppliers of equipment and materials. However, immigrants provide most of the labour in construction works. (ii) benefits for local communities are often transient due to the time limited stimulus construction economy. However, a careful project planning might enhance the boom-phase and lead to long-lasting development. (iii) dam-related infrastructure can lead to a connection of local economies to national markets. Long-term employment is generated for the maintenance and management of the dam facility. In any case, impacts of large-scale dams heavily depend on individual project design and the way how they are implemented. Impacts on the poor depend on the structure and diversification and linkages of the economy.

---

[17] According to the International Commission on Large Dams (ICOLD), a large dam is 15 m or more high (from the foundation). If dams are between 5-15 metres and have a reservoir volume of more than 3 million cubic metres they are also classified as large dams. Using this definition, there are more than 45000 large dams around the world (WCD, 2000).

[18] The following chapter draws on the WORLD COMMISSION ON DAMS Report (WCD, 2000).

Table 2.1   Impacts of Large-Scale Dams by Region

Local impact	National impact
- Loss of valley-bottom land	- Capital investment
- Resettlement	- Electricity provision
- Income from employment directly related to the dam	- Energy intensive sectors
- Indirect effects from increased local demand for food and services	- Flood control in downstream areas
- Environmental impacts	- Employment for migrant labourers
- Compensation payments	- Demand for equipment and materials
- Change in production systems: irrigation, fishery	
- Transportation infrastructure	
- Growth effects caused by changes in incentives for innovations and investment	

Source: own table, based on WCD, 2000

The cost-breakdown of a typical hydropower dam budget is about 60-70 percent for civil works, 25-35 percent for equipment and 5-10 percent for engineering (WCD, 2000). Theoretically, civil works could be provided by local firms and thus contribute to the local economy. Practically, however, the scale of the project is beyond local firms' capital and capacity resources (WCD, 2000). The majority of the jobs created directly occur in the construction and transportation sector through the activities on the dam, electricity plants and roads. However, despite the huge investment normally associated with hydropower projects, direct occupation effects tend to be moderate and limited to the period of construction. This is due to the lack of professional local service providers. Moreover, both road construction and the local production of construction materials have often no significant effect since they are not available in the necessary quantity and quality. Since a low industrial base allows only limited supply with locally produced intermediates, the value generated through their purchase is also limited (WCD, 2000).

Indirect employment creation can be expected through the demand for non-residential workers for food and services such as in mini-hotels, restaurants, food shops and entertainment. Dams might also lead to employment opportunities in tourism. The WCD report cites cases, where dams have led to job creation in tourism-related service sectors from few hundred to thousands (WCD, 2000, p.121). The agricultural sector can benefit through increased demand for basic food products such as rice, vegetables and meat might individually cause a considerable rise in income, a significant demand effect on the agricultural sector, however, can only be achieved by investments in this sector. In addition to the direct and indirect effects of the construction of dams, cost and benefits for the economy occur through the provision of irrigation and flood control. The economic benefit of irrigation depends upon incremental net financial/economic benefit, which depends on physical indicators such as additional area irrigated, productivity increases and cropping patterns (GITTINGER, 1982). Besides incremental production effects, indirect or multiplier effects occur through increased agricultural processing activities, trade private consumption etc. Due to the predominant role of the agricultural sector in rural areas, dam infrastructure development that considers the requirements of this sector has potentially high returns and can therefore make a major contribution to alleviating underemployment and poverty in rural regions (DFID, 2002; WORLD BANK et al., 2003; JBIC, 2003). The main parameter in assessing the benefits of flood control is the extent to which flood peaks in areas with considerable settlements, infrastructure and (agro-) economic activities in the flood prone zones can be reduced.

In combination with the above discussion, three conclusions clearly emerge in the context of dams and poverty. First, local and national impacts are distinct; positive impacts such as electricity provision and flood mitigation largely occur on the national level. Positive impacts on local poverty can therefore not be automatically expected. Second, labour and material for large-scale dams tends to be imported to the region, since local labourers and industries often lack skills and quality. Third, many impacts cannot be classified as good or bad per se. Impacts of large-scale dams heavily depend on individual project design, the way how it is implemented and the structure of the local economy. At the end of this chapter, Table 2.2 summarises some of the results discussed in sections 2.2.2 to 2.2.4.

Table 2.2   Overview of Results from Selected Studies

	Observed effect	Source
Investment in roads	Doubling of transport costs reduces trade volumes by 45 percent	LIMAO AND VENABLES (2001)
	Poor households living in communes with paved roads have a 67 percent higher probability of escaping poverty	GLEWWE et al. (2002), Vietnam
	85.5 of communes without access to roads were poor	FAN et al. (2004), Vietnam
	10 percent increase in market access leads to an increase in labour productivity of 6 percent	DEICHMANN et al. (2000) for Mexico
	Road investment increases	BINSWANGER et al. (1993)

	Observed effect	Source
	agricultural output with an elasticity of 0.20	for India
Investment in dam	Value added multiplier of 1.83, where 33 of the additional cents stem from direct and 50 cents from indirect effects.	BHATIA et al. (2003)
Investment in agricultural productivity	A one percent agricultural productivity growth lifts 0.56 percent of poor above the poverty line[19]	FAN et al. (2004) for Vietnam
	One unit increase in road investment increases agricultural production value by about three	FAN et al. (2004) for Vietnam
	Agriculture has a multiplier of 1.96 as compared to 0.37 in non-agriculture	TIMMER 1994 as cited by MELLOR 1999

2.3 Comparing Modelling Approaches and Choice

2.3.1 Tools for Infrastructure Investments Assessment

In general, public investments should benefit the people and contribute to regional or national economic development. The following two axioms can give helpful guidance on public investment decisions. The *Pareto principle* states that an investment is desirable, if it makes at least one individual better off and by the same time nobody worse off. In that sense, Pareto-improvement is theoretically also given, if those individuals that gain from a public investment project are able and willing to compensate the losers. In practice, however, the lack of financial resources or the nature of negative effects occurring from the project often restricts the complete compensation of incurred losses. The *Kaldor-Hicks principle* takes this reality into account by stating that the net benefit of a project is positive, if the winners would theoretically be able to compensate the losers. Several measures exist to evaluate the impacts of investment projects, which are presented subsequently.

The *Incremental Capital to Output Ratio (ICOR)* is used as an aggregate indicator of how efficiently public capital is invested. It is the amount of

---

[19] Road investment has the second largest return in this study, education ranks number one.

additional investment required to increase gross domestic product (GDP) by one unit or the reciprocal of the marginal product of capital. This aggregate indicator can also be used to assess the sectoral or regional performance of public investments. Given the availability of data, ICOR can thus provide important insights into the performance and efficiency of public investments. However, it can not provide insights into distributional and poverty impacts of investment projects. A more micro-level appraisal tool to infrastructure investments are *cost benefit analyses* (CBA). In fact, they are standard tools and appraisal agencies often rely on standard indicators such as the net present value (NPV) or the internal rate of return (IRR) (WORLD BANK et al., 2004). Project appraisals have become more comprehensive over time and look beyond financial aspects. Especially for large-scale infrastructure projects they consider environmental, cultural, social and other impacts. DEVARAJAN et al. (1995) argue that traditional project appraisals fail to take private sector responses and fiscal impacts into account. A major drawback of these tools is thus their inability to take macroeconomic and indirect impacts into consideration.[20] The understanding and quantifying of indirect impacts, however, can contribute to the designing of such large-scale infrastructures in order to achieve their full development potential.

Econometric analysis in the field of infrastructure and its impacts on the economy extends the conventional production function and makes use of cross-country and cross-regional data. According to this approach, output is not only a function of labour, capital and land, but also of infrastructure. FAN et al. (2004) extend this approach in the context of rural infrastructure and poverty by modelling poverty in a simultaneous equation system. Poverty is a function of growth in agricultural production, changes in rural wages, growth in rural non-farm employment and changes in agricultural prices. The second equation models agricultural production as a function of conventional inputs and public investment variables such as high-yield crop varieties, irrigation, roads etc. Finally, rural wages and non-farm employment are modelled as functions of growth in agricultural production as well as public investment variables (FAN et al., 2004). It is thus possible, to get insights into the relative impacts of different infrastructure variables on economic growth and poverty. Such analyses can give important insights into specific relationships and causal links. However, econometric studies using such production or cost function approaches are not able to capture indirect effects.

All three analytical tools presented above are partial models. ICOR, CBA and econometric models can not capture general equilibrium effects. An economy-wide model is needed in the landscape of economic tools for public

---

[20] See FITZGERALD (1978) for a comprehensive discussion of appraisal tools for public sector investments, GITTINGER (1982) for agricultural project assessment and WCD (2000) for financial, economic and distributional analysis of dams.

investment assessments. The WCD (2000) underlines this need exemplarily for dams by stating:

"A simple accounting for the direct benefit provided
by large dams, the provision of irrigation water, electricity,
municipal and industrial water supply and flood control
often fails to capture the full set of social benefits
associated with these services. It also misses
set of ancillary benefits and indirect economic (or multiplier)
benefits of dams projects"
(WCD, 2000, p.129)

These *ancillary and indirect economic impacts* do also exist for other kinds of infrastructures such as roads (section 2.2.3). In addition to the indirect effects, public investments and large-scale infrastructure projects have long term impacts on capital formation, on the cost of capital, the tax system and foreign trade patterns. From a regional perspective, such investment induced changes might have substantial influences on redistribution flows and regional development perspectives. Macroeconomic price and sectoral policies, which make no explicit reference to spatial dimensions, can thus be the most powerful influences between regions (TACOLI, 1998). Consequently, taking macro and indirect impacts of public investments into consideration can give additional important insights. I therefore suggest the use of the CGE framework. CGEs are in many regards predestined for such kind of analysis, since they can capture the inter linkages between production, commodity and factor markets, institutions and the recurrent state and trade and investments.[21]

2.3.2 Computable General Equilibrium Models

CGE models are able to quantify economy-wide changes of exogenous shocks by capturing transactions and transfers between different sectors and agents in the economy. Most importantly in the context of infrastructure investments, CGE models take indirect and macro economic effects into consideration. *Second-round effects or multiplier effects* are captured by CGE models, which is of particular importance in rural areas, where inter-sector and consumption linkages often have strong impacts on income distribution and poverty (BAUTISTA, 2000; BREISINGER and ECKER, 2006; WINTERS et al., 2004). In addition, macroeconomic variables such as balance of payments and government

---

[21] This suggestion has also been made by and FAN, 2003; BHATIA et al., 2003.

budget constraints can be captured by the model. Spatial aspects as well as distributional and poverty impacts of investments can be incorporated.

CGE models are in the tradition of input-output and linear programming models. Contrary to these planning models, CGEs incorporate *nonlinear relations* and *behavioural parameters* to define the behaviour of all agents in an economic system. In essence, CGE models use social accounting matrices as their parametric databases, defining the linkages and interactions between production activities, commodities, factor markets and institutions by linear and nonlinear equations. CGE models are thus powerful and comprehensive tools. However, their major strength of incorporating all major elements of an economy and link them with behavioural functions leads also to weaknesses. A *major criticism* is the use of constant elasticity parameters for consumption behaviour, substitution between factors and assumptions regarding trade. This weakness necessitates sensitivity analyses of simulation results, where the use of different elasticities and the comparison of alternative results can substantiate the results (SHOVEN AND WHALLEY, 1984). Another criticism of CGE models is the fact that results can not be statistically controlled. A solution to this problem could be the estimation of model parameters by using time-series data. However, such data is often not available in the required detail (BOWEN et al., 1998).

The theoretical structure of a comprehensive CGE model has been firstly presented in DERVIS et al. (1982). Early *application* of CGE models include ADELMAN AND ROBINSON (1978) for Korea and LYSY AND TAYLOR (1980) for Brazil. More recent applications of this type of model include WOBST (2001) who studied the impact of structural adjustment on Tanzania and LÖFGREN et al. (2004) who assessed prospects for growth and poverty reduction in Zambia. In general, CGE models have been applied to a wide range of issues, including tax policies, exchange rate policies and carbon dioxide emissions (CHAN et al., 1998; SCHWEICKERT et al., 2005; BEAUSÉJOUR et al., 1995). DIAO et al. (2005) use an inter-temporal CGE model to assess international spillovers, productivity growth and openness in Thailand. An example for the application of the CGE framework at the village level is provided by KUIPER (2005), who analyses the impact of rural-urban migration in China. The field, where CGEs have been most widely used is international trade. Examples include HERTEL AND WINTERS (2005) that analyse the poverty impacts for a dozen of countries under a potential Doha Round Agenda. ANDERSON (2004) and IANCHOVICHINA AND MARTIN (2004) analysed several WTO accession scenarios for China. In the Vietnamese context, JENSEN AND TARP (2005) incorporate a spatial dimension to assess the impacts of further trade liberalisation on poverty.

The main line of CGE models follows the *representative household approach* (RHA). RHA models incorporate households endogenously and as aggregate units into the model. A major criticism of this approach is that it neglects the intra-household group distribution of income and is thus not suitable for poverty analysis. As a consequence, several extensions of the basic model have been proposed in the context of poverty analysis. In general, micro-simulation and general equilibrium simulation with post-simulation analysis can be differentiated. The basic difference between these two approaches is that the micro-simulation approach incorporates the households endogenously, while the post-simulation or macro-micro synthesis uses two separate models in sequence.

Micro-simulation models incorporate large numbers of households endogenously into the macro-model. COGNEAU AND ROBILLARD (2000) use this approach by including 4500 households into a CGE model for Madagascar. Post-simulation analysis of impacts on household models varies in complexity on the household-model side. The basic idea behind this approach is to use the results of the macro model and to link them to a household model (REIMER, 2002). Generally such approaches have the advantage of incorporating a large number of households. One example is a study by DAUDE (2005) that links liberalisation results from the CGE model of the Global Trade Analysis Project (GTAP) to household survey data. Limitations of such studies include the fact that price transmission within a country is largely neglected, multiplier effects within the regional context are ignored and macroeconomic consistency does not exist.

BOURGUIGNON et al. (2003) compare results of an advanced version of a micro-simulation model with a RHA approach for different kinds of shocks and find that results might differ substantially. Their paper concludes that results and the nature of the bias vary depending on the circumstances and that the choice of the model once again depends on the specific case. It thus remains unclear, whether the higher costs of micro-simulation can be justified by more accuracy of results. The present dissertation uses a two-region CGE model combined with a post-simulation micro-accounting module for regional poverty analysis as presented in chapters 4.2 and 4.3, respectively. The two-region nature of this model overcomes major drawbacks of post-simulation analysis by incorporating regional differences in production, consumption and factor endowments.

CGE models that analyse the impacts of *investments*, however, are scarce. CONRAD AND HENG (2000) analyse aspects of bottlenecks in road infrastructure and assess congestion costs for the German economy. DUMONT AND MESPLÉ-SOMPS (2000) analyse the impact of an increase in public infrastructure spending on competitiveness and growth in Senegal. They model public spending via an increase of factor productivity (FP) and find that the choice of the method of financing is an important determinant for domestic price impacts. HADDAD AND PEROBELLI (2005) employ a spatially disaggregated CGE to assess the role of transportation costs for different regions of Brazil. SEUNG AND KRAYBILL (2001) use a CGE model for assessing the impacts of public investments on private investment, employment, output and household welfare. One rare example of a CGE model that explicitly takes poverty into account captures linkages between foreign aid, public investment, growth and poverty. By calibrating the model to Ethiopia, the amount of foreign aid to reach the MDG goals for the county is estimated (AGENOR et al., 2005).

The present analysis takes these studies one step further: first it combines spatial impacts explicitly with a poverty analysis module. Second, it concentrates the analysis of a specific sector (transportation) and a specific project (large-scale dam) to assess the impacts of infrastructure investment on regional poverty. The structure of the model used in this study is presented in chapter 4.

Summing up this chapter, it can be said that comprehensive assessments of the poverty impacts of public investments have to be informed by a variety of analyses. The above presented economic tools are *complementary* rather than substitutes for each other. For example, insights from econometric analyses on specific relationships and causal links can be used in the setup of more normative models. CBA can give information on actual financial costs of projects. CGEs can thus be used as a platform to incorporate insights and results from different data sources and conventional infrastructure appraisal tools. With this study, I attempt to contribute to the development of such a CGE approach to a comprehensive infrastructure appraisal tool.

3 Understanding Socio-Economic Development in Vietnam

The following chapter provides an overview of Vietnam's performance in economic growth, income distribution and poverty reduction on the national and regional level over the past two decades. Besides the generally positive developments that are usually highlighted in articles about the "emerging tiger" several concerns regarding growing regional disparities and future growth are discussed. A key issue in the allocation of public investments is whether to invest in regions, where returns to capital or where returns to social benefit are highest, respectively. The answer to this question depends on a number of factors, including the developmental state of a country, country specific patterns of growth, social and regional disparities and redistribution mechanisms. Against this background the chapter starts by reviewing developments in growth and poverty reduction by analysing the factors behind the successful development and potential weaknesses for future development. (section 3.1). Section 3.2 addresses the regional disparities, which are one of the major challenges for Vietnam's future development. The final section (3.3) of this chapter examines current public spending patterns in Vietnam and the PIP.

3.1 Was Growth Pro-Poor in Vietnam?

Vietnam emerged from a politically and economically isolated and poor country to a success story in economic development. The initialisation of the transition from a centrally planned to a market-oriented open economy was caused by a situation of huge budget and trade deficits, high inflation and critical food supplies in 1986. The Sixth Party Congress passed a reform package in December 1986, the "doi moi" program, which was characterised by decollectivisation of land, privatisation, legalisation of FDI, removal of price controls and trade liberalisation.[22] These reform measures led to an impressive development of Vietnam's economy, e.g. average GDP growth of 7 percent over the last two decades, trade volume increases of 9,400 percent between 1985 and 2002, FDI that accounts for about 40 percent of total investment and an export/GDP ratio of 59 percent (EIU, 2004; WORLD BANK et al., 2003). Weighted average tariffs of 15,9 percent (DIMARANA AND MARTIN, 2005) give an indication of the relative openness and advanced state of integration into the world economy. This integration process was accompanied by the accession to several trade agreements such as the ASEAN Free Trade Area in 1995, the

---

[22] See e.g DOANH et al. (2002) for further information economic development in Vietnam.

Asian-Pacific Economic Cooperation (APEC) in 1998 and a bilateral trade agreement with the United States of America (USA) in 2000. In addition, Vietnam is a WTO accession candidate (WTO, 2005).

However, the biggest success of the reform policies is the rate of poverty reduction that went along with the transition process. Vietnam achieved the *most rapid poverty reduction* among developing countries over the past 15 years. The average annual growth rate of 7 percent was translated into a national poverty rate reduction from 58 to 29 percent between 1993 and 2002 (WORLD BANK et al., 2003). Using the one dollar a day purchasing power parity (PPP) threshold, the percentage of population living below the poverty line was 13.6 percent in 2002.[23] If applying the 2USD PPP/day threshold, poverty in Vietnam stood at 58.2 percent in 2002. Taking these poverty rates and comparing them to a set of other developing countries, Vietnam ranks in the middle. Using the 1USD PPP/day measure, poverty in Thailand stood at 2 percent, in China at 16.1 and in India at 34.7 percent (WORLD BANK et al., 2003).

Figure 3.1 summarises major development trends in Vietnam between 1984 and 2002. Three major trends are observed: economic growth ranged between 5 percent in the early 1980's, peaked short before the Asian crisis and stabilised at around 6-7 percent from 2001 onwards. Poverty has dramatically decreased, but to a slower extent. Inequality, measured by the Gini-coefficient, rose from a low level of 0.32 percent in 1993 to 0.35 in 1998 to 42 percent in 2002 (WORLD BANK et al., 2003).

This development can be mainly explained by the relatively constant rate of GDP growth, rapid export and manufacturing growth, macroeconomic stability and healthy private investments as (DAPICE, 2003). However, regarding future developments several *weaknesses* and worrisome trends are observed. They include modest FDI inflows in comparison to the 1990's and the neighbouring country China, high corruption rates, sluggish financial and state owned enterprise (SOE) reform, major inefficiencies in investment allocation and increasing gaps in information technology developments (DAPICE, 2003). In addition, growing regional disparities between the growth hubs Hanoi and Ho Chi Minh City and the mountainous regions pose challenges for the future and are separately addressed in section 3.2.

---

[23] To be able to put poverty in Vietnam into an international perspective, it is necessary to use an expenditure threshold that is comparable across countries. A frequently used threshold is the one and two dollar a day line, which is measured at PPP. This measure takes differences in prices across countries into consideration. For Vietnam, the PPP deviation is about five, which means that a dollar in Vietnam buys as much as five dollars in the USA (WORLD BANK et al., 2003).

Figure 3.1 Vietnam - Key Developments in Growth, Poverty Reduction and Inequality

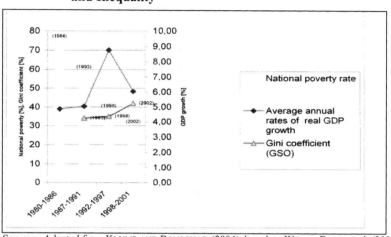

Source: Adopted from KLUMP AND BONSCHAB (2004), based on WORLD BANK et al. (2003)

However, for all its achievements, Vietnam gets a lot of attention from researchers, development institutions and private investors alike. One of the interesting questions for development economists is to identify the driving factors behind this success story and to extract lessons for less well performing countries and regions in the world. To shed light on this question, Vietnam's economic development can be divided into two phases: while in the first time span the redistribution of land and growth in the agricultural sector were the driving force, in the second time span gains were associated with job creation in the private sector and integration into international markets (WORLD BANK et al., 2003).

Major *reasons* for the successful development are seen in expanding choices and opportunities for people, carefully managed opening-up of the economy, favourable international commodity prices throughout the 1990's and considerable investments in health and education prior to reform (UN, 2002). In addition, the following factors are regarded as supporting factors in the transformation process: experiences from China, where economic transformation had been practiced since the end of the 1970's were used and learned from; favourable starting conditions including existing experiences with market economies in the south of Vietnam did exist and substantial financial support from expatriates and the favourable geographic location in one of the most booming regions of the world (KLUMP AND BONSCHAB, 2004).

Regarding the success in poverty reduction, GLEWWE et al. (2002) identify education, location and agricultural productivity increases as significant factors in the context of poverty reduction during the 1990's. LITCHFIELD AND JUSTINO

(2004) identify regional differences, access to institutions, infrastructure and education as key determinants for people to move out of poverty. Equally interesting is the analysis, to which extent economic growth in Vietnam has been pro-poor over the last two decades.[24] As the GIC in Figure 3.2 shows, all population percentiles experienced growth of income during the period of 1993 to 2002 between 5 and 9 percent. Even though the fourth and fifth quintile (with the highest income) experienced higher growth rates than the other population groups, per capita annual growth among the poorest quintile still grew between 5 and 7 percent. It has to be pointed out, however, that since the GIC accounts for percentage changes in income, absolute gains among the poor are relatively smaller. Following the weak definition of PPG, growth in Vietnam was clearly pro-poor. A poverty elasticity to economic growth also confirms the pro-poor growth nature of growth in Vietnam that was greater than -1 (KLUMP AND BONSCHAB, 2004).[25]

Figure 3.2   Growth Incidence Curve for the Period of 1993-2002

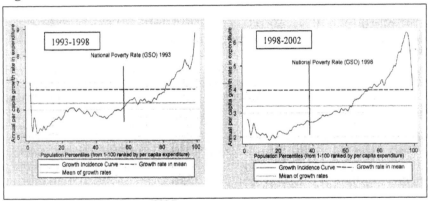

Source: KLUMP AND BONSCHAB (2004)

To continue this development path of high growth and poverty reduction, the Vietnamese Government announced in its CPRGS the target to bring the national poverty rate below 20 percent (SRV, 2003). This would put Vietnam ahead of schedule to achieve the MDG 1, which is to halve poverty by 2015. However, there are signs of decreasing growth elasticities to poverty reduction. High growth came at the price of widening regional disparities and little growth

---

[24] according to the weak definition of PPG (see chaper 2.1)

[25] KLUMP AND BONSCHAB (2004) calculate the poverty elasticities of growth for two periods (1993-1998 and 1998-2002) by using different poverty measures including the national and the food poverty line.

in remote poor regions. The CPRGS thus emphasises the important role of the mountainous regions. The high incidence of poverty suggests that Vietnam should put more emphasis on its mountainous region if it wants to further reduce poverty and reach the localised MDGs by 2015. The following chapter addresses this development at two levels and puts it into the context of geography and infrastructure.

3.2 Regional Disparities

Poverty in Vietnam is strongly associated with *geographic location*. To reduce national poverty rates, poverty has thus to be addressed where it is located. The objective of the following chapter is therefore to identify and characterise these poor regions. Vietnam is divided into 8 regions and 64 provinces. These regions from North to South are: the North-West, the North-East, the Red River Delta (with Hanoi), the North Central Coast, the South Central Coast, the Central Highlands, the South East (with Ho Chi Minh City) and the Mekong River Delta. This regional division follows geographical, climatic and structural criteria, which are highly diverse across the regions.

Figure 3.3 shows, poverty across all regions decreased between 1993 and 2002. However, differences in initial levels of poverty and the rate of poverty reduction vary strongly. While the North-East region showed the most impressive and constant performance, in five of the regions poverty reduction rates slowed down in the second period of 1998 to 2002. Poverty remains particularly persistent in the mountainous North-West region, where 68 percent of the population live below the poverty line and 28 percent suffer from malnutrition (WORLD BANK et al, 2003; GSO, 2004).s Poverty in this region fell only by 13 percent between 1993 and 2002, or 1.3 percent on an average annual rate.

On the other hand side, the Red River Delta, the South East and South Central Coast regions, where the three growth centres Hanoi, Da Nang and Ho Chi Minh City are located, have the lowest poverty rates in Vietnam. These three growth centres account for an impressive 54 percent of total GDP and 60 percent of GDP growth. They attract 89 percent of domestic investment, 96 percent of foreign direct investment and account for 80 percent of exports and 67 percent of government revenue (DOANH et al., 2002).

Figure 3.3   Poverty Rates by Region in Vietnam (1993-2002)

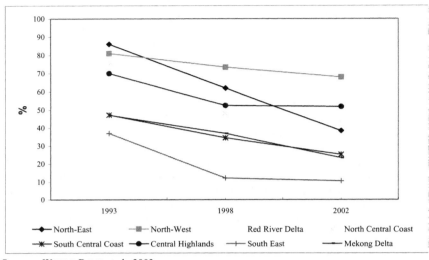

Source: WORLD BANK et al., 2003

A poverty map of Vietnam confirms that disparities in economic development are closely linked to geographic location. It suggests that the overall economic success does not seem to trickle down to all regions. These regional disparities are aggravated by the high share of ethnic minorities living in these regions. (MINOT, 2000; BAUTISTA, 2000; GLEWWE et al., 2002; WORLD BANK et al., 2003). In addition to their geographic isolation, these groups are characterised by a low level of education, a shortage of capital, slow adoption of technical innovations and insufficient and untargeted government policies contribute to the weak economic performance of ethnic minority groups. Furthermore, language and cultural barriers lead to a "different income generation model" and a "culture of poverty" (DAO IN BAULCH et al., 2002; THU AND WINTERS, 2001; VAN DE WALLE AND GUNEWARDENA, 2001).

Two different "paths to prosperity" for ethnic minority groups in Vietnam can be observed: the first is a strategy of economic and cultural assimilation that leads to the most successful economic performance. Groups that pursue the second path integrate economically, while retaining their cultural identity. Complete isolation leads to stagnant economic development and exclusion from rising living standards (BAULCH et al., 2002).

To address these *disparities*, region and group specific policies are required to include remote areas into the national socio-economic development and to prevent the increase of inter- and intraregional development gaps (VAN DE WALLE AND GUNEWARDENA, 2001; BAULCH et al., 2002). To combat poverty in the mountainous region of Vietnam, the WORLD BANK et al. (2003) suggest to learn from the experiences of China that faces similar problems in its mountainous regions. To tackle its problems in the mountainous regions China has introduced a multitude of policies, e.g. multi-sectoral rural development projects to include an integrated investment program: in: (i) upland agricultural development to increase upland agricultural productivity; (ii) labour intensive construction of rural roads, drinking water systems, small scale irrigation, and other rural infrastructure; (iii) provision of off-farm employment opportunities through a system of voluntary labour mobility for the upland poor; (iv) institution building and poverty monitoring; and (v) rural enterprise development. Improved access to basic education and health, and micro credit components, are included in some donor-supported projects (WORLD BANK, 1999A).

The United Nations (UN) also suggest to focus on the mountainous regions as a way to for Vietnam to achieve the MDG. The UN report (2002) "bringing the MDGs closer to the people" emphasises that a further reduction in poverty becomes increasingly difficult not only due to geographic, but also social, ethnic, linguistic and access to information. They calculated a provincial MDG index on 17 variables that measure different social and governance dimension underlying the MDGs (UN, 2002). The resulting index ranks provinces on a scale from 1 for good performance to 0 bad performance. The resulting indicators confirm the results of the poverty map. All of the three North-West provinces rank among the lowest quintile of the list, with Son La province ranking on the last place with a MDG index of 0.171.[26] In addition to its high poverty rate, this province is of special interest and thus in the focus of this dissertation. Son La is expecting large public investments in a hydroelectric dam and transportation infrastructure. It is expected that these investments will fundamentally transform the region and its economy. Using Son La as an example for a geographically disadvantaged and poor region, the analytical part of this study will address three major questions: first, how will market access, induced by improved rural and urban transportation infrastructure, affect economic growth and poverty. Second, which regional and national impacts can be expected from dam investment? Major characteristics of the study region and the respective scenarios that shed light on these questions are presented in chapter 5.

---

[26] The University of Hohenheim is cooperating with the Hanoi Agricultural University, the Thai Nguyen University of Agriculture and Forestry, the Vietnam Agricultural Science Institute and the National Institute of Animal Husbandry in a long-term interdisciplinary research program aimed at developing innovations that can contribute to sustainable land-use practices and rural development activities in the mountainous regions of Northern Vietnam. This research project known as "The Uplands Program" is focused on Son La province.

3.3   Public Investments and Infrastructure

To address regional disparities, the *allocation of public investments* is an important tool for governments. However, the spatial distribution of public investments in developing and developed countries faces a dilemma: should public capital be invested in fields where the returns are highest or the need is greatest? This trade off is also very critical to Vietnam's investment strategies. On the one hand, by international standards, Vietnam has high public investment/GDP ratios (WORLD BANK et al., 2004). On the other hand, regional disparities are increasing and poverty is persisting particularly in remote areas. Given the overall objective of poverty reduction, two major options arise from economic theory: the first is to favour investment choices with high financial returns and to redistribute government income resulting from high economic growth. The second approach is to judge investments according to their social returns to capital. Applied to Vietnam, the choice would either be to invest in the three growth centres Hanoi, Danang and Ho Chi Minh or in the mountainous regions. Regarding the agricultural sector, the choice would be between the delta regions (Red River Delta, Mekong Delta) and the mountainous regions. In addition to the spatial dimension of investment choices, trade-offs exists between the sectors in which to invest. Evidence from many countries suggests to gear investment more towards poor regions where infrastructure investments are less cost-effective or affordable (WORLD BANK, 1999A).

Public investments made a large contribution to economic growth and poverty reduction in Vietnam. The PIP is allocated according to 5-year plans. The PIP is a compilation of investment projects that are supported by line ministries, provincial governments and SOEs. They are funded by a combination of ODA, budget credits, banking loans and reinvested profits from SOEs (WORLD BANK et al, 2003). The sheer size of the PIP, which is one fifth of annual GDP, vastly more than the spending on target programs and more than the combined spending on health and education stress the importance of high quality and well targeting of PIP (WORLD BANK et al., 2003). The amount of public investments in Vietnam in relation to GDP has been steadily increasing from 6 percent in 1991 to 16 percent in 1999 and 20 percent in 2002 (WORLD BANK et al., 2003). Government spending by sectors in 2002 was allocated as follows: 4.4 percent of GDP was spent on transport and education, respectively. Public investments in transportation increased steadily, reflecting the huge infrastructure needs and the effort to accelerate economic growth (WORLD BANK et al., 2004). 87 percent of public expenditures in transport went into road infrastructure. 1.4 percent of GDP was allocated to rural development and 1.2 percent was spent on health (WORLD BANK et al, 2004). The agricultural sector in Vietnam receives 6 percent of public spending, yet accounts for 22 percent of GDP, 30 percent of exports and 60 percent of employment (WORLD BANK et al., 2004). Within the agricultural sector, irrigation investments made up 64 percent of the budget allocated in 2003, while forestry received 15 percent of total spending. Figure 3.5 presents two maps that indicate the per capita public spending and public investments.

Figure 3.4 Government Spending on Infrastructure and Services

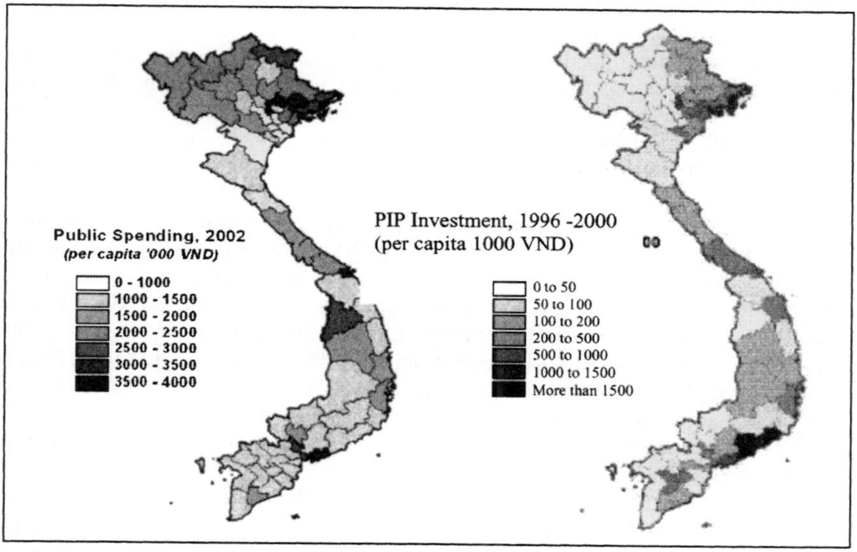

Source: WORLD BANK et al. (2004)

Large regional differences and a strong relationship between high poverty rates, high transfer payments and low public investments with growing distance to the three growth centres can be observed in all categories. Per capita public spending was highest in the Red River Delta and the Central Highlands. In the Northern Mountainous Region (North-West and North-East) public spending ranged between 1.5 and 2.5 million VND, which is about between 98 and 164 USD per capita. For public investments, the situation is even more distinct: while investments in the Red River Delta were highest, the North-West received between 0 and 80000 VND per capita. Regarding budget transfers, there are obviously also large regional differences. As expected, the growth hubs are not only the biggest recipients of public spending, but also the biggest contributors to this budget. The poorest provinces led by the North-West and the Central Highlands are the biggest net recipients.[27] Therefore, Vietnam seems to pursue a

---

[27] As indicated in Figure 3.4, data for the compilation of the different maps stem from different periods of time.

strategy of investing in the growth hubs where returns to investment are highest, compensating the poorer provinces via the returns of this investment. However, this approach might not be time consistent, since ever-growing productivity and income gaps will require growing transfer payments over time (WORLD BANK et al, 2003). Given the uncertainty of the long-term willingness of the growth areas to support the poor regions, it might be a more sustainable strategy to invest in poorer regions despite lower returns. However, attempts to scale up this contribution will have to focus more on targeted planning rather than the quantity of investments. Mainstreaming PIP on poverty issues at the project level can contribute to this process (WORLD BANK et al., 2003). Investments in large-scale infrastructure projects is regarded as key driving force in the Vietnamese industrialisation and modernisation process and as a fundamental support in combating poverty (DFID, 2002; JBIC, 2003; SRV, 2003). In addition to reducing poverty, especially transport and energy projects in Vietnam seem to have remarkable returns to investment of up to 30 percent (WORLD BANK, 2000).

Accordingly, the role of public investments in general and the role of infrastructure in particular have been given high priority in the CPRGS, which explicitly focuses on electricity, transport, irrigation and information access (SRV, 2003).[28] The original CPRGS was actually expanded to include a separate section on LSI, following a general trend of increased awareness of opportunities and risks for poverty reduction associated with LSI. The CPRGS defines LSI as "major important construction projects and investments serving production, business activities and social life, which can create strong and long lasting socio-economic development on a large scale" (SRV 2003, p. 67). The LSI section further states future directions for LSI in Vietnam. According to that, investments in infrastructure have to be designed to ensure spill-over effects, to contribute to the reduction of regional disparities, to be linked to socio-economic development goals, to increase accessibility of the poor to infrastructure services, to base project selection on regional, sectoral and socio-economical impact analysis (SRV, 2003).

Infrastructure is one prerequisite for PPG and the key question for Vietnam is how to expand the quality and quantity of infrastructure and at the same time choosing between different infrastructure options (WORLD BANK, 1999A). The present study will thus address two types of infrastructures that are highly topical in Vietnam: road infrastructure and large-scale dams.

---

[28] The CPRGS comprises seven parts: (i) Socioeconomic settings, current poverty situation, achievements and challenges (ii) Objectives and tasks of socio-economic development and poverty reduction for the period up to 2005 and 2010 (iii) Creating an environment for rapid, sustainable development and poverty reduction (iv) Large-scale infrastructure development for growth and poverty reduction (v) Major policies and measures to develop sectors and industries to promote sustainable growth and poverty reduction (vi) Mobilising and allocating resources for economic growth and poverty reduction (vii) Implementation, monitoring and evaluation of the poverty reduction and growth strategy.

4   Modelling Spatial Impacts of Infrastructure Investments

Intra-country disparities are not only on the rise in Vietnam, but are characteristical for many developed and developing countries. With the overall goal of reducing poverty, policy makers have an increasing interest in *regional development*. PRSPs are "rolled out" to provincial levels and MDGs are "localised" to account for region-specific characteristics and efficient targeting of policy measures and investments. The design of analytical tools to address spatial impacts is thus highly topical. The incorporation of spatial dimensions into CGE models can make them very useful tools to evaluate regional impacts of national policies as well as nation-wide impacts of regional policies. In addition, the combination of CGE models with micro-accounting models allows for poverty analysis. The construction and application of such a multi-region CGE with poverty module to infrastructure investments is innovative and presented in the following chapter.

The chapter has two sections: section 4.1 presents the compilation of the underlying model database, i.e. the SAM in detail. Section 4.2 introduces the specification of the CGE model, which is presented by concentrating on its specific features. Section 4.3 describes the structure of the micro-accounting module for poverty analysis and section 4.4 puts forward the technical details of the scenarios.

4.1   Constructing the Database

To identify key sectors and to analyse economic interlinkages between economic activities and institutions, SAM -based models are widely recognised tools (PYATT AND ROUND, 1977; ISARD et al, 1998). They combine macroeconomic consistency with household data and shed light on the structure of the economy, revealing transactions and transfers between production activities, commodities, factor markets and institutions. Indirect impacts like multiplier effects that arise in certain key sectors have a significant potential to contribute to the overall development of the economic system under consideration can be captured by SAM-based models.

Table 4.1   Basic Structure and Linkages of the multi-region SAM

	A-R	C	F-R	H-R	E-R	G	S&I	ROW	TOTAL
Activities by region (A-R)		Marketed outputs		Home consumption					*Gross output*
Commodities (C)	Intermediate inputs	Trans-action costs		Private consumption		Government consumption	Investment	Exports	*Demand*
Factors by region (F-R)	Value added							Factor income from ROW	*Factor income*
Household by region (H-R)			Factor income household		Distributed profits to households	Transfers to households		Transfer from ROW	*Household income*
Enterprise by region (E-R)			Factor income enterprise			Transfers to enterprises		Transfer from ROW	*Enterprise income*
Central Government (G)	VAT, producer tax	Sales tax, tariffs	Factor income government, factor tax	Direct taxes	Enterprise tax, revenues from state enterprises			Transfer payments	*Government income*
Savings and Investment (S&I)				HH savings	Enterprise savings	Government savings		Foreign saving	*Savings*
Rest of the world (ROW)		Imports	Factor income			Transfer to ROW			*Foreign exchange outflow*
TOTAL expenditure (exp)	*Activity exp*	*Supply exp*	*Factor exp*	*Household exp*	*Enterprise exp*	*Government exp*	*Investment*	*Foreign exchange inflow*	

Source: LÖFGREN et al. (2002)

The SAM is a comprehensive and consistent representation of macro and meso-economic accounts of a socio-economic system that captures the transactions and transfers between all economic agents. Table 4.1 shows the square tabular format of the SAM, where entries along the rows represent income of each account and entries along the columns correspond to expenditures. Total income and total expenditures of the same account are always equal. The function of each cell is described in the table and represents the relationship between a row and respective column account.[29] A detailed description of the SAM framework can be found in PYATT AND ROUND (1985), THORBECKE (1985, 1998), REINERT AND ROLAND-HOLST (1997) and ROUND (2005).

Despite their strength of providing a comprehensive database, SAMs are rarely constructed for the regional level mainly because of missing and insufficient data.[30] However some regional SAM exist and include, IFPRI (2003), BAUTISTA (2000) and BREISINGER AND HEIDHUES (2004) for Vietnam. The former comprises 16 provinces of Northern Vietnam for the year 2000 and has been derived from a national SAM. The paper concludes that Northern Vietnam is well below its potential for more diversified agricultural activities and finds scope for substitution of staple crops with more marketable and profitable crops. BAUTISTA (2000) built a SAM for the Central Highlands Region for the year 1997. The paper emphasises the role of macroeconomic policy in supplying equitable growth in Central Vietnam. BREISINGER AND HEIDHUES (2004) present a SAM for 2002, which is the first that concentrates on a single province in Vietnam. This SAM constitutes the basis of the database developed in the present dissertation and is further described and elaborated in the following.

In the setup of the provincial SAM, I follow ISARD et al. (1998). They describe "hybrid" SAMs as models that combine secondary data available at the regional level with national account data in order to compensate for the lack of regional data. In this context, a simple mean average analysis for Son La province reveals that the overall provincial intermediate consumption (IC) is 19 percent lower when comparing provincial data with national average data. Interregional production structures tend to vary significantly. The estimation of provincial SAMs in developing countries thus poses challenges as well as offering advantages compared to their nation or region-wide counterparts. Advantages include the relatively simple structure of the economy and the fact that major import goods are easily identifiable due to the lack of regional production (machinery, fuel, fertilizer etc. in the case of Son La). Moreover, export goods are often limited to primary products. Due to the small number of

---

[29] For instance, the top left cell entry in the matrix characterises the intermediate inputs, which constitute an expenditure for activities and an income for commodities.

[30] On the national level, many SAMs have been constructed to serve as basis for a wide range of impact analyses (cf. WOBST, 2001; TARP et al., 2002). See also section 2.3.

enterprises in key sectors, enterprise data can be directly incorporated into the SAM.

The regional SAM for Son La province is structurally comparable to a single-country standard SAM, i.e. the province is treated like a country, where the rest of the world includes both the rest of the country (ROC) and the rest of the world (ROW). The main difference is that markets are all regional, as are the institutions including households and the government. The disaggregation of production activities for the region and information on households is informed by regional input-output tables and representative household survey. The linkage to the "outside the region" is represented and accounted for by the ROC as well as the ROW. Interaction with ROC and ROW include trade in goods and services (imports and exports), factor payments (to and from outside the region), remittances to the region, transfers to and from enterprises and government transfers. This provincial SAM will serve as one part of the two-region Vietnam CGE model.

For the Son La SAM, a macro SAM has been built as the basis for a more disaggregated micro SAM in the first step. This SAM represents a snapshot of the economy in the year 2002. The micro SAM for Son La was subsequently set up in two steps. The first version made use of a variety of sources, including the Statistical Yearbook of Son La (GSO SL, 2003A), the Yearbook of Commercial Statistics for Son La (GSO SL, 2003B), the Agricultural Yearbook for 2000 (GSO SL, 2001), the Tableau of Provincial Intermediate Consumption and Value Added Data (GSO SL, 2003C), the National Input-Output Table for 2000 (GSO, 2003), the Handbook for the Implementation of the System of National Accounts (SNA) in Vietnam (GSO, 1998), the Vietnam Household Living Standard Survey (GSO, 2004) for the years 1997/1998 (GSO, 1998), a preliminary data survey of the Vietnam Household Living Standard for the year 2002 (GSO SL, 2003D) and the national accounts, bank finance and enterprises for Son La (GSO SL, 2003E).

The second version of the 2002 Son La SAM makes use of the full version of the Vietnam Household Living Standard Survey (VHLSS) 2002 (GSO, 2004) conducted by the General Statistics Office (GSO), Hanoi. I extend the rural/urban household disaggregation by a further subdivision according to ethnicity. The VHLSS 2002 for Son La Province comprises income and expenditure data of 350 representative households, including 45 urban and 305 rural households. Additionally, I disaggregate the original account 'crops' into the activities 'paddy rice', 'coffee', 'tea' and 'other crops' and subdivide the factor account 'self-employed labour' into an 'agricultural labour' account and a non-agricultural 'self-employed labour' account.

The Son La SAM comprises 28 provincial production activities, 32 commodities, four factor types, six household groups and private and public enterprises. The government receives income from two tax accounts and the rest of the world includes intra-national and international transactions. The SAM captures distinct ethnic characteristics by dividing the six household groups according to their ethnicity and rural/urban location. The ethnic groups defined here are Kinh (ethnic Vietnamese), Thai, Hmong and other ethnic minority groups in rural areas, and Kinh and ethnic minorities in urban areas. This household disaggregation results from the high share of ethnic minorities in the study region and their distinctive group-specific differences. Regarding factor markets, the SAM distinguishes between capital, skilled and unskilled labour. In the following section, I present the macro SAM entries. The next section describes the micro SAM entries.[31]

4.1.1 The Regional Macro SAM

Table 4.2 shows the Son La macro SAM. The respective entries are presented subsequently.

- Activities-Commodities: Marketed production (VND 3,852,700 million)
The gross output figure as reported in GSO SL (2003c; p.1) is used directly in the macro SAM. Within the double entry accounting system, this transaction corresponds to the total value of sales in the activity row at producer prices.
- Commodities-Activities: Intermediate consumption (VND 1,342,028 million)
Intermediate consumption for the province is taken straightforwardly from GSO SL (2003c; p.1).
- Commodities-Households: Private consumption (VND 1,937,499 million)
The figure for private consumption is derived from the balance sheet of the gross domestic product as documented in GSO SL (2003a; P. 26). It comprises the GDP share of households and cooperatives. An upward adjustment of VND 0.1 billion has been made in order to balance the SAM. This adjustment is in line with results of the VHLSS 2002 for the province that suggests a private consumption figure of VND 2.18 billion.
- Commodities-State: State consumption (VND 623,163 million)
State consumption is reported in the GDP sheet (GSO SL, 2003a; p.26).
- Commodities-Savings/Investment: Investment (VND 902,099 million)
Capital formation is documented in GSO SL (2003a; p.131).
- Commodities-ROW: Exports (VND 552,928 million)
Regional export figures to the ROW are available in GSO SL (2003a; p.162) reported as VND 72,274 million. However, supply and demand ratios of the micro SAM suggest this figure to be VND 552,928 million.

---

[31] These sections draw on the SAM presentation as documented in Breisinger and Heidhues (2004).

- Factors-Activities: Value added (VND 2,466,332 million)

Data to calculate the total value added for the province is documented in GSO SL (2003C); p.1). It is calculated as the sum of the compensation of employees (labour income from salaries, premiums and mixed income), depreciation, operating surplus and production taxes.

- Households-Factors: Compensation of employees (VND 2,114,667 million)

Wages, salaries and other benefits are reported in GSO SL (2003C; p.1), comprising mixed income and compensation of employees.

- Households-Enterprises: Distributed profits (VND 106,256 million)

Distributed profits are documented as 'premiums' in value added in GSO SL (2003C; p.1).

- Household-Government: Direct subsidies (VND 9,579 million)

Direct transfer payments (particularly pensions) are reported in the government expenditure balance in GSO SL (2003A; p.31). However, data from the preliminary VHLSS 2002 suggests that this figure underestimates the real transfers to households (GSO SL, 2003D). This issue will be further developed in the process of micro SAM estimation.

- Enterprises-Factors: Returns to capital (VND 210,692 million)

Gross profits are calculated by adding the operating surplus and the payments for depreciation (consumption of fixed capital) as presented in GSO SL (2003C; p.1).

- Enterprises-State: Enterprise subsidies (VND 34,732 million)

Subsidies for state enterprises are documented in GSO SL (2003E; p.74). No information is available for private enterprises.

- State-Activities: Value Added taxes (VND 44,340 million)

Value added taxes are reported in GSO SL (2003A; p.30).

- Government-Commodities: Trade taxes (VND 108 million)

Trade taxes are recorded in GSO SL (2003A; p.30).

- Government-Factors: Factor taxes (VND 22,271 million)

Factor taxes include land use tax, land transfer fees and other factor-related fees (GSO SL, 2003E; p.69).

- Government-Households: Income taxes (VND 7,951 million)

Personal income taxes are reported in the government revenue tableau (GSO SL, 2003A; p.30).

- Government-Enterprises: Enterprise taxes (VND 69,537 million)

Government revenue from enterprises includes income from direct enterprise taxes as well as income from state-owned enterprises (GSO SL, 2003A; p.30).

- Government-ROW: Transfer payments (VND 1,070,633 million)
By far the largest portion of regional government income stems from transfer payments from ROW (GSO, 2003/1, p. 30).

- Savings/Investment-Institutions: Institution savings (VND 902,099 million)
Total household savings are documented in GSO SL (2003E; p.62) as being VND 240,426 million. Enterprise savings are adapted to VND 69,631 million and provincial government savings are estimated at VND 547,366 million in order to balance the SAM.

- ROW-Commodities: Imports (VND 1,504,859 million)
Direct imports to the province are documented in GSO SL (2003A; p.165). Imports to the province are residually calculated as the difference of regional supply and demand of goods and services. This approach is supported by the fact that important commodities like chemicals, machinery and fuel are not produced in the province.

- ROW-Factors: Payments to ROW (VND 118,702 million)
Payments to ROW – including payments to other provinces in Vietnam (ROV) – consist of payments to centrally managed SOEs in the province (GSO SL, 2003C, p.1).

This yields the 2002 Son La macro SAM as presented in Table 4.2.

Table 4.2   2002 Son La Macro SAM (in billion VND)

	A	C	F	H	E	G	S&I	ROW	TOT
Activities (A)		3,853							**3,852**
Commodities(C)	1,342			1,938		623	902	553	**5,358**
Factors (F)	2,466								**2,467**
Households (H)			2,115		106	10			**2,231**
Enterprises (E)			211			35			**246**
Government(G)	44	0.1	22	8	70			1,071	**1,215**
Savings and Investment(S&I)				285	70	547			**902**
Rest of the World (ROW)		1,505	119						**1,624**
TOTAL(TOT)	**3,852**	**5,358**	**2,467**	**2,231**	**246**	**1,215**	**902**	**1,624**	

To gain more insights into distributional aspects within production activities, consumption patterns and institutions, a more disaggregated structure is required. Therefore, the macro SAM is disaggregated into 28 provincial production activities, 32 commodities, four factor types, six household groups and three enterprise types. Table 4.3 shows the SAM disaggregation in detail. Although, the locally provided data covered a lot of the necessary ground, it is obvious that imbalances occur in micro SAM building. Various methods of SAM balancing exist ranging from simple iteration procedures (RAS technique)[32] to more elaborated algorithms like cross entropy methods.[33] Alternatively, a third method is based on the modeller's knowledge of the local economy that allows her or him to adjust cell values within the SAM in order to balance rows and columns. For the present provincial SAM, the latter approach is preferred for the following reasons: the economy is relatively simply

---

[32] For more information, see THORBECKE (1998).

[33] The cross entropy method allows for incorporating errors in variables, inequality constraints and the modeler's prior knowledge about any SAM account. For further information see ROBINSON et al. (2001).

structured; trade can be assumed for the most part as supply - demand ratios and enterprise data can be used to substantiate adjustment decisions. When making adjustments this way, one starts at the top left of the SAM table, pushing the imbalances to the bottom right. Data on activity rows and columns is consistent in the case of the Son La SAM. The assumption of supply-demand equalisation via trade balances the commodity accounts. The savings account on the expenditure side and the account ROW on the income side were used to adjust the institution accounts. Those accounts were additionally chosen since complete and consistent data were not available here.

Table 4.3   2002 Son La Micro SAM Disaggregation

Activities/ commodities	Financial Services
Rice	Science and Technology
Coffee	State Management
Tea	Education and Training
Other Crops	Health
Livestock	Other Services
Forestry	**Factors/Value Added**
Fishery	Skilled Labour
Mining	Unskilled Labour
Food Processing	Capital
Textiles, Garment, Leather	**Households**
Forestry Products	Urban Kinh Household
Publishing and Printing	Urban Ethnic Minority Household
Other Goods	Rural Kinh Household
Cement	Rural Thai Household
Other Construction Material	Rural Hmong Household
Metal	Other Rural Household
Chemicals	Enterprises
Machinery	State owned Enterprise
Electricity, Gas, Water	Private Enterprise
Fuel and Lubricants	**Taxes**
Agricultural Services	Value Added Tax
Construction	Direct Taxes
Trade and Repair	
Restaurant and Hotel	**Government**
Transport	**Savings and Investments**
Post and Communication	**Rest of the World (ROW)**

The result of this estimation process is a fully balanced Micro SAM for Son La Province. The setting up of activity, commodity, factor, savings and investment and institutional accounts is discussed in the following section.

4.1.2 The Regional Micro SAM

• Activities-Commodities: Marketed production
Gross output for Son La Province is available for 43 sectors, including 12 agricultural, 3 forestry, three fishery, 16 industrial (incl. mining) and 19 service sectors (GSO SL, 2003A). An aggregation of those sectors yields to the 25 sectors of the micro SAM.

• Commodities-Activities: Intermediate consumption
Data for Son La exist for the year 2002 on IC by 20x4 sectors, a higher level of aggregation than the 25-sector classification of the provincial SAM. In disaggregating intermediate consumption, an important step is therefore the apportionment of IC across the 25 activities. IC data aggregates manufacturing to one single account. For the disaggregation, I rely on output shares of the relevant manufacturing activities and calculate their respective IC share from national average. The disaggregation of the 4-activity vector to 25 activities is a more demanding task. Again, I rely on the national 2000 input/output (I/O) classification of IC (GSO, 2003). In this process, the values of the local 4-sector vector (the respective provincial sub-sector totals) and the 112x112 national vectors are used to fit the provincial production structure. This is possible since the I/O accounting methodology on the provincial level resembles the one on the national level and is based on the System of National Accounts (SNA) (GSO, 1998). Intra-sectoral intermediate input use might vary on the provincial and national level. This variation within the 4-sector vector is assumed not to influence the results significantly. The disaggregation of the 'crops' account is documented separately in section 3.

• Commodities-Households: Private consumption
The disaggregation of the household accounts and the corresponding home consumption accounts that capture the opportunity value of the consumption of self-produced goods (valued at producer prices) used data from the VHLSS 2002. In Son La, 350 households were representatively interviewed for various living standard indicators including both income and consumption expenditure data. The additional survey of communities distinguishes between urban and rural areas and was merged with the household survey. Of the 45 urban households interviewed, 26 were Kinh households, while the remaining households were grouped into the urban ethnic households account. A decomposition of the latter according to their ethnic identity was not feasible since the sample size of the living standard survey of each urban ethnic household group was too small to obtain realistic results. In order to base the

analysis on a large sample size and thus to avoid overall distortions, the consumption expenditures of the ethnic households was calculated as the difference between the aggregation of all urban households less those of urban Kinh households. The VHLSS 2002 sample size of rural households consisted of 305 households, which incorporated 41 rural Kinh, 152 rural Thai and 35 Hmong households. Again, the difference in the consumption expenditures between all rural households and that of the named households groups was assigned to other rural households.

- Commodities-State: State consumption

State consumption is documented for 20 sectors in GSO SL (2003E; p.70ff) and straightforwardly applied to the micro SAM. State consumption of manufacturing goods was disaggregated according to respective output figure shares.

- Commodities-Savings/Investment: Investment

Investment defined as net capital formation is defined for 20 sectors in GSO SL (2003A; p.131). Manufacturing is again disaggregated according to output shares. This is a simplifying assumption. However, it is not assumed to affect analytical results as long as they do not directly deal with investment patterns in manufacturing sub-accounts.

- Commodities-ROW: Exports

Exports to the ROW are documented in GSO SL (2003A; p.162). Furthermore, I assume that excess local production is exported to the rest of Vietnam (ROV). Major export goods are limited to primary products, mainly tea, coffee and. maize. Trade flows to ROV and ROW cannot properly be differentiated and are therefore merged to one single trade account, i.e. ROW.

- Factors-Activities: Value added

Value added data is straightforward to apply for labour (including salaries and income from self-employment) and capital, namely in the form of operating surplus, depreciation and production taxes across 20 sectors. Only for the manufacturing sector, no disaggregated data was available. Income was shared out according to the number of employees and capital was distributed to the sub-sectors according to their share of gross output. Operating surplus and depreciation in manufacturing was estimated by using enterprise data. The mapping of factor incomes into the account 'crops' is documented separately in later in this chapter.

Alternatively, labour is divided in skilled and unskilled labour. This disaggregation facilitates comparisons with the national SAM and is more useful for analytical purposes. However, there is no value added data on the provincial level available that differentiates by skill. I therefore assume that the labour shares by skill and across sectors equal respective national averages. National averages are derived from the national SAM (TARP et al., 2002). Land is not explicitly defined in value added data. I make the assumption that in the case of the agricultural sector, value added of capital equals value added land. Capital expenditure of activities is therefore directed towards the newly created land account. This approach can be justified on two grounds: (1) agriculture in Son La province is very capital extensive (2) most of the capital is sector specific and immobile and thus closely linked to the land.

• Households-Factors: Compensation of employees

For the disaggregated factor income matrix, I rely on the VHLSS 2002 (GSO, 2004). The figure in the macro SAM varies from those of employed, self-employed and agricultural labour to households in the micro SAM (GDP at factor cost). Income from self-employment and from employment was directly calculated from the VHLSS 2002 for the six household groups. Alternatively, labour income of households is disaggregated by skill. I use the education level of the household level, classifying household heads with no or only primary education as "unskilled" and from lower secondary on as "skilled". Household income from capital and land lease is originally summed up in the capital account. Income from land is not straightforward since a land lease market does virtually not exist in Son La province. I therefore make the following assumption: only rural households earn income from land. Consequently, value added from capital is redistributed to land among rural institutions. Some upward adjustment is made across all rural households to reflect the match the value added data on land. The 'Savings & Investment' (S&I) account was subsequently used to equalise imbalances of household income and expenditure.

• Households-Enterprises: Distributed profits

No information was available. Distributed profits are therefore assumed to be included in the factor payments of enterprises to households.

• Household- Government: Direct subsidies

Direct transfer payments from the state, namely pensions and other subsidies, are listed in the VHLSS 2002 and are straightforward to apply to the household groups.

• Enterprises-Factors: Returns to capital

Operation surplus and consumption of fixed capital is available for 20 sectors from the GSO SL (GSO SL, 2003c). Manufacturing, again, had to be disaggregated relying on gross output shares. Income from the government was given an upward adjustment to balance the enterprise account.

• State-Activities: Taxes

Government revenue in taxes is defined in GSO SL (2003a; p.37) and GSO SL (2003e; p.10). Detailed information is available for the value-added tax across the 20 commodities, activity taxes across 26 activities and enterprise taxes for state-owned and private enterprises. The direct tax share between the household groups is derived from the VHLSS 2002. Other income includes subsidies from the national government (GSO SL, 2003A; p.10), which is accounted as transfers from ROW and from capital.

• Government -ROW: Transfer payments

The income from the ROW figure also includes annual payments of the neighbouring Hoa Binh Province. In practice, it is the compensation for the Hoa Binh hydroelectric power plant and its impacts on Son La Province (GSO SL, 2003E; p.69).

• Savings/Investment-Institution: Institution savings

Income from savings is derived from the macro SAM and adopted in order to balance the micro SAM.

• ROW-Commodities: Imports

Trade can be subdivided into trade with ROW and trade with ROV. Direct imports from ROW are documented in the Statistical Yearbook of Son La (GSO SL, 2003A; p.165-167). The imports from ROV including indirect imports are calculated as residuals from the supply-demand balance sheet. This assumption holds, if I assume that stocks do not change. Major import goods are easily identifiable due to the lack of regional production as demand-supply ratios (machinery, fuel, fertilizer, etc.). Again, trade with ROV and ROW is merged to one single account due to data constraints (i.e. ROW).

• Agricultural activity disaggregation

The disaggregation of the original SAM production activity account 'crops' in 'paddy rice', 'tea', 'coffee' and 'other crops' was not straightforward. The lack of economic data in Son La necessitated some assumptions and derivation from national sources. The task behind disaggregating this account was to maintain close alignment with existing provincial data in order to achieve a high degree of realistic correspondence. Furthermore, the methodology of adjusting the national average data on the provincial level was designed to guarantee transparency and avoid inter- and intra-account distortions. Thus, the reference values are the gross output (GO) of agriculture as total, the GO of the single cropping systems, and the total IC as well as the total value added (VA) of each cropping system. The income and expenditure distribution within each IC and VA account was adapted to these values.

The Statistical Yearbook 2002 of Son La Province provides data on GO, IC and VA for crop cultivation as an aggregated account as well as explicitly the GO for rice. Further provincial data is available for the production output in quantity units of all cultivated crops including coffee, tea and sugar cane. Production outputs multiplied with the producer prices, which were obtained from the VHLSS 2002, lead to the respective GOs. The relative GO share of sugarcane compared to that of the remaining crops is needed to reflect the intra-IC and intra-VA structure of the account 'other crops' at the provincial level.

On the national level, a highly disaggregated I/O classification based on producer prices with a 112 x 112 vector IC coefficient matrix exists for 2000

(GSO, 2003). Since newer detailed I/O-data was not available, it is assumed that the intra-IC did not change considerably within two years. The I/O classification includes the relevant national average values for the agricultural production accounts 'paddy rice', 'coffee', 'tea', 'sugarcane' and 'other crops', which were used to apportion the IC shares of the provincially cultivated crops. The total provincial IC and VA of the account 'other crops' in the Son La SAM were obtained by aggregating the total IC of sugarcane, which is explicitly listed in the national I/O matrix, and that of other crops of the national I/O-table according to their GO shares. This aggregation assumes that the provincial composition of the 'other crops' account is similar to that on the national level.

The 112-sector IC of the national I/O matrix is subsequently assigned to the 32-sector IC of the 2002 Son La SAM and the 4-sector national VA to the 3-sector provincial VA. The total IC of each crop was calculated according to the proportional distribution on the total IC of all crops. This distribution is in turn derived from the relative share of the total IC on the total GO of each crop on the national level and adapted according to the GO of each crop on the provincial level. As a result of this adjustment procedure, the proportional intra-IC structure of the 2002 Son La SAM is consistent with the intra-IC structure of the national I/O matrix. The relative share of the VA from the GO is the difference between the relative share of the IC and the total GO. It yields a share of the total provincial IC from the total provincial GO of each crop, which is about 32 percent lower than the nationwide proportion. This implies that agricultural production in Son La Province is more labour intensive.

In order to incorporate the substitution of capital by labour, the proportional intra-VA structure of the 2002 Son La SAM is not derived from the national I/O matrix. Instead, it is oriented on the original distribution of labour and capital in the aggregated account of crop cultivation before disaggregation. Due to the lack of appropriate data for distributing the VA share between labour and capital, the proportional distribution of the total crop cultivation was allocated to each crop account. The subdivision of employment in employed labour and self-employed labour in the SAM, which does not exist in the I/O matrix, necessitates a further assumption. The share of employed labour from total employment amounts to only 1.5 percent in cropping activities, while that in rice cultivation can be set at zero since rice cultivation in Son La is traditionally practised by household-own labour. Consequently, 1.5 percent of the total VA share of employed labour in the coffee and tea production account is transferred to the account 'self-employed labour'. One can argue that it is doubtful that the provincial IC (and VA) of each crop production account is proportionally lower (and higher correspondingly) than the respective national account. Another argument might be that the intra-IC (and VA) structure can differ significantly between provincial and national average data. Particularly tea and coffee production processes in aggregate Vietnam do not differ considerably from those in Son La Province. Natural conditions and cultivation methods in other regions of Vietnam (mainly mountainous areas of Central and Northern Vietnam) are essentially similar. However, critical differences between national and provincial production data do exist in the cultivation of paddy rice. This is mainly caused by the high contribution of the large delta regions to total rice production in Vietnam. Both the total yield per year and the yield per harvest in those regions are higher. The focus on gross output data and the fact that the cultivation of paddy rice in Son La is mainly practised on fertile fields, however, minimises the distorting impact of the use of national IC and VA shares.

The result of the SAM construction documented in this chapter is a comprehensive and consistent representation of macro and meso-economic accounts of a provincial economy – a fully balanced SAM for Son La, Vietnam. It reveals the structure of the economy and key linkages between production activities, factors, institutions and the rest of the world. The Son La SAM is thus used to describe the socioeconomic baseline of the study region in chapter 5.

4.1.3 Multiplier Model

In order to further characterise the economy, multipliers can be calculated from the Son La SAM. Multiplier models specify which variables are exogenous and endogenous and link them through a set of mathematical relations.[34] The basic assumption in transforming a SAM into an economic model is that all relations are linear and that prices are fixed. SAM-based multiplier models first require the division of the matrix into endogenous and exogenous accounts. All exogenous accounts, i.e. the institution accounts 'enterprises' and 'government', the account of savings and investments, and the account of imports and exports from and to other provinces and nations, are aggregated into a single account recording a cumulative set of injections (x). The matrix comprising the endogenous accounts – production activities (1), production factors (2), and households (3) – constitutes the transaction matrix T. The transaction matrix is converted into the corresponding matrix of average expenditure propensities A by dividing each element by the corresponding column total y (total expenditure) so that $T = Ay$ holds. Since total income and total expenditures of each account are equal, the incomes of endogenous accounts (row sums) can be expressed by a series of linear identities, which is given in general form as $y = Ay + x$. Derived from the structure of the transaction matrix, matrix A represents a composed set of expenditure coefficients of the three endogenous accounts determined by:

---

[34] this section draws on BREISINGER AND ECKER (2006).

$$A = \begin{bmatrix} A_{11} & 0 & A_{13} \\ A_{21} & 0 & 0 \\ 0 & A_{32} & 0 \end{bmatrix}$$
(1)

The submatrix A_{11} includes the input-output coefficients, in other words, the intermediate consumption pattern of each production activity for commodities and services. The subset A_{21} represents the relative distribution of value added in each production activity on the used production factors. According to the provision of production factors, the relative distribution of factor remuneration on household groups is shown in submatrix A_{32}. The submatrix A_{13} comprises the pattern of consumption expenditure for commodities and services of household groups that allocates income onto the production activities. Submatrices, which show no transactions, are recorded as zero.

The series of linear identities which determines the income of production activities (y_1), production factors (y_2), and households (y_3) generated by an exogenous injection in production activities (x_1) is thus given as:

$$y_1 = A_{11} y_1 + A_{13} y_3 + x_1$$

$$y_2 = A_{21} y$$

$$y_3 = A_{32} y_2$$
(2)

that leads to:[35]

$$y_1 = (I - A_{11})^{-1} A_{13} y_3 + (I - A_{11})^{-1} x_1$$

$$y_2 = A_{21} y_1$$

$$y_3 = A_{32} y_2$$
(3)

The last set of relations (3) is graphically represented in Figure 4.1 that illustrates how a positive exogenous injection in a certain production activity generates endogenously a circular flow of income driven by the multiplier effect. An exogenous income increase x_1 in a certain production activity results in a boost of its corresponding output of $(I - A_{11})^{-1} x_1$. The employment of the additional production factors to produce this output generates a stream of value added $(A_{21}y_1)$ that constitutes an additional factor income amounting to $y_2 = A_{21}y_1$. This is distributed among household groups according to their endowment

---

[35] I describes the identity matrix.

with the employed resources (A_{32}). The income increase of the household groups is thus determined by $y_3 = A_{32}\, y_2$. These allow them additional consumption according to their consumption expenditure pattern (A_{13}). The household expenditures on commodities and services accumulate to production activities through the input-output production pattern (A_{11}). Finally, the total additional income of production activities amounts to $y_1 = (I - A_{11})^{-1} A_{13}\, y_3 + (I - A_{11})^{-1} x_1$. The final income multiplier effect on a production activity thus includes two components: a consumption ($(I - A_{11})^{-1} A_{13}\, y_3$) and a production effect ($(I - A_{11})^{-1} x_1$). The consumption effect is composed of the initial injection (x_1) and its multiplication via production linkages ($(I - A_{11})^{-1}$).

Three general types of multipliers evolve from this type of SAM-based multiplier analysis: first, the gross output multipliers, which report the increase in gross output of provincial production activities, second, the value added multipliers, which represent the gain in provincial GDP, and third, the household income multipliers, which indicates the income rise in household groups. The complete multiplier matrix for Son La province including the sums of the gross output multipliers, the value added multipliers, and the household income multipliers is presented in appendix 2 and discussed in chapter 5.

Figure 4.1 Exogenously Induced Income Multipliers in the Circular Flow of Income

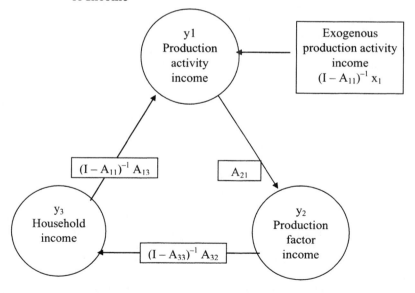

Source: Breisinger and Ecker (2006), adapted from Thorbecke (1998)

SAM-based multiplier analyses have some shortcomings. First, the assumption of fixed prices leads to the fact that the model is only driven by quantity changes. Second, the use of Leontief technology for production activities assumes fixed relations at the top of the technology nest (between intermediate consumption and value added). Similarly, the substitutability between different factors of production are also modelled as Leontief functions, respectively. The multiplier model does therefore not allow for non-linear substitution effects. Third, the absence of factor supply constraints assumes unlimited factor supplies at fixed prices. Finally, the static nature of the model can not capture dynamic effects. These shortcomings can be overcome by CGE models. The following section presents such an approach for Vietnam.

4.2   Structure of Two-Region CGE Model

The two-region CGE model presented in this chapter uses the regional SAM and a national SAM as its database. The national SAM was assembled for Vietnam (VIETSAM) at the Central Institute for Economic Management (CIEM) and covers 97 activities, 97 commodities, 14 factors of production and 16 household types. In addition, it contains 3 enterprises, accounts for the government, savings and investments. Information on foreign trade flows is disaggregated by 88 trading partners. The construction and detailed structure of the SAM is documented in TARP et al. (2002). Key features of the Vietnamese economy are derived from the VIETSAM and presented in section 5.1.

The basic idea behind the construction of a multi-region CGE model is to capture interregional differences that stem from factors such as geographic location, infrastructure and capital endowments. In the one-region type provincial SAM described in the previous chapter, linkages and interactions of the province were captured via the trade account. Imports and exports to and from the region are not differentiated by origin. Practically speaking, the SAM does not differentiate, if a commodity is imported from the rest of Vietnam or the rest of the world. With such type of database, it is hard to analyse impacts that go beyond regional boundaries. On the other side, national SAMs cannot capture regional differences in production costs, factor markets and institutions. The construction of a hydropower plant can exemplify the point: since the construction of the dam and related infrastructure has both local and national impacts, only a multi-region model can properly reflect impacts by region such as the inundation of land (local) and the provision of electricity (national).

The core model database represents the structure of the regional as well as the national economy and consists of two SAMs. Additional information includes a set of elasticities on trade, production and consumption, demographic characteristics, government policies and information on costs and benefits of dam construction and productivity increases. To build this 2-region CGE model, I first merge the VIETSAM with the regional SAM (REGSAM), which effectively represents a sub-region of the VIETSAM. The following steps are taken to merge the two datasets and derive a database that differentiates between a specific region (REG), the rest of the country (ROC) and the rest of the world (ROW).

In a first step, both SAMs are aggregated to the same dimensions, including the number of activities, commodities, factors and institutions to facilitate the merging process. In the case of this dissertation, I choose a 30 sector, 4 factor, 2 households and 3 enterprises disaggregation.[36] The SAM aggregation module (samagg. gms) in the IFPRI standard model is used to perform the task.[37] The SAMs represent different base years (2000 and 2002). It has thus to be considered to make adjustments in one of the SAMs to account for inflation, economic growth and structural changes.[38] However, each attempt to adjust the two databases to the same year bears the risk of undermining their consistency. In the present case, where REGSAM only accounts for a marginal share of VIETSAM data, the trade-off between temporal and internal consistency favours the use of the original SAMs.

To derive a SAM that describes a rest of the country region from the perspective of the province, the respective regional matrix entries are subtracted from the national SAM entries. The result is a SAM that describes the economy of the ROC.

$$SAM_{National} - SAM_{Regional} = SAM_{ROC} \tag{4}$$

Merging the region and the ROC SAM results in a 60 activity, 60 commodity, 6 factor and 6 institutions SAM. The regional and ROC savings and investments, the government and the ROW are added up, respectively. Calibrating the model to the SAM, where the SAM provides the coefficients for the model equations and solves for equilibrium reproducing the base year SAM. The resulting SAM serves as a basis for the CGE model described below. It is based on the standard CGE set up and used at IFPRI. The following presentation of the model thus draws on the documentation of LÖFGREN et al. (2002) and concentrates on major features of the model. The theoretical structure of the comprehensive CGE model has been presented in DERVIS et al. (1982). Following this tradition, LÖFGREN et al. (2002) have complemented the model with features such as household consumption of self-produced and non-marketed goods, explicit treatment of transaction costs for nationally and internationally marketed goods and the ability of one commodity to be produced

---

[36] For the secor mapping between the 112 commodities documented in the national I/O table and the national SAM to 30 sectors see Appendix 1.

[37] IFPRI's Standard CGE model is documented in LÖFGREN et. al. (2002).

[38] This would practically mean to build a new SAM, either a national SAM for 2002, or a 2000 SAM for Son La province.

by different activities and vice versa. All of these features are of particular relevance for policy analysis in developing countries.

The two-region Vietnam CGE explains all the payment flows between activities, commodities, factors and institutions in a set of linear and non-linear equations (Figure 4.2). Activities, factors and households are region-specific, while the commodities are traded on a single national market. Each region thus has its local production activities, factors and households and the major linkage of the model is the interregional (intra-country) trade on a perfectly competitive commodity market. Linkages in the factor markets represent the flows of capital and the movement of labour and capital across regions. The assumption of the basic model is that the factor markets are segmented, effectively excluding the possibility of migration. This assumption is relaxed in several scenarios to estimate the impact of labour mobility on model results and further discussed in section 5.5.

Figure 4.2   Flowchart of Two-Region Vietnam CGE Model

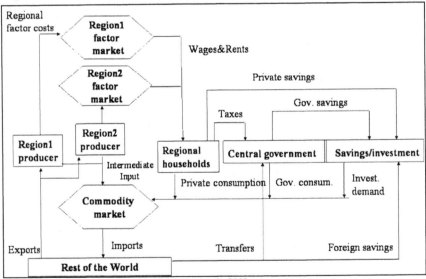

Source: Own illustration, based on LÖFGREN et al., 2002

The equations describe the behaviour of the different actors, partly following simple rules using fixed coefficients, partly capturing behaviour by non-linear, first-order optimality conditions. The model equations also ensure that macro and micro constraints are satisfied, including factor and commodity markets, the savings investment balance, the government and the current account with ROW. To determine these flows, behaviour of actors and competition between regional production activities have to be modelled.

4.2.1 Production and Factor Markets

The CGE requires functional forms and additional parameters that govern production activities, trade and household consumption. The main regional feature is the separation of production activities including their imperfect substitutability, which reflects differences in timing, quality and location. Regional production and the flow of marketed commodities are presented in Figure 4.3. Regional producers maximise profits according to prices and a production technology, which at its top level uses a Leontief production function to make the decision between the substitution of intermediates and factors of production. The second choice of how to combine different factors of production, i.e. value-added is modelled as a constant elasticity of substitution (CES) function; aggregate intermediate inputs are determined by a Leontief function of sectoral intermediate inputs. There is a one to one mapping between production activities, except for the case, where no regional production of the respective commodity takes place.

Figure 4.3 Region-Specific Production Structure

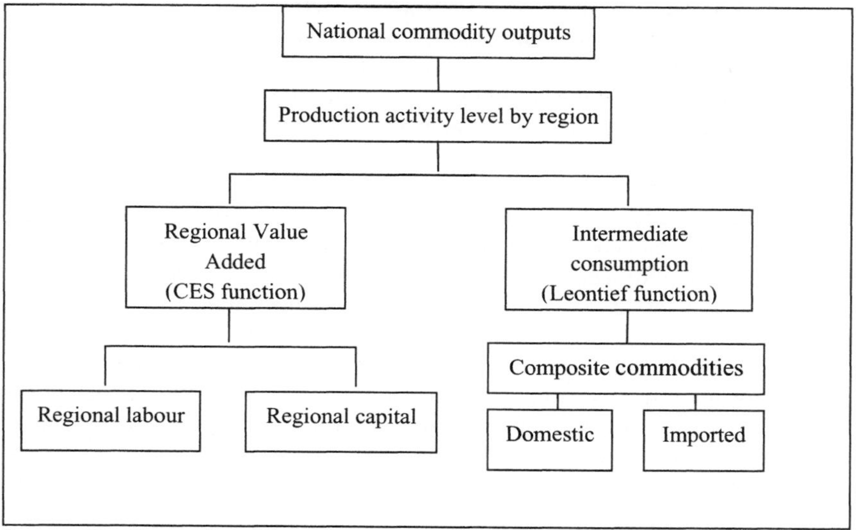

Source: Own figure; adopted from LÖFGREN et al., 2002

In both cases, aggregate intermediate inputs are determined by a Leontief function of sectoral intermediate inputs. There is a one to one mapping between production activities, except for the obvious case, where no regional production of the respective commodity takes place. The behaviour of producers and institutions and the set up of the macroeconomic balances in scenarios are equal. The model allows for different mechanisms that equilibrate supply and demand in the factor market. The three factor market specifications are as follows:

- The first closure fixes the quantity of supply of each factor, representing a case, where the factor is fully employed. An economy-wide wage is free to adjust to assure that the sum of factor demands equals supply. Wages are activity specific. The wage is the product of the economy-wide wage and an activity-specific wage distortion term. This distortion term is fixed in this closure.
- The second setting addresses segmentation and sectoral immobility of labour markets and employs a closure of activity-specific factors, implying that demand for the respective factors and their economy-wide wage is fixed, while supply is flexible. Therefore, factor income can only change through changes in activity output and prices. It reflects quality differences in labour markets that exist regarding education and location.
- To account for un- and underemployment, the third labour market setting allows for unemployment in alternative categories. Each activity can employ any desired quantity at its fixed and activity specific wage. It assumes labour mobility among activities and serves as an indication of the impact of a more flexible labour market. The elasticity of substitution between factors and the elasticity of substitution between aggregate factor and intermediate inputs reflect the levels of substitutability.

For the analyses in chapter 5, I use the first setting (i) for skilled labour and the third for unskilled labour (ii). This best reflects the situation in the study region, which is characterised by un- and underemployment among low skilled workers. Each activity can employ any desired quantity at its fixed and activity specific wage. It assumes labour mobility among activities and serves as an indication of the impact of a more flexible labour market. However, labour can not upgrade skills and cannot migrate between the regions. The impact of allowing for migration is examined in section 5.3. The elasticity of substitution between factors and the elasticity of substitution between aggregate factors and intermediate inputs are set at 1.2 and 0.8 in all simulations to ensure comparability.[39] Sensitivity analyses using different values for these

---

[39] These values are chosen in accordance with a standard setting in IFPRI's model.

substitution elasticities in a previous study have shown that higher elasticities can have strong effects on the magnitude of impacts. However, the direction and relative distribution of benefits remained consistent.[40] Sensitivity analysis for the present model and its impact on the results are discussed in section 5.6. Capital is assumed to be fully employed and mobile in all scenarios.

4.2.2 Commodity Markets and Trade

The functioning of the commodity market on the supply side is determined by a two-step procedure. First, except for home-consumed goods, all commodities enter the market place. In a second step, aggregated output is divided between regional sales and exports to ROV/ROW. A constant elasticity of transformation (CET) function is used to determine this decision. It assumes that producers maximise their sales revenue for any given output level subject to imperfect transformability between exports and domestic sales. In the regional context, the small country assumption is used for the case of exports, implying that demand from ROV/ROW is indefinitely elastic at constant national market prices. Prices received by regional producers are adjusted by transaction costs and taxes. On the demand side, imports and domestic goods form a composite good, for which the demand is derived from the assumption that domestic consumers minimise costs subject to imperfect substitutability, captured by a CES function. Given the regional focus, it is again assumed that supplies of imported goods are infinitely elastic.

Each commodity can be produced by different regional activities. The national market is thus served by regionally produced goods and services. In the case of regionalised production, output from regional activities is imperfectly substitutable due to differences in e.g. timing, quality and geographic location. The first step in Figure 4.4 thus shows that a CES function is used to aggregate production output from different regions (QXAC (ROC, REG)). In a second step, aggregate national output (QXD) is divided between national sales (QD) and exports (QE) to ROW. A constant elasticity of transformation (CET) is used to determine this decision. Aggregate producers maximise their sales revenue for any given output level, subject to imperfect transformability between exports and domestic sales.

---

[40] See BREISINGER (2005).

Figure 4.4   Flow of Marketed Commodities: 3-Market and Region-Specific Production Activity

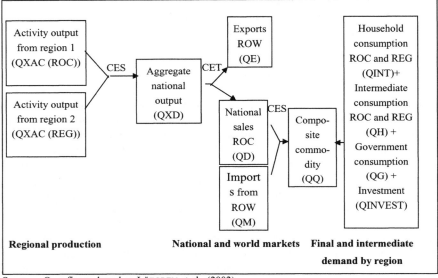

Source: Own figure, based on LÖFGREN et al., (2002)

The small country assumption is used for the case of exports, implying that demand from ROW is indefinitely elastic at constant world market prices. Prices received by producers are adjusted by transaction costs and trade taxes. A composite commodity (QQ) is demanded from region-specific households and intermediate consumption as well as from aggregate government consumption and investment. Demand for this composite is determined by the assumption that domestic consumers minimise costs subject to imperfect substitutability, captured by a CES function. The Armington assumption is used for the specification of trade flows (ARMINGTON, 1969). Sectoral exports are determined by CET[41] and sectoral imports by CES functions.[42] The model assumes a uniform substitutability between REG and ROC products and the ROW. CET is set at 1.5 for primary and secondary sectors and to 0.5 for services. CES are set at 3 for the primary and secondary sectors and to 0.5 for services. This setting reflects the fact that Vietnam is a relatively open country

---

[41] Elasticity of transformation for domestic marketed output between exports and domestic supplies (SIGMAT in IFPRI Standard model).

[42] Elasticity of substitution bw. imports and domestic output in domestic demand (SIGMAQ in IFPRI Standard model).

(see section 3.1). The lower values for the service sector, are due to the fact that services are mostly local in their nature, and tradability therefore lower. [43] The consumer price index (CPI) is the model numeraire. The CPI is one measure of inflation, and nominal changes in prices and incomes have to be interpreted in the context of the CPI.

Table 4.4 summarises the trade and production related parameters.

Table 4.4 Overview of Model Parameters (Trade and Production)

	Trade elasticities		Substitution elasticities between production factors	Substitution elasticities between factors and intermediates
	CES	CET		
Primary and secondary sectors	3.0	1.5	1.2	0.8
Services	0.5	0.5	1.2	0.8

4.2.3 Institutions

A RHA is chosen for the model. Geography is implicitly included by the regional focus of the model. In addition, each region's households are split into rural and urban. The regional households receive income from the factors of production, transfers from the government and remittances from the rest of the country/rest of the world. On the expenditure side, household consumption differentiates between products, purchased at market prices and self-produced items valued at producer prices. Total household consumption is allocated across market and home-consumed commodities according to linear expenditure system (LES) demand functions. Expenditure elasticities by commodity and household are derived from IFPRI (2003). Elasticities for agricultural products classified by rural and urban were estimated by IFPRI, 2003 for the northern mountainous region and used for parameter specification. The following elasticities are used for agricultural products: rice: 0.100 for rural and 0.344 for urban households, coffee and tea: 1.185 for urban and 1.167 for rural households, other crops are set at unity for all households, livestock: 1.096 for urban and 1.302 for rural households, fishery: 0.699 for urban and 0.931 for rural households, processed food: 1.123 for urban and 1.370 for rural

---

[43] These value are also oriented on standard values used in CGE modelling (see e.g. LÖFGREN et al., 2002).

households. For industrial and service products it is assumed that they are uniform across commodities and set at unity for all households. Furthermore, households pay ad valorem taxes and save. Savings of all households are fixed. The Frisch parameter, which determines the subsistence spending of households, is set at -2 for all households.

The regional government receives its income from regional taxpayers and from the rest of the country, representing the central government. Taxes are fixed at ad valorem rates and government savings are flexible. Government consumption is fixed in real terms and government transfers to households and enterprises are indexed to the CPI.

4.2.4 Macroeconomic Settings

The macroeconomic closure rules determine how an equilibrium is achieved in the trade balance, the government balance and the savings-investment account. In the present model, the real exchange rate is fixed, which allows the trade balance and foreign savings to vary. Savings drive investment. Savings of households and enterprises are fixed. The quantity of each commodity in the investment basket is multiplied by a flexible scalar to equal investment costs and savings value. Savings-driven investments, which practically mean that marginal savings propensities are fixed, investment demand quantity adjustment factors and absorption shares for investment demand are flexible. For the government closure, all tax rates are fixed and government savings are flexible.

4.2.5 Simulation Variables and Parameters

In order to use the CGE model explained and defined in chapter 4 to conduct policy analysis, a set of scenarios has to be defined and implemented. Depending on the type of the exogenous shock to be induced, model variables and parameters have to be changed exogenously. In the following technical description, I will concentrate on the variables and parameters relevant for the analysis conducted in the context of the present study. These are transaction costs, the capital stock and FP. The respective simulation file is available upon request from the author.

- Transaction costs

The CGE model includes transaction costs in the prices paid by demanders, reflecting the cost incurred for moving the commodity from the domestic supplier to the demander, or in the case of exported goods and services from the producer to international markets. In the following equation, the parameter $icd_{c'c}$ describes the trade input of c per unit of commodity cp produced and sold domestically.

$$PDD_c = PDS_c + \sum_{c'\in CT} PQ_c * icd_{c'c}$$ (5)

where, PDD_c denotes the demand price of domestic non-traded goods, PDS_c the supply price for commodity c produced and sold domestically, PQ_c the price of composite good c. Demand for transportation and trade is a fixed coefficient per unit of sold goods or services. A reduction of $icd_{c'c}$ thus leads to lower demander prices and benefits producers (through lower costs for intermediate goods) and consumers of the respective commodities.

- Factor productivity

In several scenarios, FP is changed exogenously. Equation 6 states that the quantity of value added for each activity is a CES function of disaggregated factor quantities. Simulations involving a change in FP therefore allow each factor unit to produce one unit more value added in the production process. The formalisation is as follows:

$$QVA_a = \alpha_a^{va} * \left(\sum_{f\in F} \delta_{fa}^{va} * QF_{fa}^{-p_a^{va}} \right)^{-\frac{1}{p_a^{va}}}$$ (6)

where QVA_a is the quantity of aggregate value added, α_a^{va} is the efficiency parameter in the CES value added function, δ_{fa}^{va} the CES value added function share parameter for factor f in activity a, QF_{fa} the quantity demanded of factor f from activity a, and $-p_a^{va}$ is the CES value added function exponent.

   Practically, a one percent increase in the simulation enables each unit of the production factor to produce one percent more value added. There is no substitution between factors and intermediates, since I use a Leontief function at the top of the technology nest. FP increases change the productivity of all factors including labour, capital and land. Substitution between factors in this process is determined at the bottom of the technology nest by the elasticity of substitution. The mechanisms through which markets are influenced by FP increases depend on demand elasticities, trade elasticities and factor market equilibrating rules. A FP increase in activity a will lead to increased output in this sector. Depending on domestic and international demand, prices for commodity a decrease, but due to higher quantities sold, labour income rises. Rising income leads to an increase in income and consumption and thus a reduction in poverty. These trends can be expected to be more poverty reducing, the more poor people are employed in the targeted sector or enjoy the benefits of relatively higher incomes.

Regarding the labour market, there are three possible settings, which influence the effects of FP increases: assuming constant elasticities of factor substitution, in the case of unemployment and fixed wages, an increase in FP will lead to an increase in demand for labour. Since wages are fixed, new workers can be employed at fixed costs. Assuming full employment in the baseline, higher demand for a certain labour factor leads to higher wages and thus higher costs for the production activity. The same can be expected in the third possible setting, where labour is assumed to be activity specific and thus immobile. FP increases are expected to have the strongest impacts on poverty, where both supply-side effects of increased income and demand- side effects of lower product prices affect a large share of the poor population.

- Increase in capital stocks

The capital stock as part of the value added is an endogenous variable in the model and represented by the term QF_{fa}.

$$QVA_a = \alpha_a^{va} * \left(\sum_{f \in F} \delta_{fa}^{va} * QF_{fa}^{-\rho_a^{va}} \right)^{-\frac{1}{\rho_a^{va}}} \tag{7}$$

To manipulate an increase/decrease in the amount of activity-specific capital, stocks have to be fixed and are thus made exogenous. Output of the targeted activity will increase/decrease and additional capital will induce a substitution of labour. The size of the substitution is determined by the elasticity of substitution between the different factors. Its setting depends on the respective simulation.

This comprehensive two-region model is used to analyse the impacts of different infrastructure scenarios, which are further developed in chapter 5.2. To analyse poverty impacts, a micro-accounting module is presented in the following chapter that uses the results of the macro-model for post simulation analysis.

4.3   Micro-Accounting Module

Poverty reduction is on top of the international development policy agenda. To define and assess poverty impacts of policies, adequate measurement methods are required. The CGE model presented in the previous chapter is complemented by a micro-accounting module to better capture intra-household group distributions. Before defining the poverty line for Vietnam and presenting the micro-accounting module, the following section introduces the general concept of poverty.

4.3.1   Concepts of Poverty

Poverty is increasingly seen as a multidimensional problem with various dimensions that interact and reinforce each other (WORLD BANK, 1990; MCCULLOCH et al., 2001; WORLD BANK, 2000). It is very difficult if not impossible to find a single index for these multifaceted and multidimensional aspects of poverty and the combination of different qualitative and quantitative approaches might be the most adequate way of measuring poverty. In the following, I concentrate on the main approaches used to measure economic poverty and shortly present strength and weaknesses of these approaches.[44]

Figure 4.5 structures several quantitative poverty measures.[45] The Human Development Index (HDI) of the UN is a practical example of a multidimensional approach. It includes life expectancy, infant mortality and levels of education as indicators. More recently, also concepts of vulnerability, powerlessness and a lack of voice are used to describe poverty (KANBUR AND SQUIRE, 2001). In that spirit, the Vietnam Development Report 2004 gives a comprehensive definition of poverty stating that "Poverty is a state of deprivation involving multiple dimensions. Limited income, or limited opportunities to generate income; lack of assets to protect consumption in difficult times, and vulnerability in the face of adverse shocks; few possibilities to convey demands and grievances to those who could address them, and to participate in collective decision making; a sense of humiliation, and a lack of respect by others...all these are aspects of poverty" (WORLD BANK et al., 2003, p.7).

---

[44] More extensive discussions on advantages and disadvantages of these approaches can be found e.g. in ZELLER (2004).

[45] Contrary to quantitative measures, qualitative poverty measures focus on subjective judgments of people by using purposive sampling (WORLD BANK, 1990). Application of a variety of such measures for Vietnam can be found in the WORLD BANK et al. (2003).

Figure 4.5   Classification of Poverty Measurement Approaches

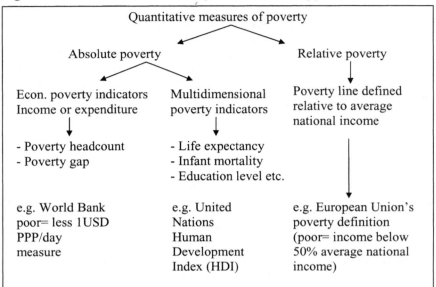

Source: Own illustration

However, the most widely used approach is to use income or expenditure per capita information from household surveys and compare them against a poverty line (headcount approach). RAVALLION (1996) regards the simplicity and easy digestibility as the main reasons for the widespread use of the headcount approach.[46] From a theoretical perspective, it can be argued that the expenditure variable summarises many other variables that improve the quality of life such as consumption of food, payments for education and health (WORLD BANK, 2000). In fact, income, health and education variables are interdependent and causality not easy to determine. As a result, broadening the poverty definition does not influence significantly who is counted as poor (KANBUR AND SQUIRE, 2001).

The poverty line is a threshold and households or individuals falling below this line are defined as poor. According to a cost of basic needs approach, LIPTON AND RAVALLION (1995) define the poverty line as the minimum value of expenditures required per capita to satisfy defined basic needs. This line can be defined as a food poverty line, which is calculated by the money needed to buy a certain amount of calories, or as threshold that allows for the consumption of a

---

[46] RAVALLION (1996) also presents an extensive overview of advantages and disadvantages of different poverty measures.

predefined basket of goods. The resulting incidence of poverty is a headcount index and comprises the share of population whose income is below this poverty line.

However, one of the first critics of the poverty line was put forward by SEN (1976). Major criticisms include the fact that the depth of poverty is totally neglected and dynamics around the poverty line are disregarded. This leads e.g. to effect that once people fall below the poverty line, they are classified as poor. If they become even poorer this cannot be captured any more. SAITH (2005, p.4601) shares this view that might lead to "a misidentification of the poor and subsequently to the adoption of targeting, monitoring and evaluation criteria, which are equally narrow".

An improvement that partly addresses this criticism is the additional measure of the poverty gap. The poverty gap represents the difference between the levels of consumption or income and the poverty line can thus be defined as the amount of money necessary for households or individuals to escape poverty (KANBUR AND SQUIRE, 2001; ZELLER, 2004). The poverty gap is thus a very useful indicator in addition to the poverty line since it provides important complementary information on poverty properties. It accounts for the case that some population groups are characterised by a high poverty incidence but a low depth – when relatively numerous households are clustered just below the poverty line – and others vice versa – when relatively few households are below the poverty line but with extremely low levels of income (COUDOUEL et al., 2002).

Following this argumentation and deciding for the poverty line concept, the next general distinction can be made between using income or expenditure data to define the poverty line. Expenditure is often preferred for a number of reasons: it shows the current actual standard of living and it smoothes out irregularities and thus better reflects long term average well-being (ZELLER, 2004). It thus summarises many things that improve the quality of life, such as food consumption, education and health. Major weaknesses of the income indicator include: first, income only affects welfare, when it is actually used for consumption purposes. Second, another disadvantage frequently mentioned is the fact that income (especially semi-official) income is underreported and some parts of income such as income from informal activities, home agricultural production are hard to observe. The major advantage of the income approach is the lower cost of data collection, which is about a fifth of expenditure data (ZELLER, 2004).

The most well known and most frequently used poverty measure is the 1 USD a day threshold calculated in PPP (WORLD BANK, 1990). Its obvious advantage is its comparability across countries. Shortcomings include the neglect of intra-country price differentials and the lack of accounting for home produced and consumed goods (KANBUR AND SQUIRE, 2001). On the national level, national poverty lines are thus often preferable. Such thresholds take country-specific characteristics and distributional aspects into account.

Measuring poverty in Vietnam is done in a variety of ways. The Ministry of Labour, Invalids and Social Affairs (MOLISA) uses an income poverty line and the National Center for Social Sciences (NCSSH) computes a HDI on the provincial level. The GSO relies both on income and expenditures to calculate the poverty rate. The definition of the poverty line is based on the cost of a consumption basket, including country-specific food items to secure 2100 calories per day and person and non-food items[47].

4.3.2 Defining the Poverty Line

The study uses a poverty line calculated, which is documented in the VDR 2000 (WORLD BANK, 1999A). The following description of the method concentrates on the relevant features of this approach and describes the updating procedure used for the spatial and temporal adoption of the poverty line in the context of the present study.

The poverty line refers to a consumption basket necessary to ensure the daily intake of 2100 calories, an indicator defined by the World Health Organisation (WHO). This consumption basket was derived from household data of the Vietnam Living Standard Survey (VLSS) 1992/93 and consequently updated to 1998 by using the same basket of goods and accounting for price changes. Additionally to this food poverty line, a general poverty line was calculated that represents non-food items plus the amount of money necessary to purchase the 2100 calories. In the following, I refer to this general poverty line and use it for the calculations. To calculate the non-food poverty line, households were divided into quintiles and the average value of the third quintile including use values of durable goods and imputed rent from owner-occupied housing was used to determine the non-food poverty line. Since the third quintile consumed slightly less than 2100 calories, adjustment were made for consistency reasons. However, taking the food and non-food poverty lines together, the general poverty line for 1993 amounted to 1.160.363 VND per capita. This value was updated taking commodity-specific price changes for food items into account and using inflation rates for the non-food items. This yielded a poverty line of 1.789.871. I use the latter poverty line for the analysis and update it to the year 2002.

A critical point in the calculation of the expenditure basket is the valuation of housing and other fixed assets. Most of the households in the VHLSS for Son La province live in their own houses. Opportunity costs for housing could be calculated by using regional rental prices. However, property rent markets are underdeveloped or not existent. Alternatively, the opportunity costs of housing

---

[47] For a more detailed presentation and discussion see HÄUSER (2005) and the VDR (WORLD BANK et al., 2003).

can be calculated as the ratio of the estimated house value and other non-food expenditures (WORLD BANK, 1999A). .According to this calculation the housing value (HV) of is set at 3 percent of total expenditures for Vietnam (WORLD BANK, 1999A). The calculation of housing costs in this dissertation follows the same approach, assuming that the ratio did not change between 1992/93 and 2002.

Additionally, regional price deflators were calculated for seven regions of Vietnam (WORLD BANK, 1999A). Weights used for these regional price indices were taken from the price questionnaire and include food and non-food items. The index is expressed relative to national prices and amounts to 0.9930 for rural and 1.0178 for urban households in the northern uplands (WORLD BANK, 1999A).[48] I assume that this relation has not changed and derive the regional poverty line for 2002 and the study region as follows:

$$PL(Y_0) * I_n * D_R = PL(Y_1) \tag{8}$$

where PL is the poverty line, Y is the year, I_n is the inflation index in period n and D_R is the region-specific deflator. This yields a poverty line of 2,005,726 VND for urban households and 1,956,853 VND for rural households.[49] For poverty measurement I use the Foster, Greer and Thorbecke (FGT) measure (FOSTER et al., 1984). The denomination is as follows:

$$P_{\alpha} = \frac{1}{n} \sum_{y_{it}=0}^{z_t} (\frac{z_t - y_{it}}{z_t})^{\alpha} \tag{9}$$

where α is a poverty aversion parameter, n the number of households, y_{it} is household i's consumption in period t, z_t is the poverty line in period t. In this equation, $\alpha = 0$ yield the headcount ratio and $\alpha = 1$ yields the poverty gap index. I calculate these measures for each representative household (urban and rural) group in Son La province. Poverty impacts on households outside the region are not accounted for.

---

[48] WORLD BANK (1999A) reports that the adjustment factor for rural areas for Northern Vietnam is with 1.0178 higher than the one for urban areas (0.993). This seems illogical. The fact that for all other regions the rural adjustment factors are lower than the urban factors support the thesis that these two figures were changed. HÄUSER (2005) rightly adds to this point that if the Northern region was really an exception, it would have certainly been discussed in the report.

[49] Annual inflation rates (CPI, Jan. 1995=100): for Vietnam: 1998: 7.8; 1999: 4.3; 2000: -1.6; 2001: -0.4; 2002: 4.0 (WORLD BANK et al., 2003).

4.3.3 Micro-Accounting of Poverty

The CGE model presented in section 4.2 is only of limited use for assessing poverty impacts of infrastructure investments, since the RHA can not capture differences in intra-household group distribution of expenditure. To take these intra-group distributional patterns into account and to analyse changes in poverty levels that stem from exogenous shocks induced by infrastructure investments, I use an macro-micro approach. This approach allows for connecting the CGE model with more disaggregated household data. Base run and simulation results of the CGE model are used to calculate this micro-accounting model. AGÉNOR et al. (2004) suggest the following general steps to build such a micro-accounting module:

- The sample from the household survey is classified to fit the representative household categories of the macro model.
- Growth rates of consumption and/or income per capita are retained from the simulation results of the macro model for the different household groups.
- These growth rates are separately applied to the per capita income or consumption expenditure of each single household in the household survey. Absolute income or consumption changes levels can thus be derived in the post-shock situation.
- Poverty lines can then be adjusted using changes in the CPI as derived from the macro model. This can be done in a region- specific way or by differentiating between rural and urban areas. After calculating these new nominal levels of income or expenditure, the headcount index, poverty gap and other measures can be derived.
- Finally, these new poverty levels can be compared with the baseline values to assess the impact of the shock on the poor.

Such micro-accounting method overcomes the shortcoming of assuming uniform intra-household group distributions. It uses the distribution of income or expenditure derived from actual households using representative household surveys. As documented in section 4.2, the macro model includes four aggregated households, two of which are classified as REG and two as ROC. In addition, the households in REG and ROC are classified as rural and urban. The micro-accounting module concentrates on poverty impacts in REG and incorporates household expenditures of all rural and urban households included in the VHLSS for Son La province. All incorporated expenditure items follow the initial items of the VLSS 1992/93, of which the original poverty line for Vietnam was calculated.

In the next step, the micro accounting model uses the real per capita consumption changes obtained from results of the CGE model for urban and rural households. These results of the macro model expressed as percentage changes are imposed on each single member of all urban and rural households. Consumption expenditure changes are thus calculated per capita to account for the largely varying household size in the sample. Differences in intra-household distribution, i.e. between different members of the household are not accounted for. To account for inflation, real household expenditures changes (CPI adjusted) are used and compared to the baseline results.[50] Table 4.5 gives an overview of main characteristics of the 350 household's average household size, average per capita expenditure and sample size. The baseline expenditures of all households can be found in the appendices 3 and 4.

Table 4.5   Overview of Household Characteristics for Micro Accounting

	Population in Son La province	HH in VHLSS (2002)	HH size	Average expenditure per capita (1000 VND)	Exp. Max	Exp. Min
Households total	941901	350	5.6	2.223		
Urban	103764	103	4.2	4.465	19.117	1.849
Rural	838137	247	5.8	1.893	6.866	0.321

Source: GSO, 2003; GSO, 2004
Notes:
HH: Household
Exp. max: maximal expenditure per household in sample (in 1000 VND)
Exp. min: minimal expenditure per household in sample (in 1000 VND)

---

[50] One could also use absolute changes in expenditures and adjust the poverty line for inflation as suggested in AGÉNOR et al. (2004). The results are the same.

5 Analysing Regional and National Impacts of Infrastructure Investments

Based on the discussion of the theory and empirical database this chapter presents selected model results. Section 5.1 discusses the baseline solution and the structure of the two regional economies. Section 5.2 presents three scenarios: road investment, a large-scale dam investment scenario and poverty reducing effects of economic growth. Section 5.3 tests the robustness of the model.

5.1 Baseline: The Structure of the Economy

Qualitative and quantitative analyses of the baseline model shed light on the economic structure of the two regions that are included in the model: Son La province and the rest of Vietnam.[51] Special emphasis is placed on the real economy, particularly production, consumption and investment. Furthermore, the poverty focus requires a detailed analysis of factor markets and households.

5.1.1 Macroeconomic Structure of the Two Regions

Specific information on sectoral distribution and trade is presented in the following discussion by referring to the baseline solution of the model. Total real absorption defined as the total demand for goods and services by all residents stood at 453.4 trillion VND. Household consumption contributes the largest share to absorption with 276.8 trillion VND. About 131 trillion VND are contributed by investment and 45.6 trillion VND by government consumption. Private savings amounted to 25 percent and government savings to 4.2 percent of GDP (Table 5.1).

---

[51] In the model, Son La province is also referred to as REG and the rest of Vietnam as ROC. These terms will also be used in the further discussion of results.

Table 5.1   Structure of the Vietnamese Economy: Macro Table Baseline

Economic indicators	BASE
Absorption*	453.4
Household consumption*	276.8
Investment*	131.0
Government consumption*	45.6
Private (household + enterprise) savings**	25.0
Foreign savings**	0.5
Government savings**	4.2
Import tax revenue**	3.1
Direct tax revenue**	8.9

Notes:
* in trillion VND
** as percent of GDP

Production output, GDP and trade are analysed by four aggregate sectors. Table 5.2 presents the absolute numbers, while Table 5.3 reports the data as percentage shares. The ROC economy is dominated by services and industry, which contribute 37 percent and 32 percent to GDP, respectively. Agriculture contributes 26 percent to GDP and 16 percent to total ROC output. The contribution of construction to GDP has an almost equal share in ROC and REG and stands at 6 and 7 percent of both regions' GDP, respectively. Regarding trade, 38 percent of total industrial production is exported. At the same time, most of the imports occur in this sector, leading to a negative trade balance in industrial goods. The trade balance of agriculture is positive. 16 percent of agricultural production is exported, as compared to 2 percent of output value that is imported. Construction is not internationally traded.

GDP of the REG economy stood at 2.516 trillion VND or 165 USD per capita, which is considerably below the nationwide average of 437 USD and an average figure for Hanoi of 945 USD (GSO, 2004). As compared to the secondary sector-dominated structure of the ROC economy, agriculture plays the most important role in the contribution to GDP in REG. The economy is simply structured with a low level of diversification in production sectors. In 2002, 59 percent of the total GDP was generated by the primary sector (agriculture, forestry and fishery), 11 percent by the secondary sector (industry and construction) and 31 percent by the tertiary sector (services).[52] The structure of the REG economy will be further investigated and analysed in section 5.1.2.

---

[52] Annual GDP of the Son La Province in 2002: Total: VND 2,502 billion; primary sector: VND 1,426 billion; secondary sector: VND 292 billion; tertiary sector: VND 793 billion (GSO SL, 2003A).

Table 5.2   Structure of the Economy by Region and Sector (in Trillion VND)

	Output		GDP		Trade	
	ROC	REG	ROC	REG	E	I
AGR	155.7	1.9	100.2	1.5	25.3	3.5
IND	440.2	0.3	124.1	0.1	165.9	182.9
CONSTR	87.0	0.6	21.8	0.2		
SERV	261.3	1.1	143.4	0.8	33.8	25.1
TOTAL	944.3	3.9	389.6	2.5	225.0	211.5

Notes:
E: Exports
I: Imports
GDP: at factor cost (real)

Table 5.3   Structure of the Economy by Region and Sector (as Share of Total)

	Output		GDP		Trade	
	ROC	REG	ROC	REG	Ei/Yi	Mi/Yi
AGR	0.16	0.49	0.26	0.59	0.16	0.02
IND	0.47	0.08	0.32	0.04	0.38	0.42
CONST	0.09	0.14	0.06	0.07	0.00	0.00
SERV	0.28	0.29	0.37	0.31	0.13	0.10
TOTAL	1.00	1.00	1.00	1.00	0.24	0.22

Notes:
Ei/Yi: share of exports in total value of output in sector i
Mi/Yi: share of imports in total value of output in sector i
GDP: at factor costs (real)

Transaction costs play a vital role in the functioning of domestic markets and the participation in the global economy. The model accounts for domestic transaction costs and for transaction costs for exported goods, respectively. Table 5.4 shows that the share of transaction costs in Vietnam for exported goods as compared to the share of transaction costs of domestically traded goods is lower for both agricultural and industrial commodities. Especially the difference for industrial goods is substantial. The share of transaction cost for exports accounts for 8 percent of the total export value as compared to a 14 percent share for domestic transaction costs of domestically marketed output. This might be counterintuitive at first glance. However, it can be explained by the fact that a large share of exported industrial goods is produced around the three export hubs Hanoi, Danang and Ho Chi Minh City. All three exports centres are located close to the sea, have good export infrastructure and therefore comparably lower transaction costs.

For agricultural commodities, domestic transaction costs for export and domestic use are almost similar (9 percent and 10 percent, respectively). This is in line with the general characteristics of the transportation network. Once the agricultural commodities are moved out of rural areas with generally weak infrastructure, transaction cost to export hubs are on average as high as to other domestic markets.

Table 5.4   Overview of Transaction Costs by Sector

	MM-E	MM-D	MM-E/E	MM-D/Y
	billion VND	billion VND		
AGR	2502	14844	0.09	0.10
IND	14396	56693	0.08	0.14

Notes:
MM-E: transaction costs for exports
MM-D: domestic transaction costs
MM-E/E: transaction costs for exports as a share of total exports
MM-D/Y: domestic transaction costs as a share of total domestic production

5.1.2 The Son La Regional Economy

5.1.2.1 Son La Economy in the National Context

Son La ranks fifth out of 64 provinces of Vietnam in surface area. Its population, however, accounts for only 1.2 percent of the total population of Vietnam and, as the following section will show, its economic importance in the national economy is limited. Linkages between Son La province and the rest of Vietnam include flows of commodities, factors and government transfer payments. Imports to the region are dominated by manufacturing and industrial goods, while exported goods are mainly agricultural and processed food products. Financial flows include remittances from migrants, transfers from the central government and private and public investments from outside the province. Since revenues of the regional government are negligible, the provincial budget is largely financed by transfers from the central government. To quantify major contributions of Son La province to the national economy and to further place the Son La province into the national context, Table 5.5 calculates some structural shares from the 2-region model, namely the respective value added and trade shares of regional production to the national economy.[53]

Table 5.5 Contribution of Son La's Value Added and Trade as a Share of Total National Value Added and Trade (in Percent)

	Labour skilled	Labour unskilled	Capital	E	M
AGR	0.00	0.65	0.05	0.29	0.63
IND	0.01	0.02	0.00	0.00	0.07
CONST	0.01	0.28	0.02	0.00	0.00
SERV	0.10	0.08	0.03	0.05	0.16

Notes:
E: exports
M: imports

It becomes clear that the province contributes less than one percent to national trade and value added in all categories as compared to its population share of 1.2 percent. The share of unskilled labour contribution of Son La province to national agricultural value added in unskilled labour is highest and stands at 0.65 percent. In skilled labour and capital, these shares are remarkably lower and range from zero to 0.28 percent of the national total across all categories. Total agricultural exports account for 0.29 percent of the national total, while imports account for 0.63 percent of total national imports. Similarly, Son La's share in imports is higher in the industrial, construction and service sectors as compared to its share in exports. Despite this limited importance for the national economy, Son La province represents a typical mountainous province in Vietnam and is thus a key region for national poverty reduction strategies. The following chapter therefore predominantly takes a closer look at this province.

---

[53] In the case of imports and exports, contributions to national trade might be overestimated. This is due to the fact that the provincial trade balance also includes intra-country trade with ROC.

5.1.2.2 Production and Investment

Section 5.1.1 has presented an aggregate view on Son La's economy. The following section further investigates sector-specific information and investment patterns. The diversification of the regional economy is low. Industry is dominated by food processing and construction materials. Major intermediate goods including machinery, chemicals and fuel are not produced locally. The tertiary sector in the province comprises a high share of public services. Other relevant services include construction, trade, hotels and restaurants.

The trade balance defined as the ratio of trade between the province and the rest of Vietnam plus the rest of the world is negative and accounts to about 45 percent as a percentage of GDP. On the import side, processed food, machinery, rice, chemicals, fuel and textiles make up 56 percent of total imports to the province. 61 percent of the output value of the major staple food rice is imported. Table 5.6 shows that imports of processed food and textiles exceed local production by about 296 and 879 percent, respectively. Exports out of the province are largely concentrated in the agricultural and forestry sector. 65 percent of marketed crop output and 36 percent of forestry products are exported.

**Table 5.6   Structure of Regional Economy: Son La Province, 2002
(Selected Sectors)**

	Y	GDP	Ei/Yi	Mi/Yi	P
Rice	0.08	0.10	0.02	0.61	1.24
Other Crops	0.23	0.30	0.65	0.00	1.19
Livestock	0.07	0.06	0.20	0.06	2.00
Forestry	0.09	0.11	0.36	0.00	1.21
Fishery	0.01	0.01	0.00	0.41	1.41
Food Processing	0.03	0.01	0.03	2.96	3.75
Textiles	0.00	0.00	0.00	8.79	4.85
Cement	0.01	0.00	0.19	1.40	5.12
Oth.Constr. Material	0.01	0.01	0.00	0.57	3.18
Civil Construction	0.07	0.03	0.00	0.02	3.28

Notes:
Y: Sectoral gross output as a share of total gross output of Son La province
GDP: GDP at factor cost as a share of total provincial GDP at factor cost (real)
Ei/Yi: share of exports in total value of output in sector i
Mi/Yi: share of imports in total value of output in sector i
P: Productivity as ratio between activity output and the composite factor

Base year factor productivities across sectors are calculated as the ratio between activity output and the composite factor. Productivity is highest in the cement and textile sectors, followed by food processing. Agricultural productivity is comparatively low, ranging between 1.2 and 2.0. Annual growth rates in the province averaged 9 percent between 1990 and 2002.[54] The primary and secondary sectors grew by 8 percent over that period, whereas the service sector showed average growth rates of 11 percent. However, in the period from 1996 to 2002, growth in the primary sector remained constant, whereas growth in the secondary and tertiary sectors reached annual increases of 12 percent and 14 percent respectively. These growth rates can largely be explained by public investments in infrastructure and the expansion of public services. For the interpretation of the results in section 5.2, it is important to note that percentage changes are additional to these long-term growth trends.

Table 5.7 analyses the contribution of the different factors of production to the total value added of different sectors. It becomes clear that unskilled labour is the dominant factor across all sectors. It has its highest share in agriculture, followed by construction and services. Skilled labour accounts for 24 percent of value added in the service sector, while the share in agriculture is still a remarkable 14 percent. Capital constitutes 27 percent of value added in industry, 18 percent in services and 13 percent in construction.

Table 5.7   Sectoral Value Added by Factor (as Share of Total Sectoral Value Added)

	Skilled labour	Unskilled labour	Capital	Land	TOTAL
AGR	0.14	0.80	0.03	0.03	1.00
IND	0.20	0.53	0.27	0.00	1.00
CONST	0.21	0.66	0.13	0.00	1.00
SERV	0.24	0.58	0.18	0.00	1.00

Total public and private investments in Son La province for the year 2002 amounted to 1.3 trillion VND (GSO SL, 2003A). The sectoral distribution of this investment is as follows: 19 percent went into the agricultural sector, 3 percent into construction. The share of public investment was 56 percent. Private investment, including households and private enterprises accounted for 36 percent. FDI played a minor role with 0.3 percent of total investments (GSO SL, 2003A). Table 5.8 compares per capita investments by type between Son La and national averages. Large discrepancies occur in all three categories. While the

---

[54] Measured at constant 1994 prices (GSO SL 2003A).

amount of public investments per capita is half the national average, private investment is only about 10 percent of the national average and FDI is virtually not existent.

Table 5.8   Investment by Type (USD per Capita)

	Public investment (USD)	FDI (USD)	DPI (USD)
Son La	39.00	0.00	2.11
Vietnam	74.46	26.34	22.03

Source: GSO SL, 2003A; DAPICE, 2003
Notes:
FDI: Foreign direct investment
DPI: Domestic private investment
Public investment are displayed for the year 2000, domestic private investment for the year 2001, FDI
        for 2002

5.1.2.3 Households and Factor Markets

To better understand poverty in the region, the following section discusses relevant characteristics of households and factor markets. Son La has 942,000 inhabitants compared to 77,685,000 of Vietnam's total population (GSO SL, 2003A). In 2002, 89 percent of the inhabitants were identified as rural and 11 percent as urban. Table 5.9 indicates that disparities between urban and rural households in the province are distinct. In the baseline, annual per capita expenditure of urban households is about 2.4 times higher than of rural households. Accordingly, poverty rates among rural households are much higher. While 63 percent of all rural households are below the poverty line, only 2 percent of their urban counterparts are below that line.[55]

Substantial differences also exist in the depth of poverty, measured by the poverty gap indicator. While the distance between expenditure levels and the poverty line for urban households was 112,000 VND, the poverty gap of rural households was almost 5 times higher. Differences also exist in household size. It varies from 2 to 18 household members, with a clear tendency of larger household sizes in rural areas. Finally, subsistence levels are clearly higher in rural areas. While 95 percent of goods and services consumed by urban households originate from markets, this share for rural households is only 57 percent. The relatively high share of home produce and a low share of imported

---

[55] Base year expenditures by rural and urban households are listed in Appendix 3 and 4.

goods in the consumption basket of households among rural households should therefore buffer the direct impacts of price changes of traded commodities.

Table 5.9 Poverty Characteristics of Households

	Population (in 1000)	Average HH size	EXP (1000 VND)	HC/TC (%)	POV (%)	POVGAP (1000 VND)
Urban	104	4.2	4.465	0.05	0.02	112
Rural	838	5.8	1.893	0.43	0.63	537
Total households	942	5.6	2.223	0.34	0.55	

Notes:
EXP: expenditure per household
HC/TC: home consumption of self-produce as a share of household consumption
POV: headcount poverty rate
POVGAP: poverty gap

Education levels among the province' inhabitants are generally very low. 76 percent of the total population aged between 16 and 60 years have no or only primary education. This education level is much more alarming in rural areas, where 85 percent of the population has received no or only a very low level of education (GSO, 2004). Even more alarming is the situation among ethnic minorities. The rate of uneducated or only poorly educated people stands at 87 percent among rural Thai people of whom 62 percent have received no education. The rate of uneducated or only poorly educated people among Hmong people stood at 99 percent of the sample. 88 percent had no school qualifications and the illiteracy rate among them is 69 percent (GSO, 2004).[56]

Accordingly, unskilled labour dominates the factor market. The contributions of the different factors towards total value-added is 73 percent for unskilled labour, 23 percent for skilled labour, 1 percent for capital and 2 percent for land. Table 5.10 shows that 82 percent of the rural households earn their income from unskilled labour. Their share of income from skilled labour accounts to 14 percent. In addition, rural households generate 1 percent of their income from capital and three percent from land. Urban households earn 59 percent of their income from skilled labour and 38 percent from unskilled labour.

---

[56] The sample for Hmong households in the VHLSS comprises only 26 households, figure on education are thus not representative and have to be interpreted with care.

Table 5.10 Factor Income Distribution for Son La Households (as a Share of Total)

	Total (billion VND)	Skilled labour	Unskilled labour	Capital	Land
Urban	421	0.59	0.38	0.03	0.00
Rural	1,608	0.14	0.82	0.01	0.03

The unemployment rate within Son La's workforce is estimated to be at 8 percent, amounting to 30 percent among the urban and 5 percent among the rural population, respectively (GSO, 2004). The underemployment rate in rural areas amounts to 31 percent at a mean shortfall of 15.45 hours per person and week.[57] However, the actual rates might even be higher. The ECONOMIST (2006A) refers to an Asian Development Bank (ADB) report that puts these official underemployment figures much higher. According to that source, underemployment in rural areas of Vietnam stands at 56 percent.

5.1.2.4 Regional Economy from a Multiplier Perspective

In addition to the descriptive analysis of base model results, the multiplier perspective confirms the early stage of development of Son La's economy.[58] The analysis confirms that gross output-, GDP- and income multipliers are the highest in agriculture, indicating that the agricultural sector has large potential to drive economic growth.

Inspections of the multiplier matrix reveal large multiplier values predominantly in the primary sector activities (column (1) – (8) of the multiplier matrix in the appendix 3).[59] In the agricultural sector (including forestry and

---

[57] In rural areas of Vietnam, overcapacity of the labour force is measured according to the underemployment rate, which is defined as the percentage of employable population working less than 40 hours per week (GSO, 2004).

[58] The multiplier model is estimated as a single region model for the Son La province.

[59] In general, three types of multipliers can be derived from such analysis. The gross output multiplier reports the total effect on provincial gross output, which results from an income increase of a one monetary unit (MU) of a SAM account i. It is calculated by summing up all production activity elements in the multiplier matrix along the column of account i. The value added or GDP multiplier is derived analogously by adding up the factor elements along the column of account i. The respective sum represents the total increase in provincial GDP resulting from an exogenous injection of one MU. Similarly, the household income multiplier is composed of the combined income of all household groups in account i and indicates the impact of an exogenous 1 MU injection in account i on provincial household income.

fishery) the total multipliers vary between 3.5 and 5.3. The crop accounts 'paddy rice', 'coffee', and 'tea' have gross output multipliers of 1.9, 2.4, and 2.4 respectively. The gross output multiplier of livestock production amounts to 2.7, that of forestry to 2.6, and that of fishery to 2.1. Compared to that, gross output multipliers in the secondary and tertiary sectors are significantly lower. These are between 1.1 and 2.0 in the secondary sector and between 1.2 and 2.3 in the service sector. Value added multipliers in the crop production sector range from 0.8 to 1.4. In industry and manufacturing, they are significantly lower with values between 0.04 and 0.5. In the service sector, value added multipliers range from 0.1 to 1.1. Differences in household income multipliers are distinct, too. They are highest in the agricultural sector in a range of additional income for all households between 0.7 and 1.3 as compared to 0.03-0.3 and 0.08-0.9 in the secondary and tertiary sectors. The high shares of imported goods in these sectors mainly lead to the comparably low multiplier values in manufacturing and industry.

These findings suggest that the agricultural sector has the highest potential to contribute to economic growth thus should be one of the prime target for interventions. In the poverty reduction scenario in section 5.2.3, I will therefore concentrate on agricultural growth as the main driver of regional growth and poverty reduction.

5.2 Assessing the Impacts of Infrastructure Investments and Economic Growth

Scenario 1 shows how improved infrastructure and access to markets can contribute to economic growth and poverty reduction. Scenario 2 analyses the multidimensional impacts of a hydropower dam on the regional and the national level. Scenario 3 estimates the impacts of economic growth on poverty. Figure 5.1 shows the organisation of the three scenarios.

Each scenario presentation (sections 5.2.1, 5.2.2, and 5.2.3) consists of different simulations and is structured in three parts: the specific motivation and background of the scenario is followed by the presentation and the implementation of the single simulations. The third part presents the results. The results of all scenarios are presented in four categories. These include macroeconomic changes, structural changes by economic sectors, changes in factor incomes and changes in household performance. The macroeconomic table refers to the national level, without differentiating between the two regions. Due to the focus of the study, special attention is given to trade, investment and household related indicators in the discussion of results by economic sectors. The sectoral perspective presents the results aggregated by agriculture, industry, construction and services. Changes in output and GDP are given by region, while the imports and exports refer to international trade of the two combined regions. Changes in factor incomes consider all factors, including the two labour categories, capital and land.

Figure 5.1 Organisation of Scenarios

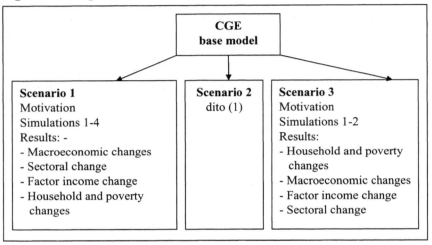

The table on household expenditure indicates changes for urban and rural households in REG and ROC. All changes are given in real terms, measured at base year prices. The poverty analysis, however, concentrates on REG. Poverty changes are given as the new incidence of poverty and as the absolute number of poor crossing the poverty line. In addition, household results include changes in the poverty gap indicator.

Finally, it should be noted that the following discussion of results largely relies on comparing the size of impacts within and across simulations rather than quoting exact numbers. This is due to the nature of CGE models, which are intended to indicate directions rather than produce point-specific results (McCulloch et al., 2001). In the case of poverty analysis the presentation also relies on numbers to better illustrate the impacts, while interpreting them carefully.

5.2.1 Road Infrastructure

5.2.1.1 Motivation

Roads are vital drivers of growth and the adequacy of road infrastructure plays a key role in the participation and empowerment of remote regions in the successful development of Vietnam. An aggregate view on road infrastructure in Vietnam reveals that Vietnam has an average road density of 0.63 km per square km of surface, which is about the average of other ASEAN countries (WORLD BANK et al., 2004). Paved roads account for 84 percent of all roads and the number of communes without access to district centres has been reduced to 2.6 percent (WORLD BANK et al., 2004). This is the result of an increasing share of public spending that was allocated towards road networks. Investments grew at 13.5 percent per annum (FAN et al., 2004). However, investments into interregional and rural road networks and other large-scale infrastructure systems are still not sufficient and fail to meet international quality standards (SRV, 2003). In addition, higher investments in roads mean lower expenditure allocated for recurrent expenditures. This leads to a neglect of operation and maintenance costs (FAN et al., 2004). Given the limited resources, the CPRGS thus emphasises the upgrading of existing road networks while assessing new projects according to their impact socio-economic development (SRV, 2003).

Road density and economic development in Vietnam are clearly interlinked. Statistics show that 85.9 percent of communes without access to a road network were poor; in the Northern Mountains poor communes without road access accounted for 18.5 percent of the total poor communes (FAN et al., 2004). For Son La province 8 out of the 201 communes are not accessible by bus (GSO SL, 2003A).[60] In addition, seasonally impassable roads, an insufficient number of physical market places, market information and a lack of a sound legal framework for buyers and sellers function as trade barriers and increase transaction costs. This leads to substantial price differences of traded goods compared to other regions of Vietnam (CUONG, 2005).

To address the strong disparities in both infrastructure endowments and poverty in urban and rural areas it is important to differentiate between rural and urban road investments. This differentiation can give insights into the impacts of the respective road types and add an economy-wide perspective on this issue to the existing literature.

---

[60] More exact data on road accessibility and road condition for the province was not available. According to personal experience there is definitely scope for road improvement and the reduction of transaction costs.

5.2.1.2 Simulations

Improvements in road infrastructure are implemented through two different mechanisms, the reduction of transaction costs and increases in FP. To account for the strong rural/ urban disparities, I differentiate between investments in rural roads and urban roads by assuming that rural roads benefit mainly the agricultural sector and urban roads benefit mainly the industrial sector. In both cases, a reduction of transaction costs will benefit producers through lower costs of production and consumers through lower demand prices. Simulation TRADE1 takes a national perspective and reduces domestic transaction costs of agricultural commodities by 20 percent, while simulation TRADE2 reduces transaction costs of industrial and manufactured goods by 20 percent.

Simulations TRADE3 and TRADE4 look at the impacts on the regional level. To implement the simulations, I follow the empirical evidence that improvements in physical infrastructure increase the FP. Again, to compare investments in rural and urban roads, TRADE3 looks at the impacts of FP increases in agricultural production activities, while TRADE4 examines the case of manufacturing and industry. The comparison of results within the categories can be expected to give interesting insights not only in the size of impacts but also to the direction of impacts. This is due to the fact that they use different approaches of implementing the simulation. Finally, it is important to note that the objective of these simulations is to capture the economy-wide impacts of investments. Quantifying the cost of reducing transaction costs and increasing FP is beyond the scope of this thesis.

Table 5.11 Overview of Road Simulations

Scenario 1: Investments in road infrastructure	
TRADE1	Investment in rural roads: 20 percent reduction in domestic and export transaction costs for agricultural commodities
TRADE2	Investment in urban roads: 20 percent reduction in domestic and export transaction costs for industry, manufacturing and construction
TRADE3	Investment in rural roads: 20 percent FP increase in regional agriculture
TRADE4	Investment in urban roads: 20 percent FP increase in regional industry, manufacturing, transport and trade

In general, the model reacts to these shocks as follows. The reduction of transaction costs lowers the costs for moving the commodity from domestic suppliers to the demanders, or in the case of exported goods from the producer to international markets. A reduction of transaction costs thus leads to lower prices and benefits producers (through lower costs for intermediate goods) and consumers of the respective commodities. Higher productivity leads to higher output, which meets increased domestic demand of consumers. Since both the domestic producer and consumer benefit, overall impacts on the domestic economy are expected to be positive. Losers in this process could be the service providers of transactions, including traders, transportation services etc. This sector might shrink, if the net effect of additionally created trade and the forgone income caused by more efficient transactions is negative. In addition, domestic economic growth effects depend on changes in the current account balance. Since the model assumes a fixed nominal exchange rate, the trade balance is the major determinant for the balance of payments.

5.2.1.3 Results

Table 5.12 shows macroeconomic changes for the simulations TRADE1 to TRADE4. Table entries indicate percentage changes as compared to the baseline. The comparison of macroeconomic indicators between rural and urban roads on the national level (TRADE1 and TRADE2) reveals that size and direction of impacts vary strongly. Rural roads lead to an increase in private consumption and spark investment. This leads to a rise in the domestic demand and the domestic price index and a lower PPP of the VND compared to foreign currencies. The trade deficit grows, since real exports decrease and real imports increase. Imports increase due to an increase of domestic demand and domestic prices for non-tradeables. Urban roads have a positive influence on the trade balance and reduce the deficit. This effect is due to both increasing exports and decreasing imports. Real household consumption increases by about the same percentage than under the rural road simulation. However, real investment is shrinking, which can be explained by the increase of the real exchange rate combined with lower foreign savings. Government consumption remains constant, while government savings slightly increase. Revenues from imports and direct taxes only slightly change. Simulations TRADE3 and TRADE4 look at the impacts of roads from a one-region perspective (REG), which explains the generally much lower national macroeconomic impacts and impacts on ROC sectors and households. Only rural roads in REG have sizeable impacts on the national level. Total absorption, household consumption, investment and imports increase, other macroeconomic indicators remain unchanged.

**Table 5.12 Macroeconomic Changes of Road Investment Scenarios
(Percentage Real Change from Base)**

	TRADE1	TRADE2	TRADE3	TRADE4
Absorption	4.1	1.1	0.1	0.0
Household consumption	2.3	2.4	0.1	0.0
Investment	9.3	-1.4	0.2	0.1
Government consumption	0.0	0.0	0.0	0.0
Exports	-2.3	1.9	0.0	0.0
Imports	2.4	-0.9	0.1	0.0
PPP real exchange rate (LCUs per FCU)	-0.9	0.4	0.0	0.0
Domestic (non-tradables) price index	0.9	-0.4	0.0	0.0
Private (household + enterprise) savings	-0.1	0.0	0.0	0.0
Foreign savings	2.5	-1.5	0.0	0.0
Trade deficit	2.2	-1.6	0.0	0.0
Government savings	0.2	0.1	0.0	0.0
Import tax revenue	0.0	-0.1	0.0	0.0
Direct tax revenue	0.0	0.1	0.0	0.0

These macroeconomic changes are not substantial and only of limited importance for the analysis of structural changes and poverty impacts of roads. There are other mechanisms at work such as trade policies, exchange rate policies and capital market regulations that have much more influence on these macroeconomic indicators. This depicts a certain dilemma: incorporating other policy developments into infrastructure analyses would contribute to the understanding of the overall macroeconomic development. But at the same time, such an approach would not allow to isolate infrastructure induced impacts. However, taking these effects into account provides a sound basis and a good starting point for further analysis of changes in economic sectors.

The sector perspective confirms the positive impacts of roads and provides further interesting details between the impacts of rural and urban roads (Table 5.13 and Table 5.14). As can be expected, rural roads lead to a strong output and GDP growth in agriculture. This growth is substantially higher in REG, indicating that the marginal benefit of rural roads in poor agriculture-based regions is higher. Agricultural growth leads to increasing real income of the rural population. Due to this substantial increase in purchasing power and the high income elasticities of demand for primary products, the demand for agricultural products grows. This increasing demand it partly satisfied through a substitution between exports and domestically marketed goods. This decrease in exports is not sufficient to satisfy demand and is accompanied by an increase in agricultural imports. However, it is not only the agricultural sector that benefits from rural roads.

Table 5.13 Changes by Economic Sector TRADE1 (Percentage Real Change from Base)

	Output		GDP		Trade	
	ROC	REG	ROC	REG	E	I
AGR	1.5	5.9	1.4	5.8	-4.4	6.2
IND	0.5	4.8	-0.2	4.3	-2.0	2.7
CONST	9.2	13.4	9.2	13.4	0.0	0.0
SERV	-2.6	-1.1	-2.3	-1.0	-2.1	-0.4
TOTAL	0.6	4.9	0.0	4.2	-2.3	2.4

Table 5.14 Changes by Economic Sector TRADE2 (Percentage Real Change from Base)

	Output		GDP		Trade	
	ROC	REG	ROC	REG	E	I
AGR	0.6	4.0	0.5	4.0	-4.5	10.7
IND	4.7	4.1	2.7	4.2	3.4	-1.1
CONST	-1.4	-0.5	-1.4	-0.5	0.0	0.0
SERV	-2.9	-0.7	-2.6	-0.5	-2.2	-0.3
TOTAL	1.4	2.0	-0.1	2.3	1.7	-0.8

Industry is growing at almost the same pace as agriculture in REG, although less in ROC. Construction shows strong growth in the case of rural roads and a modestly recessive trend in the case of urban roads.[61] Besides the construction sector in the case of urban roads, services can not benefit from the reduction of transaction costs and even show decreasing outputs. This is due to two reasons: the database structure and the model structure. Even though service activities use trade and transportation services as inputs, no information is available for national and international transaction costs of services. Consequently, the model does not account for potential benefits for the service sector from roads. The actually incurred losses stem from the fact that reduced transaction costs lead to reduced demand for related services. This result is a

---

[61] This finding is counterintuitive, since a decrease in transaction costs through improved roads is associated with road construction works. However, this decrease might be caused by the private rather than the public construction and due to generally shrinking total investments in TRADE2.

rather short- to medium term interpretation caused by the static nature of the model. In the longer run, benefit for services should occur through an increasing demand of other sectors and institutions that benefit from the road investments.

In sum, rural roads lead to higher aggregate GDP growth, which is about twice as high as in REG as that induced by urban roads. This result is surprising for two reasons: first the industrial sector's output value is about three times higher than in the agricultural sector. One might thus expect stronger impacts of lower transaction costs. Second, initial domestic transaction costs as a share of output for industrial goods are higher as the costs of agricultural goods. The marginal benefit of a percentage reduction of these transaction costs could therefore be expected to lead to higher overall effects. However, results indicate that marginal benefits of improvements of urban roads are smaller than those of rural roads indicating that the initial quality and quantity determines the size of the impacts.[62] Strong intersectoral effects and strong linkages of agriculture with the rest of the economy particularly in REG lead to the effect that industrial sector is growing by the same rate in the rural road simulation than in the urban road simulation. On the contrary, urban roads do not benefit the rural sectors to same extent. This finding underlines the importance of taking economy-wide effects into account. The following two simulations aim at substantiating these findings. In the following simulations, roads are simulated by increasing the FP of rural and urban production activities in REG (Table 5.15 and Table 5.16).

Table 5.15 Changes by Economic Sector TRADE3 (Percentage Real Change from Base)

	Output		GDP		Trade	
	ROC	REG	ROC	REG	E	I
AGR	0.0	27.7	0.0	28.4	0.5	-1.0
IND	0.0	1.0	0.0	0.6	-0.1	0.1
CONST	0.2	-0.2	0.2	-0.2	0.0	0.0
SERV	0.0	-1.0	0.0	-1.0	0.0	0.0
TOTAL	0.0	13.3	0.0	16.4	0.0	0.1

---

[62] This finding is confirmed for the impacts of roads on access to credit in Cameroon (HEIDHUES and SCHRIEDER, 1993).

Table 5.16   Changes by Economic Sector TRADE4 (Percentage Real Change from Base)

	Output		GDP		Trade	
	ROC	REG	ROC	REG	E	I
AGR	0.0	-0.1	0.0	-0.1	0.0	0.1
IND	0.0	12.9	0.0	14.9	0.0	0.0
CONST	0.0	11.7	0.0	11.7	0.0	0.0
SERV	0.0	8.0	0.0	7.6	0.0	0.0
TOTAL	0.0	5.0	0.0	3.6	0.0	0.0

These simulations confirm the results of TRADE1 and TRADE2. Rural roads induce higher economy-wide growth and lead to higher multiplier effects. However, a closer look at the results reveals some differences. Due to the relatively small size of the regional economy, roads in REG do not have big impacts on ROC sectors or foreign trade. Only the strong growth in agriculture caused by rural roads slightly changes the agricultural trade balance by increasing national exports and reducing imports. In addition, there are substitution effects in the construction sector, where the ROC construction sector is taking shares from the REG construction.

Sectoral changes in the region are more pronounced than in TRADE1 and TRADE2. Rural roads lead to almost 30 percent GDP growth in the agricultural sector. However, the regional industry stagnates, which can be explained by the fact that major intermediate consumption goods of agricultural production such as fertilizer, fuel and pesticides are not produced in REG. In addition, many investment and consumer goods, e.g. machinery, chemicals, are imported to REG. On the contrary, due to its local nature, the service sector can benefit from rural roads and substantially contribute to overall growth.

Urban roads lead to GDP growth of about 13 percent in the industrial sectors. Also construction and services gain from the performance of the industrial sector. The relatively bad performance of agriculture compared to services is based on the local nature of most services, which are often related to urban areas. Industrial growth does therefore not seem to trickle down to rural areas. A reason for this could be the relatively small size of the sector, which does not allow for relevant intersectoral effects. Consequently, total regional GDP grows only modestly. This result suggests that broad growth has to come from agriculture, since both aggregate growth and trickle down effects are substantially bigger.

Major channels through which economic shocks are transmitted to households are factor markets. For the rural population in REG, unskilled labour markets are of special relevance since they receive about 82 percent of their income from that factor. In addition, most of the rural people are farmers and generate income from land. Table 5.17 shows that rural roads generally have positive impacts on all factor categories. Results confirm that unskilled labour and land benefit most from rural roads. The impacts on REG unskilled factor markets in TRADE1 and TRADE3 are quite similar, ranging around an increase of 10 percent and are major drivers of poverty reduction. Urban roads have the strongest effect on skilled labour at the national level, followed by unskilled labour. Urban roads on the regional level equally benefit skilled and unskilled labour, followed by capital and land.

Table 5.17 Changes in Factor Income (Percentage Real Change from Base)

	TRADE1	TRADE2	TRADE3	TRADE4
LUSK-ROC	5.3	2.3	0.1	0.1
LUSK-REG	9.8	-0.6	8.4	3.7
LSK-ROC	3.9	2.8	0.1	0.0
LSK-REG	6.9	-0.6	5.0	3.7
CAPI-ROC	4.9	2.1	0.1	0.1
CAPI-REG	5.6	-1.3	2.1	2.9
LAND-ROC	6.6	0.9	0.1	0.1
LAND-REG	9.3	0.1	9.7	2.8

Notes:
LUSK: Unskilled labour
LSK: Skilled labour
CAPI: Capital
LAND: Land

The macroeconomic table at the beginning of this chapter showed increasing real household consumption for rural and urban roads. The following section takes a closer look at these positive effects by taking a regional and urban/rural perspective to get insights into distributional and poverty effects of roads. It thus comes to the final step in this scenario analysis and presents the results of the micro-accounting poverty module (Table 5.18).

In line with the results presented above, there is no tendency that rural households only benefit from rural roads and urban households from urban roads. In 14 out of 16 cases, urban and rural households can increase their real expenditures. The major linkages of mutually increasing expenditures are labour markets that link urban and rural regions and households. Multiplier effects of increased demand for goods and services from private households and production activities lead to spillover effects to other sectors. For both rural and urban REG households expenditures increase from roads. The benefits range from 3.4 to 3.8 percent in the case of urban and 5.6 to 11.5 percent in the case of rural households. As compared to that, urban roads lead to expenditure changes of between 1.6 and -0.2 for urban and 3.1 to -0.2 for rural households. The slightly negative impact of TRADE4 stems from the small GDP decrease in agriculture, which can not be compensated by growth in the other sectors.

Table 5.18 Changes in Real Household Expenditure and Poverty

		EXP		POV		POVGAP	
		ROC	REG	%	No.	(1000 VND)	%
Urban	TRADE1	2.1	3.4	2.2	0	47.3	-57.6
	TRADE2	2.4	1.6	2.2	0	81.4	-27.1
	TRADE3	0.1	3.8	2.2	0	39.7	-64.4
	TRADE4	0.0	-0.2	2.2	0	115.5	3.4
Rural	TRADE1	2.5	5.6	54.4	71448	536.9	0.1
	TRADE2	2.4	3.1	58.4	38472	533.7	-0.5
	TRADE3	0.1	11.5	49.5	112668	507.2	-5.5
	TRADE4	0.0	-0.2	63.0	0	539.4	0.5

Notes:
EXP: Real expenditure change (as percent from base)
POV: Poverty. % expresses the new poverty rate under the respective simulation. No. indicates
    changes in the number of poor people.
POVGAP: Poverty gap. % shows the percentage change in the poverty gap as compared to the base
    poverty gap (see also definition poverty gap in chapter 4.3).

In ROC, however, rural and urban households benefit almost equally from rural roads and urban roads. In REG, rural households have higher percentage increases in expenditure in all simulations. This result is somewhat surprising at a first glance. An explanation for this outcome can be found in linkages in labour markets, especially rural unskilled labour employed in urban industrial sector contribute to this outcome. In addition, rural households benefit from the growth in the agricultural sector. However, due to their substantially lower initial expenditure, the absolute changes are generally lower for rural households. The real changes in welfare can best be analysed by taking poverty effects into account. It should be noted that initial poverty among REG households was distinctively different between urban and rural households. While the poverty rate among urban households is at 2 percent, 63 percent of rural households were classified as poor. The poverty gap for rural households was almost five times higher, 112,000 VND per capita for urban households as compared to 537,000 VND per capita for rural households. It should be kept in mind that the poverty impact analysis only refers to REG.

The results show that roads do not significantly contribute to the eradication of urban poverty. The poverty rate remains at 2 percent in all four scenarios. However, the poverty gap is shrinking between 57.6 percent and 64.4 percent in the case of rural roads and 27.1 percent in TRADE2. Only TRADE4 leads to a slight increase in the poverty gap by 3.4 percent. These results indicate that rural roads can have positive impacts on urban poverty reduction, which are even bigger than the impacts of urban roads. The impacts of both rural and urban roads on rural poverty are much more pronounced. The results display that especially rural roads can strongly contribute to poverty reduction. Poverty among rural households is reduced by 8.5 percentage points to 54.4 percent in TRADE1 and 13.4 percentage points in TRADE3. This amounts to a total number of people between 71,448 and 112,668 who can be lifted out of poverty by rural roads. The impacts of urban roads on rural poverty is less pronounced, ranging between zero and 38,472 people.

Despite these positive impacts, the examination of the poverty gap index reveals some worrisome results with far reaching policy implications. The impacts on the poverty gap are much lower than on poverty incidence - the changes range between an increase of 0.5 percent to a decrease of 5.5 percent. The poverty gap remains very high and in all cases above 500,000 VND per capita. This means that roads can contribute to lifting a substantial number of people out of poverty, but these tend to be people who live close to the poverty line. For the large majority of the poor, the relatively small absolute gains do not contribute much to improve their economic situation.

In summary, results of the model confirm that roads *are* vital elements in the engine of growth. In addition, model outcomes suggest that roads can also contribute to poverty reduction. The metaphor can thus be extended to "roads are vital elements in the engine of *pro-poor growth*". Furthermore, the differentiation between urban and rural roads confirms the findings of empirical studies that rural roads have higher potentials to contribute to poverty reduction than urban roads by increasing output and trade volumes. Substantial multiplier effects can be observed at the sector, factor and household level emphasising the importance to take these effects into account when analysing infrastructure investments.

5.2.2 Large-Scale Hydropower Dam

5.2.2.1 Motivation

The key problem and one of the major challenges surrounding large-scale dams are its diametrical spatial impacts. While costs in the form of inundated land have to be carried largely by the local population, benefits such as flood mitigation and electricity availability are mostly enjoyed by urban centres and industry (WCD, 2000). The objective of the following scenario is to examine the impacts of a specific dam project, the Son La Hydropower dam, from both a regional and a national perspective.

Son La dam is a key project in the electricity sector strategy of Vietnam (SRV, 2003). The energy policy of Vietnam pursues a development strategy of power sources with priority given to renewable energies, namely hydroelectric power (EVN, 1999). The nationwide economic boom in Vietnam has led to a massive increase in demand for energy and the north-western mountainous province of Son La was selected to be the site for a large hydroelectric power plant. The Son La dam is build on the Da River, a tributary of the Red River, about 250km upstream from its confluence and 170km upstream of Hoa Binh dam. Total public investments are estimated at 38 billion VND or 15 times the annual provincial GDP of Son La province (EVN, 2001). This biggest hydroelectric dam project in Vietnam is planned to have an installed capacity of 2,400 MW, spread over eight engine complexes with 300 MW each. It will provide an average energy of 9.2 billion kWh/annum, which is equal to the current volume consumed annually in Northern Vietnam. The dam will be 136m high and the reservoir's full supply level will be 215m. Construction of the dam started at the beginning of 2005 and the dam is expected to start operating fully in 2015. It is designed as a multi-purpose dam. While its core benefit is electricity generation, other expected benefits include flood mitigation (EVN 1999; EVN, 2001).

80 percent of the construction material and workers are imported from the rest of Vietnam to the project region, while 20 percent of the materials and workforce will be provided by the province (EVN, 2001). Dam construction needs qualified staff, which is not available in Son La province. One third of the total sum has been earmarked for the resettlement of families living in the 44,700 hectares to be flooded by the reservoir. The remaining 25.3 trillion VND (1.7 billion USD) are used for construction.

5.2.2.2 Simulations

Four simulations estimate the impact of the Son La hydropower dam on economic growth and poverty, whereby two of the simulations address isolated impacts of single shocks and two simulations look at combined impacts. Scenario 2 is structured as follows: the simulation of dam construction (DAMCON) and decrease in land (LANDDECR) look at the two major regional effects, the construction and the inundation of land.

Table 5.19   Overview of Large-Scale Dam Simulations

Scenario 2:

Investment in hydropower dam

DAMCON	Short-term impacts of dam construction: increase in capital stock of regional and national construction
LANDDECR	Short and medium-term impacts of dam construction: Loss of land and capital in agriculture and forestry sector
DAMREG	Net regional short to medium term effects of the dam: 2-part simulation including effects construction boom and loss of land.
DAMNAT	National impacts of the dam: increase in energy availability and flood control leads to a 10 percent FP increase in energy intensive industries (cement, metal, chemicals and electricity). Benefits of flood control lead to a reduction of losses thus FP increase in ROC agriculture (rice and other crops).

• DAMCON

The simulation DAMCON is modelled by exogenously increasing the capital stock of construction activities. The respective capital stocks are adjusted according to the annual cost of construction. The CGE model includes four construction accounts, two REG and two from ROC. The civil construction account includes various types of public construction including dam, roads and electricity grids as defined in the I-O table (GSO, 2003). The annual size of the shock is calculated by using the information of ELECTRICITY OF VIETNAM (EVN, 2001). Total investment is divided by the number of construction years. The resulting capital investment is distributed 2:8 between REG and ROC construction. By taking the "fresh" capital as a share of existing capital stock, which is 11 billion for the REG civil construction and 4,639 billion VND for the ROC civil construction activity, the coefficients that shock the model are derived as 23.0 in the case of regional and 1.2 in the case of national capital stock. It is assumed that the construction boom leads to an increase in demand for agricultural goods, transportation, restaurants and trade services. This demand is implemented by increasing the respective FP of the sectors by 10 percent.

The capital stock increase in construction modifies the production function for construction activities. At the same time, increased demand leads to an upward shift of the demand function. Labour is substituted by capital, construction output grows. Due to the increase in demand, total labour income increases. This partial perspective can explain substitution effects and subsequent changes in output and factor markets. However, it neglects three important aspects taken into account by the 2-region CGE model. First, supply and demand for capital and labour are determined on economy-wide rather than sector-specific factor markets. Second, construction can be supplied by two construction activities (REG and ROC), which have different production functions. Third, multiplier effects caused by increasing household incomes and respective changes in commodity and factor markets are taken into account in the CGE model.

- LANDDECR

The scenario is motivated by the fact that damming the Da River will involve the inundation of large parts of land. Inundation leads to the loss of land, reduces agricultural output and thus income of farmers in the province. The simulation LANDDECR is modelled by decreasing FP in the agricultural sector. The translation of this loss of land into a reduction of agricultural production is presented in the following. To calculate a coefficient that reflects the impact of the inundation of land, the following assumptions are made: total agricultural land in Son La province is 191,310 ha and half of the inundated land is either agricultural or forestry land. Since land along the river is usually characterised by higher quality, and in the case of Son La, often equipped with irrigation systems, it is further assumed that its productivity is twice the productivity of the rest of the land in the province. Following these assumptions, 22,350ha of inundated land represent a production decrease of about 20 percent.[63]

The decrease in land modifies the production function, which leads to a decrease in agricultural output, since the loss of land cannot be substituted by other factors. In a closed economy, net effects on the income of producers depend on the demand elasticities for agricultural products and are determined by the demand function. If the demand elasticity for agricultural products is equal or bigger than one, prices will increase and compensate producers for the foregone decrease in output. This partial perspective is useful to understand underlying mechanisms of the agricultural production function. To capture real world effects in the regional context, however, one has to extend this partial perspective to a general equilibrium framework and allow for interregional and international trade. If one includes trade in the model, regional price changes

---

[63] Calculation: ((44.700/2)*2)/191310 (then rounded to 20 percent to take the lower limit). These are rough estimates. More precise data, which was not available for this study could easily be incorporated.

will depend upon the elasticity of substitution between domestically produced goods and imported goods. The higher this elasticity, the more trade will substitute for regional production shortfalls and the weaker the impacts on local prices will be.[64] From this perspective, the land decrease reduces production output and decreases the demand for labour and wages.

- DAMREG

In the next step, these two major regional effects of construction and loss of land are simulated in a combined scenario to assess their net impact. Simulation DAMREG presents a two-part experiment, where the combined effect of DAMCON and LANDDECR is estimated and thus the short to medium-term net effect of the dam is assessed.

- DAMNAT

On the national level, the two major impacts are expected to benefit the economy through flood control and improved availability of electricity. To estimate these effects, simulation DAMNAT models the two major national effects, electricity availability and flood mitigation, to quantify the benefits outside the project area. Case studies show that hydropower dams have often benefited the electricity-intensive industrial sectors and urban areas (WCD, 2000). I assume that these benefits translate into FP increases in energy-intensive sectors in Vietnam, including cement, chemicals, metal and the electricity sector itself. Since no empirical estimation is available of the size of these impacts, I assume for the present simulation that the Son La dam will increase FP in energy intensive sectors by 10 percent in ROC and REG.

The main parameter in assessing flood control benefits is the extent, to which floods are reduced in areas with infrastructure and agricultural activities in the flood prone zones located in the river basin. The purpose of the Son La dam is to minimise the probability of coincident flood peaks from tributary streams of the Da River and the Red River. It does therefore contribute to flood mitigation in the Red River delta, which is home to 20 percent of Vietnam's total rice cultivation and where most of the agricultural land of the region is located (EVN, 2001). It is assumed that flood control improves FP of crop production by 20 percent in the Red River Delta, which translates into a nationwide increase in crop productivity of 4 percent.

---

[64] As described in section 4.2, the present model uses a one commodity market approach, i.e. the elasticity of substitution between the two regions is infinitely elastic.

5.2.2.3 Results

Table 5.20 shows that due to the size of the annual investment volume of the hydropower dam as compared to the size of the economy, macroeconomic impacts are modest. However, some changes can be observed. Real investment increases by the dam itself (DAMCON). Total investment slightly decreases if the negative impacts on the regional level are accounted for (DAMREG). Strongest increases in investment take place, if the positive impacts on the national level such as electricity availability and flood mitigation are accounted for (DAMNAT). Overall negative impacts can be observed in the loss of land simulation (LANDDECR). Total investment decreases and total real household consumption also shrinks caused by the loss of land. Major positive effects for consumption demand stem from the positive national effects.

Table 5.20 Macroeconomic Changes of Dam Investment Scenarios (Percentage Real Change from Base)

	DAMCON	LANDDECR	DAMREG	DAMNAT
Absorption	0.5	-0.1	0.4	1.8
Household consumption	0.0	-0.1	-0.1	1.4
Investment	1.8	-0.2	1.7	3.0
Government consumption	0.0	0.0	0.0	0.0
Exports	0.1	0.0	0.1	0.1
Imports	0.6	-0.1	0.5	0.9
PPP real exchange rate (LCUs per FCU)	0.1	0.0	0.1	0.1
Domestic (non-tradables) price index	-0.1	0.0	-0.1	0.0
Private (household+enterprise) savings	0.0	0.0	0.0	0.0
Foreign savings	0.3	0.0	0.3	0.0
Trade deficit	0.3	0.0	0.3	-0.1
Government savings	0.0	0.0	0.0	0.0
Import tax revenue	0.0	0.0	0.0	0.0
Direct tax revenue	0.0	0.0	0.0	0.5

Changes in the trade flows can be observed in all of the simulations. Exports tend to pick up except in the case of simulation LANDDECR. However, the trade deficit increases in DAMCON and DAMNAT, which is due to a stronger increase in imports as compared to exports. This increase in imports is caused by the increasing domestic demand, which can not be fully met by domestic production. This effect can be explained by the initial trade balance for industrial goods, which is negative. Taxes are largely unaffected, only DAMNAT leads to slight increases in government revenue through direct taxes.

Table 5.21 Changes by Economic Sector DAMCON (Percentage Real Change from Base)

	Output		GDP		Trade	
	ROC	REG	ROC	REG	E	I
AGR	0.1	10.7	0.1	10.9	0.4	-0.3
IND	0.2	2.7	0.2	2.3	0.0	0.7
CONST	1.8	13.4	1.8	13.4	0.0	0.0
SERV	0.1	4.5	0.1	4.0	0.1	0.1
TOTAL	0.3	8.7	0.2	8.6	0.1	0.6

Table 5.21 reveals that the dam construction process itself leads to positive economic results for the region of the construction site and for ROC. ROC construction increases its sectoral GDP growth due to the heavy involvement of ROC construction firms in dam building. Changes in other ROC sectors are lower, but do occur in industry, followed by services and agriculture. As can be expected, impacts on the regional level are stronger due to the size of investment as compared to the size of the REG economy. Construction leads the list of growing sectors and increases GDP at a double-digit rate, followed by agriculture. The growth in agriculture occurs due to multiplier effects that stem from the increased demand for food and increased factor incomes from construction. The same effect occurs in services, which grow due to increased service demand related to the dam construction such as transport, restaurants, hotels, entertainment etc. Industry only grows modestly, which can be explained by the fact that increased demand for dam construction materials cannot be met by local supply and has to be largely imported from other regions. Regarding trade, both exports and imports from ROW increase. In sum, the model estimates that the dam construction leads to an additional 0.2 percent GDP growth at the ROC level, while adding 8.6 percent annual growth to the regional GDP.

Table 5.22 Changes by Economic Sector LANDDECR (Percentage Real Change from Base)

	Output		GDP		Trade	
	ROC	REG	ROC	REG	E	I
AGR	0.0	-26.4	0.0	-26.8	-0.6	1.1
IND	0.0	-1.2	0.0	-0.7	0.1	-0.1
CONST	-0.2	0.3	-0.2	0.3	0.0	0.0
SERV	0.0	1.2	0.0	1.3	0.0	-0.1
TOTAL	0.0	-12.6	0.0	-15.4	0.0	-0.1

The loss of land leads to strong negative economic effects (Table 5.22). The reduction of land in REG, however, has virtually no effects on the ROC economy. GDP remains unchanged, however, some sectoral shifts in the trade balance can be observed. Exports in agriculture decrease and are substituted by imports. In the project region, the inundation of land specifically hurts the agricultural sector, which shrinks by 26.8 percent. Due to this, industry also shrinks, although modestly. This modest decrease and can be explained by the high share of not locally produced intermediate inputs of agriculture. The increases in services and construction are due to increasing trade, which occurs to substitute the reduction of agricultural goods. However, the question remains, how the factor markets react and how households are affected by this shock. Before discussing this, I turn to the sectoral changes of simulation DAMREG, to estimate the combined regional effect of DAMCON and LANDDECR.

Table 5.23 Changes by Economic Sector DAMREG (Percentage Real Change from Base)

	Output		GDP		Trade	
	ROC	REG	ROC	REG	E	I
AGR	0.1	-12.8	0.1	-13.1	-0.1	0.7
IND	0.2	3.2	0.2	3.3	0.1	0.6
CONST	1.6	15.0	1.6	15.0	0.0	0.0
SERV	0.1	8.4	0.1	8.1	0.1	0.0
TOTAL	0.3	-1.4	0.2	-4.1	0.1	0.5

The simulation DAMREG has the objective to estimate, whether the local effects of the dam are positive or negative for growth and poverty reduction in the region. As can be seen in Table 5.23, the impacts of the construction process absorb some of the negative effects induced by the loss of land. This is due to the increased demand for local goods and services as well as increased employment opportunities for local population. However, total GDP in REG still shrinks, implying that the net effect remains negative. Strong growth in the construction sector accompanied by growth in services and industry can not compensate for the shrinking agricultural sector. This finding once more underlines the importance of agriculture for REG and implies that without growth in this sector, regional development will be hard to achieve.

Table 5.24 shows that the impacts of the dam from a national and medium term perspective are positive.[65] Increased availability for energy intensive sectors such as cement, metals, chemicals and electricity and the mitigation of floods in the Red River Delta, leads to equally modest additional economic growth in REG and ROC. Industry benefits from the positive impacts on energy-intensive sectors. Construction growth is strongest across all sectors for REG and ROC. ROC agriculture clearly benefits from flood mitigation, which leads to a reduction of losses or practically an increase in output.

Table 5.24 Changes by Economic Sector DAMNAT (Percentage Real Change from Base)

	Output		GDP		Trade	
	ROC	REG	ROC	REG	E	I
AGR	2.1	1.5	2.3	1.4	3.4	-2.7
IND	1.3	1.9	1.1	1.5	-0.3	0.9
CONST	3.0	4.4	3.0	4.4	0.0	0.0
SERV	0.7	1.5	0.6	1.5	-0.4	1.1
TOTAL	1.4	1.9	1.3	1.6	0.1	0.9

Substantial intersectoral effects occur and can clearly be observed in the REG agricultural sector. Agriculture almost grows at the same extend as REG industry without enjoying the benefits of electricity availability. The flood mitigation has relatively strong impacts on the agricultural trade balance. National agricultural exports increase and at the same time, imports decrease in this sector. However, increased imports of industrial goods and services lead to a slight deterioration of the overall trade balance.

---

[65] They are medium-term effects because the power plant will only deliver energy approximately 15 years after the beginning of construction works. The same applies to flood control benefits. It makes thus sense to separate these two impacts from dam construction and the loss of land.

Table 5.25 Changes in Factor Income (Percentage Real Change from Base)

	DAMCON	LANDDECR	DAMREG	DAMNAT
LUSK-ROC	0.0	-0.1	-0.1	1.7
LUSK-REG	1.3	-6.5	-3.4	2.1
LSK-ROC	0.0	-0.1	-0.1	1.6
LSK-REG	0.6	-4.0	-2.6	1.8
CAPI-ROC	0.1	-0.1	0.1	1.4
CAPI-REG	2.2	-2.0	0.4	1.3
LAND-ROC	0.1	0.0	0.1	1.0
LAND-REG	2.1	-7.2	-3.9	1.7

Before turning to the impacts of the dam on household welfare and poverty, a look at the changes of factor income of all four dam-related simulations can give further insights into distributional effects (Table 5.25). Impacts on ROC factors are modest in the first three scenarios. The nation-wide impacts of the dam, however, have a sizeable impact on both labour categories, capital and land, where labour income increases tend to be stronger than increases in the other two factors.

On the regional level, the strongest impacts can be observed in the LANDDECR simulation. The decrease in output leads to lower total factor income, where especially income from land and unskilled labour declines. This effectively leads to more unemployment in the unskilled factor market. The dam construction especially benefits capital and unskilled labour income. Net benefits of the dam on the regional level lead to factor income increases in REG capital, but to net negative impacts on all other factors. DAMNAT favours unskilled labour income in both regions, followed by income from skilled labour, capital and land. Since factor income is a strong determinant of poverty, these results give first hints regarding the size of poverty impacts of the dam simulations. The following section will explicitly concentrate on households and these poverty impacts.

In line with the distinct results of the four simulations in GDP growth and factor income, Table 5.26 reveals that impacts on households and poverty vary strongly among the four simulations. Changes in poverty rates range from a fall of rural poverty to 57 percent to an increase to 74.4 percent. Particularly the construction process of the dam has the potential to reduce rural poverty in REG. DAMCON shows that the poverty rate can be reduced by 6.0 percent points, which is equal to lifting 49,464 people out of poverty. However, these positive impacts turn out negative when considering the loss of land. Sharply increasing poverty rates are associated with the loss of land and the net regional impacts of the dam. The loss of land reduces expenditures of urban and rural households. Poverty among urban households increases from 2 to 4.2 percent or

2306 individuals. The situation for rural households is much more dramatic. The poverty rate increases by 11.5 percentage points from 63 to 74.5 percent, which amounts to almost 100,000 people. This negative effect is only partially absorbed by the positive impacts of construction. DAMREG shows that the construction effect leads to approximately halving the negative impacts of land decrease. In addition DAMREG leads to urban poverty increases by 2.2 percent points and rural poverty by 5.2 percent points. In both cases, the poverty gap substantially increases by 8.8 percent in the case of DAMREG and 15.5 percent in the case of LANDDECR.

Table 5.26 Changes in Real Household Expenditure and Poverty

		EXP		POV		POVGAP	
		ROC	REG	%	No.	(1000 VND)	%
Urban	DAMCON	0.0	1.0	2.2	0	92.8	-17.0
	LANDDECR	-0.1	-4.4	4.4	-2306	124.7	11.6
	DAMREG	0.0	-2.5	4.4	-2306	87.3	-21.8
	DAMNAT	1.4	1.8	2.2	0	77.6	-30.5
Rural	DAMCON	0.0	3.6	57.0	49464	539.0	0.5
	LANDDECR	-0.1	-12.4	74.4	-96180	619.8	15.5
	DAMREG	-0.1	-6.4	68.2	-43968	583.5	8.8
	DAMNAT	1.4	2.2	59.0	32976	540.1	0.7

Notes:
EXP: Real expenditure change (as percent from base)
POV: Poverty. % expresses the new poverty rate under the respective simulation. No. indicates
      changes in the number of poor people.
POVGAP: Poverty gap. % shows the percentage change in the poverty gap as compared to the base
      poverty gap.

Taking a national perspective (DAMNAT), some positive impacts of the dam can be expected from electricity availability and flood mitigation also for REG. DAMNAT leads to an increase in urban REG household expenditure of 1.8 percentage points. The 2.2 percentage points increase of rural household expenditure translates into a poverty reduction of rural households of 4.0 percent. The absolute number of people escaping poverty under this simulation equals 32,976 people. However, as in the case of the strong poverty reduction effect of roads, the poverty gap virtually remains unchanged. The depth of poverty can thus be regarded as a major cause for enduring poverty and highlights the need for substantial economic growth within the poor parts of the population.

Neither road investments nor the, by Son La's standards, huge public investments into the dam can be expected to substantially reduce poverty in the region. However, national and international plans oblige the Government of Vietnam to reduce poverty, particularly in the mountainous regions. The third and last scenario thus addresses the question, how much growth is needed to meet the MDG 1 goal.

5.2.3 Achieving MDG 1 on the Regional Level

5.2.3.1 Motivation

The motivation of the following two simulations is twofold. First, Vietnam is rolling out its national MDGs and PRSPs to the regional levels. This trend is due to increasing regional disparities, which are of high importance for the future economic development and social stability of Vietnam. As outlined in section 3.2 and confirmed by the baseline of model results (section 5.1), poverty in Son La remains high and the province ranks last on the MDG indicator list. This province and the whole mountainous region is thus a prime target for poverty reduction efforts of the Government of Vietnam. Second, the planned large investment in the hydropower dam could offer the opportunity to kick-start regional development. However, as indicated in the previous simulation (5.2.2), net regional effects of the dam tend to be negative and poverty tends to increase. In addition, benefits from the construction boom in Son La Province will be transitory and long-term benefits are expected to be modest. This poses the question, of what could be done to not only compensate agricultural producers for the loss of their production base but also to initiate a sustainable pro-poor growth process in the province.

In this context, empirical evidence suggests that agricultural growth has been more pro-poor than industrial growth in many developing countries. The multiplier analysis in section 5.1 confirms this finding for Son La province, indicating that agriculture has the highest potential to contribute to regional economic growth and poverty reduction. The following simulations thus address two major questions. First, what is the marginal growth and poverty reducing effect of agricultural productivity increases? Second, how much growth is needed in the agricultural sector to half poverty in Son La province?

5.2.3.2 Simulation

Scenario three consists of two simulations that address these questions. POVERTY1 simulates an increase in FP in agriculture by 1 percent. This marginal perspective has the advantage that it can be used for international and interregional comparisons. POVERTY2 takes a different approach. Rather than predetermining the size of the exogenous shock, it fixes the model outcome. It thus poses the question, what kind of shock is necessary to achieve a certain outcome, in the present case to half the rural poverty rate.

Table 5.27   Overview of MDG Simulations

Scenario 3: Achieving MDG 1 on the regional level	
POVERTY1	1 percent FP increase in agricultural productivity
POVERTY2	MDG simulation: how much agricultural FP growth leads to halving the rural poverty rate?

The model will react to this exogenously induced agricultural growth by an increase in regional output and thereby an increase of the national supply of agricultural products. In the case of inelastic demand it is theoretically possible that producers loose out due to inflating prices. This scenario for producers is unlikely to happen in the regional context of Son La province, since the local economy is relatively open and trades with the rest of the country and the rest of the world. The product-specific perspective reveals that the assumption of elastic demand holds for all major agricultural commodities. For rice, the province is a net importer. Additional supply would therefore compete with imports from other regions. Coffee and tea are export goods and the small country assumption is applies given the size of the sub-sectors.[66] The same applies to demand elasticities for forestry. It can thus be expected that prices remain stable. Demand for agricultural products increases and producers benefit from agricultural growth. This leads to higher total factor incomes, increased demand for other goods and services and ultimately to a reduction of poverty. Due to the fact that the poverty rate in rural areas is 63 percent as compared to only 2 percent in urban areas, the poverty simulations mainly concentrate on rural poverty reduction. The following section will present the actual outcome of the model.

---

[66] This argument is only valid for the regional level. For Vietnam as a whole, the country is the second largest coffee exporter in the world.

5.2.3.3 Results

Due to the set-up of the scenario and the focus on poverty, the following section of results starts with the presenting poverty impacts. Table 5.28 shows the marginal impacts of agricultural growth (POVERTY1) and the results of MDG 1 poverty reduction simulation (POVERTY2).

Table 5.28 Changes in Real Household Expenditure and Poverty

		EXP		POV		POVGAP	
		ROC	REG	%	No.	(1000 VND)	%
Urban	POVERTY1	0.0	0.2	2.2	0	107.9	-3.4
	POVERTY2	0.2	11.4	0.0	2306	0.0	-100.0
Rural	POVERTY1	0.0	0.6	62.0	8244	536.5	0.0
	POVERTY2	0.2	38.2	31.5	263807	376.7	-29.8

Notes:
EXP: Real expenditure change (as percent from base)
POV: Poverty. % expresses the new poverty rate under the respective simulation. No. indicates changes in the number of poor people.
POVGAP: Poverty gap. % shows the percentage change in the poverty gap as compared to the base poverty gap.

The 1 percent FP increase in regional agriculture affects both urban and rural regional households. Rural households can increase their expenditures three times more than urban households; the impact on the national level is too small to affect ROC households. Rural poverty in REG is reduced by one percentage point, implying a poverty elasticity of FP growth of -1. A one percent growth increase thus lifts about 8,244 rural people above the poverty line. However, the poverty gap remains virtually unchanged for urban and rural households.

POVERTY2 is based on achieving the target of the reduction of poverty in REG by half. Consequently, the poverty rate drops from 63 percent in the baseline to 31.5 percent, effectively lifting 263,807 rural inhabitants above the poverty threshold. This development is accompanied by the eradication of urban poverty. The poverty gap for urban households thus disappears and substantially diminishes for rural households from 536,500 to 376,500 VND per capita. This poverty reduction is induced by the increase in household expenditure of 11.4 percent for urban households and 38.2 percent for rural households. Economic growth and substantial welfare increase in REG also have an impact on ROC households, where expenditure grows by 0.2 percent for rural and urban households.

As in previous regions-specific simulations, macroeconomic changes are modest for both POVERTY simulations (Table 5.29). However, the results suggest that despite the relatively small size of the regional economy, poverty reduction efforts in REG do have impacts on the national level. Total investment increases and increasing domestic demand leads to an increase in imports, causing a slight deterioration of the trade balance. In addition, government income from direct taxes increases. In addition to the positive social impacts of poverty reduction and the reduction of interregional disparities, economic growth in poor regions can thus contribute to national growth and overall government income.

Table 5.29 Macroeconomic Changes of POVERTY Scenarios (Percentage Real Change from Base)

	POVERTY1	POVERTY2
Absorption	0.0	0.4
Household consumption	0.0	0.4
Investment	0.0	0.5
Government consumption	0.0	0.0
Exports	0.0	0.0
Imports	0.0	0.2
PPP real exchange rate (LCUs per FCU)	0.0	-0.1
Domestic (non-tradables) price index	0.0	0.0
Private (household+enterprise) savings	0.0	0.0
Foreign savings	0.0	0.0
Trade deficit	0.0	0.1
Government savings	0.0	0.0
Import tax revenue	0.0	0.0
Direct tax revenue	0.0	0.1

As can be expected, changes in factor markets are driven by increasing regional returns to land and unskilled labour (Table 5.30). The marginal increase leads to a 0.3-0.2-0.1-0.3 contribution of unskilled labour, skilled labour, capital and land on the regional level. In the case of POVERTY2, additional factor income from land amounts to 16.6 percent, from unskilled labour of 15.7 percent. Skilled labour increases by about 10 percent, followed by capital. Comparing these results with the baseline, substitution effects between factors can be observed, increasing the share of land and skilled labour.

Table 5.30 Changes in Factor Income (Percentage Real Change from Base)

	POVERTY1	POVERTY2
LUSK-ROC	0.0	0.3
LUSK-REG	0.3	15.7
LSK-ROC	0.0	0.3
LSK-REG	0.2	9.5
CAPI-ROC	0.0	0.2
CAPI-REG	0.1	6.0
LAND-ROC	0.0	0.1
LAND-REG	0.3	16.6

Notes:
LUSK: Unskilled labour
LSK: Skilled labour
CAPI: Capital
LAND: Land

Table 5.31 Changes by Economic Sector POVERTY1 (Percentage Real Change from Base)

	Output		GDP		Trade	
	ROC	REG	ROC	REG	E	I
AGR	0.0	1.4	0.0	1.4	0.0	-0.1
IND	0.0	0.1	0.0	0.0	0.0	0.0
CONST	0.0	0.0	0.0	0.0	0.0	0.0
SERV	0.0	-0.1	0.0	-0.1	0.0	0.0
TOTAL	0.0	0.6	0.0	0.8	0.0	0.0

Table 5.32 Changes by Economic Sector POVERTY2 (Percentage Real Change from Base)

	Output		GDP		Trade	
	ROC	REG	ROC	REG	E	I
AGR	-0.1	106.0	-0.1	109.4	1.9	-3.4
IND	-0.1	3.4	-0.1	2.3	0.3	0.3
CONST	0.5	-0.4	0.5	-0.4	0.0	0.0
SERV	0.1	-2.6	0.1	-2.7	-0.1	0.2
TOTAL	0.0	51.2	0.0	63.5	0.0	0.2

The sector perspective (Table 5.31 and Table 5.32) reveals that agricultural growth primarily benefits the regional agricultural sector, but also leads to intersectoral effects. Especially the regional industry can benefit from agriculture-led growth, while regional construction and services tend to be substituted by ROC construction activities and services. The marginal impact of FP growth in agriculture leads to a 1.4 percent growth in agricultural output and GDP. The total regional economy grows by 0.8 percent. At the national level, a small share of agricultural imports is substituted by regional production. Agricultural exports and trade in other goods and services remain unaffected.

In POVERTY2, regional agricultural output grows by 106 percent and agricultural GDP by 109 percent, effectively leading to a 63.5 percent increase of total regional GDP. Regarding the objective of the simulation to estimate the growth rate needed to half poverty, the result of the simulation suggests that a doubling of agricultural GDP and regional overall growth rates of around 60-70 percent are needed to achieve MDG1. The sheer size of these numbers pose the question, in how far these growth rates can be achieved by agricultural productivity gains, especially when taking the loss of land induced by the hydropower dam into account. It can only be assumed that a combination of technical innovation and expansion of area combined with a diversification towards high value crops have to achieve such growth rates. In addition, agricultural growth might have to be supplemented by growth in other sectors, where Son La can achieve comparative advantages. Even though the technical and policy mix to achieve this growth is beyond the scope of this dissertation, the above presented number could provide a target figure, against which the impact of technical innovations and improvements can measured.

5.3   Testing the Robustness

CGE models represent a comprehensive approach to economy-wide analyses. Their major strength of taking all sectors and agents of the economy into consideration is also their major weakness. Modelling behaviour involves making assumptions about the functioning of production, consumption, factor markets and trade flows. In addition, the macroeconomic closures including the exchange rate regime, the savings and investment balance and the government closure have to be exogenously determined in order to get an equilibrium solution.

It is therefore of crucial importance to test, whether and how these assumptions influence the model results. The following chapter takes on these sensitivity tests. Section 5.3.1 assesses the role of the assumption that factor markets are regionally segmented. Section 5.3.2 analyses the major elasticities used in the model.

5.3.1 Assessing the Role of Regionally Segmented Factor Markets

The major linkage in the CGE model between the two regions is the common commodity market. Major regional features include the differentiation between production activities and institutions. In addition, each region has its own factor markets, effectively prohibiting migration of labourers and the movement of capital between the two regions. It can thus be argued that this assumption of factor immobility does not properly reflect reality and might distort results of the model. To test the validity of this argument and to estimate the impact of inter-regional factor mobility versus segmented factor markets, Table 5.33 presents the results of a modified version of the CGE model. The difference between the models is that the new version of the model allows for perfect mobility of labour and capital between the regions. Besides testing the robustness of the model, this test can provide useful insights into the role of factor mobility and give indications of accelerator effects of the previously presented investments and interventions scenarios. Table 5.33 presents the results of the comparison of changes in GDP growth in both regions in the case, where factors are regionally segmented (FACREG) and alternatively the case of nationally perfect factor mobility (FACMOB) across all ten simulations.

Table 5.33   Comparison of Original Model Results with Model of Interregional Factor Mobility (Percentage Change)

| | \multicolumn{6}{c}{Changes in real GDP (percent)} | | | | | |
| | ROC | | | REG | | |
	FACREG	FACMOB	Diff	FACREG	FACMOB	Diff
TRADE1	-0.05	2.93	2.98	4.18	6.27	2.09
TRADE2	-0.06	3.18	3.24	2.31	4.86	2.54
TRADE3	0.00	0.06	0.06	16.37	15.67	-0.71
TRADE4	0.00	0.01	0.01	3.64	3.71	0.07
DAMCON	0.21	0.17	-0.04	8.61	8.38	-0.23
LANDDECR	0.00	-0.06	-0.06	-15.39	-14.79	0.60
DAMREG	0.21	0.23	0.02	-4.07	-6.59	-2.52
DAMNAT	1.33	2.83	1.49	1.61	3.07	1.45
POVERTY1	0.00	0.00	0.00	0.80	0.76	-0.03
POVERTY2	0.00	0.19	0.19	62.35	59.89	-2.47
AVERAGE*	0.16	0.95	0.79	8.04	8.12	0.08

Notes:
FACREG: Regional factors markets are segmented
FACMOB: Factors are mobile across regions
Diff: Difference between FACREG and FACMOB (in percentage points)
* AVERAGE: The average total difference between the two cases is calculated as the arithmetic mean
        value of percentage changes across the simulations.

The difference in results between the two models across all ten simulations is below one percentage point in GDP growth on average. This aggregate result suggests that interregional mobility of factors does only have limited impacts on model results and confirms the robustness of the model. In addition, the aggregate view shows that labour mobility has positive effects on model outcomes in most of the cases. With three exceptions, the direction of change (positive or negative) is the same. However, differences across the simulations vary. Particularly for the region-specific simulations, results are fairly robust to interregional factor mobility. The model thus well represents empirical realities in the region. In fact, only little migration does take place, which is confirmed by the relatively small size of remittances received by regional households (GSO, 2004). On the other hand, labour markets in Vietnam are characterised by a strong correlation between labour mobility and the availability of transportation, access to formal and informal networks and education levels (DANG et al., 2003). It can therefore be expected that the majority of people cannot exploit the benefits of sector-mobility of labour. It hinders especially remotely living and low-skilled households to benefit from market opening in the study region.

However, a more simulation-specific analysis reveals differences between model outcomes in several cases. Especially the nation-wide simulations TRADE1 and TRADE2 and DAMNAT show substantially differing GDP growth rates. GDP growth in all three cases is about twice as high in the model with mobile factors compared to the segmented factor market model. In TRADE1 and TRADE2, differences in growth rates of 2.1 to3.2 percent points occur in REG and ROC between FACREG and REGMOB. In both cases, mobile factors contribute to higher growth, implying that the benefits of both urban and rural roads can be altered by interregional factor mobility. Differences between the two models are also observed in the DAMNAT and DAMREG simulations. While the negative effects in DAMREG are aggravated by factor mobility, positive impacts of DAMNAT are accelerated. At the first glance it seems to be counterintuitive, why factor mobility should contribute to a further GDP decrease in DAMREG. However, it seems that ROC benefits more from mobile factors, effectively taking over some of the growth otherwise occurring in REG. In all simulations except TRADE1 and TRADE2, differences between FACREG and FACMOB range between -0.71 and +0.6 percentage points and can therefore be assumed not to distort the results of the model.

Three conclusions can be drawn from this analysis: first, the model is robust regarding the assumption of regionally segmented factor markets in the case of region-specific simulations. Second, in the case of nation-wide simulations, factor mobility does substantially enhance economic growth in both regions, implying that growth induced by infrastructure investments can be accelerated by increased flexibility in factor markets. Third, it appears that neither totally segmented nor fully mobile factor markets reflect reality well. An extension to the model could therefore attempt to model the behaviour of interregional factor flows.

5.3.2 Robustness of Elasticities

The elasticity parameters used in the model are exogenous. Their values in this study are inspired by several country case studies that use the IFPRI CGE model (LÖFGREN et al, 2002). To test the sensitivity of the model, several elasticities are changed to get a feeling for the model and to judge, whether results are robust. These elasticities concern the substitution between factors of production, the substitution between domestically produced and foreign goods, including the Armington function for imports and the CES function for exports, and the LES demand elasticities. I change the value of each of these elasticities by 20 percent in each direction, i.e. their base value is reduced and increased. This is done one by one and for four simulations. Table 5.34 to Table 5.36 show the results of these tests. Column two indicates the percentage change in the respective scenario under the initial elasticity values. The subsequent columns report the percentage changes of the respective scenario induced by the changed elasticity value, which are indicated at the top of the table. Values that differ by less than 0.1 percentage points are omitted from the table.

Table 5.34 Sensitivity Analysis for TRADE1 (in Percent)

	Result TRADE1	PRODELA1		SIGMAQ		SIGMAT		LESELA	
		0.9	1.5	3.6	2.4	1.8	1.2		
Output									
ROC	0.6		0.7			0.7			
REG	4.9	4.5	5.2		4.8		4.8	4.7	5.0
Trade									
E	-2.3	-2.0	-2.7			2.6	-1.9		
I	2.4	2.1	2.6		2.2	2.5	2.2		2.3
Consumption									
HHUr-ROC	2.1					2.0			
HHRu-ROC	2.5		2.4						
HHUR-R	3.4	3.5	3.3		3.3	3.3		3.2	3.5
HHRu-R	5.6	5.3	6.0	5.7			5.7	5.4	5.8

Notes:
PRODELA1: Elasticity of substitution between factors
SIGMAQ: elasticity of substitution between imports and domestic output in domestic demand
SIGMAT: elasticity of transformation for domestic marketed output bw. export and domestic supplies.
LESELA: LES demand elasticities

Table 5.35 Sensitivity Analysis for TRADE2

	Result TRADE2	PRODELA1		SIGMAQ		SIGMAT		LESELA	
		0.9	1.5	3.6	2.4	1.8	1.2		
Output									
ROC	1.4	1.2	1.5				1.3		
REG	2.0			1.7	2.4	2.1	1.9	1.9	2.1
Trade								0.0	0.0
E	1.7	1.2	2.1	1.8	1.5	1.3	2.0		1.6
I	-0.8		-0.9	-1.4	-0.2	-0.7	-1.0		-0.9
Consumption								0.0	0.0
HHUr-ROC	2.4			2.3			2.3		
HHRu-ROC	2.4	2.5			2.5	2.5			
HHUR-R	1.6	1.7	1.5	1.4	1.9				1.7
HHRu-R	3.1	3.0	3.2	2.8	3.4	3.0	3.1	3.0	3.2

Table 5.36 Sensitivity Analysis for TRADE3

	Result TRADE3	PRODEL A1		SIGMAQ		SIGMAT		LESELA	
		0.9	1.5	3.6	2.4	1.8	1.2		
Output									
ROC	0.0								
REG	13.3	13.1	13.5					13.0	13.5
Trade								0.0	0.0
E	0.0								
I	0.1								
Consumption									
HHUr-ROC	0.1								
HHRu-ROC	0.1								
HHUR-R	3.8	3.9	3.7					3.6	4.0
HHRu-R	11.5	11.3	11.8	11.6		11.6	11.5	11.1	11.9

This analysis shows that the model results are fairly robust to changes in elasticities across the simulations. In many cases, the deviation between initial model results and the changed values is below 0.1 percentage point. The most sensitive elasticity parameter appears to be the substitution between factors. However, a 20 percent change of the initial values does not substantially change results. The differences range between 0.5 and -0.4 percentage points. In the case of unskilled labour, which constitutes a large share of total factor income in

Vietnam, high underemployment and fixed wages contribute to this relatively modest impact and the robustness of results. As can be expected, lower values tend to decrease the size of the initial change, whereas increased substitutability increases the effects.

Trade elasticities are less sensitive on average. Most deviations occur in the flows of exports and imports and range between -0.3 and +0.4 percent points. More open borders tend to increase the expenditure across all household groups, indicating that more open markets can accelerate growth and household incomes of road investments.

Demand elasticities are fairly insensitive to changes. Most of the deviation from initial results is below or around 0.1 percentage points. The direction of changes clearly follows the model structure and is supported by intuition: higher demand elasticities lead to more consumption per unit of real income increases. This in turns leads to increased domestic demand and the associated multiplier effects.

By looking at the results from a regional perspective, it can be concluded that the region-specific simulations TRADE3 and TRADE4 are much less sensitive to parameter changes.[67] In the case of demand elasticities and trade elasticities, this is caused by the single commodity market and the small size of the REG economy. This does also play a role for the insensitivity of factor substitution elasticities. However, the low values also confirm the robustness of the model.

In conclusion, it can be noted that deviations of the chosen values for the different exogenous elasticity parameter only modestly affect the results of this study and confirm the robustness of results. In addition, increasing openness to trade and flexibility of factor markets have a clear tendency to increase and accelerate trade, production output and household welfare.

---

[67] Results for TRADE4 are not reported, since all changes are below 0.1 percent except for LESELA increase, which leads to a decrease of consumption of HHRu-R by 0.1 percentage point.

6   Major Findings, Policy Recommendations and Future Research Directions

In the following, I summarise the major findings that emerge from the economy-wide analyses of infrastructure investments in Vietnam. Chapter 1 hypothesises that a macro-micro model can improve the assessment of infrastructure investments to better account for direct macroeconomic growth effects, indirect effects (multiplier effects) and poverty impacts. Furthermore, it argues that infrastructure investments can contribute to economic growth and poverty reduction in the mountainous region of Vietnam. A review of the literature shows that commonly used appraisal tools for infrastructure are partial models disregarding indirect effects. To fill this gap in research, the study introduces a CGE model, the most comprehensive model in the class of economy-wide models. In addition, it introduces a regional dimension in policy analysis, which is important for two reasons: First, impacts of infrastructure investments cross regional boarders and influence various regions in different ways. Second, large disparities in economic growth, poverty and the distribution of public investments exist in many countries. With regard to their special relevance for the mountainous region, roads and a large-scale hydropower dam were selected as examples for public infrastructure investments.

6.1   Achievements and Major Findings

This dissertation makes two major contributions to the existing literature. First, it constructs a multi-region CGE model for Vietnam that links a mountainous province with the rest of the country and the rest of the world. In addition, a micro-accounting module complements this model to allow for an analysis of poverty effects. Second, this study applies an economy-wide model to assess infrastructure investments and thereby provides a new tool to simultaneously include macro- and microeconomic dimensions into the analyses of growth, poverty and infrastructure investments. The literature so far has not developed such an approach.

The major findings that evolve from this dissertation are assessed with the help of the two research objectives stated in the introduction. The first part refers to the added-value of such type of models regarding their contribution towards more comprehensive infrastructure assessments (hypotheses I-III). The second group of findings refers to the specific model results relevant for Vietnam (hypotheses IV-VI).

• Macroeconomic Effects

Results show that macroeconomic effects such as changes in the trade balance, the savings and investment balance and the government budget are limited and strongly dependent on the size of investment. The trade balance proves to be the major macroeconomic variable that is due to be affected by infrastructure investments. *Road investments* in particular have sizeable impacts on trade, which can mainly be explained by the market opening effect. In the road scenario, the trade of goods and services generally increases. In the case of urban roads, particularly exports grow strongly, while rural roads lead to a stronger increase of imports. Even in the case of region-specific investments and the relatively small annual investment into a *hydropower dam*, changes in national imports and exports can be observed. Investment in the hydropower dam leads to increases in both imports and exports with an overall slightly deteriorating trade balance. *Agricultural growth* leads to a substitution of imported agricultural goods by domestic production and an increase in exports of agricultural goods. Besides changes in the national trade balance, macroeconomic impacts from infrastructure investments include changes in the government balance and the savings-investment balance. Size and direction of these changes depend on the simulation and are generally small.

• Indirect Effects

Results confirm that the added-value of CGE models in analysing infrastructure investments is greatest through its ability to account for *multiplier effects*. These multiplier effects increase the size of direct impacts of infrastructure investments and comprise sectoral and regional dimensions. Particularly road investments and agricultural growth investments have substantial intersectoral impacts across all simulations. Similarly, multiplier effects that are induced by industrial growth are sizeable and lead to positive spill-over effects to the agricultural sector. These growth effects are mainly transmitted through labour markets and lead to positive impacts on household income. Consequently, rural households can benefit from investments in rural and urban infrastructure alike. Accordingly, urban household income increases by investments in urban and rural areas.

• Interregional Impacts

The spatial differentiation of the model gives interesting insights into region-specific growth and poverty effects, which would be unfeasible by looking at single-region models only. Regionally diverging impacts occur across all scenarios, but are especially relevant for the hydropower dam. While the costs of the dam in the form of loss of agricultural and forestry land have to be carried by the local population, benefits such as the mitigation of floods and improved electricity availability occur mainly in urban centres and the industrial sector. Results show that the model also captures interregional multiplier effects. For instance, growth caused by the hydropower dam outside the region leads to positive growth effects in the region of the dam. Another example for these interregional multiplier effects is the DAMNAT simulation, where agriculture in Son La grows almost at the same rate as industry in the rest of Vietnam without enjoying the benefits of electricity provision of the hydropower dam.

Several conclusions can be drawn from this first group of findings. CGE models have the ability to incorporate several dimensions of infrastructure investments and can thus contribute to the question of how to integrate investment patterns into poverty and distribution-oriented development strategies. The major advantage lies in the incorporation of *intersectoral and interregional multiplier* effects. It can therefore be assumed that the stronger these effects are, the more useful is the use of economy-wide models. It can further be concluded, that considering *macroeconomic effects* in the model provides a sound basis and a good starting point for a comprehensive analysis of changes in economic growth and poverty. However, these impacts are rather limited and they alone would not justify the use of CGE models for infrastructure investment analysis. Furthermore, CGE models cannot substitute traditional infrastructure appraisals, such as financial cost-benefit analysis, but also environmental impact assessments. These can not yet sufficiently be incorporated in CGE models. Finally, not each single large-scale infrastructure project might require a specific CGE model. Rather, lessons on the direction and size of impacts of certain investments might be transferable across regions and countries.

The second set of results refers to the application of the model to infrastructure investments in Vietnam. Despite Vietnam's pro-poor economic development over the last two decades, regional disparities persist. The CGE model therefore includes a mountainous region, which is particularly poor. Son La province ranks last on the MDG indicator list in Vietnam and rural poverty stands at 63 percent. It represents a typical region, which is geographically disadvantaged, is dominated by agriculture and has a high share of ethnic minority inhabitants. Due to the high incidence of poverty, the province and mountainous regions in general are a prime target for poverty reduction efforts by the Government of Vietnam. It appears that, in the past, Vietnam has pursued a strategy of redistribution rather than a strategy of targeted economic growth to contribute to the development of its poor regions. However, more recently, Vietnam is widening its national MDGs and PRSPs to the provincial levels, which confirms the importance of the mountainous regions for the future economic development and social stability of the country. It also underlines the need to design and assess these programmes. Due to the importance of roads and the construction of a hydropower dam for national electricity provision in the study area, these infrastructure investments were analysed. Even though these results are primarily country specific for Vietnam, they might serve as an indication for comparable infrastructure projects in other parts of the world.

• Growth and Poverty Reduction in Vietnam

Two important general results emerge from the impact analyses of infrastructure investments on growth and poverty in Vietnam. First, infrastructure investments do not always reduce poverty. While the example of road investment presents overall positive impacts for both model regions, sectors and household groups, the positive impacts of the hydropower dam are mostly found in regions other than the project region. If no appropriate measures are taken, the rural poverty rate in Son La province can increase from 63 to 74 percent because of the dam, which would effectively add 100,000 people to the poor. Even when considering positive impacts of dam construction through employment opportunities and multiplier effects, poverty in Son La is likely to increase. Second, despite the fact that the number of poor in Son La province can be substantially reduced in most infrastructure simulations, the poverty gap remains big, in most cases above 500,000 VND per capita, as compared to the poverty line of about 2,000,000 VND.

• Roads

Rural roads lead to higher aggregate output and GDP growth, which is about twice as high as that induced by urban roads. This effect is higher in Son La province as compared to the rest of Vietnam, indicating that the marginal benefit of rural roads in poor regions of Vietnam is higher. Rural roads can induce additional economic growth of between 4 and 13 percentage points in Son La province, which translates into rural poverty reduction of between 11 and 14 percentage points. Rural road induced growth is driven by agricultural growth and transmitted to households via the unskilled labour market. This household perspective underlines the importance of rural roads: while rural roads tend to benefit urban and rural households, urban roads have limited positive impacts on rural households. The benefits of both rural and urban roads can be altered by interregional factor mobility. In the case of road investments in Son La province positive effects of roads are accelerated by 60 to 100 percent.

• Agricultural Growth

Neither roads nor the dam construction alone have the potential to achieve the MDG 1 in Son La province. In addition, the depth of poverty remains high across all simulations, indicating that the eradication of absolute poverty can not be expected in the short to medium run. The question arises, how investments in infrastructure can be complemented to support a sustainable pro-poor growth process in the mountainous province can be initiated. The comparison of sectoral multipliers reveals that agriculture has the largest potential to drive regional economic growth. Further investigation shows that the poverty elasticity of agricultural FP growth in Son La province is about -1, indicating that a one percent FP growth in agriculture reduces rural poverty by 1 percent. To achieve MDG 1 in Son La province, i.e. to reduce the number of poor by 263,807 individuals, roughly a doubling of agricultural GDP (a 110 percent increase) and regional economy-wide growth rates of around 65 percent are needed.

It can be concluded that the examined infrastructure investments in Vietnam can promote economic growth and reduce poverty. However, large differences occur between the different infrastructures. *Roads* and particularly rural roads accelerate economic growth in Vietnam and can contribute to lifting a substantial number of people out of poverty in Son La province. However, these tend to be people, who live close to the poverty line. For a large majority of the poor, the small absolute gains in household income cannot contribute to the improvement of their economic situation. The *Son La hydropower dam* poses a threat and an opportunity for regional development at the same time. Without complimentary measures, poverty in Son La will increase. If the dam is regarded as an opportunity, it can be used as the starting point to induce a sustainable development processes in the province and region. Infrastructure investments are not sufficient to achieve MDG1. Agricultural GDP growth of 109 percent is necessary, or with other words, agricultural production has to be more than doubled. Given the fact that the large-scale hydropower dam will decrease the size of agricultural land, challenges become even bigger.

6.2 Policy Implications

Based on the findings of this study, several policy recommendations emerge. First, economy-wide models with regional disaggregation are useful tools for policy analysis and should be promoted. Regional SAMs constitute the basis for such models. Their set-up and maintenance for major regions of a country can thus contribute to effective and efficient policy planning and serve as the basis for analytical tools to analyse poverty reduction and growth strategies. In Vietnam for instance, they can analytically support the "roll out" of PRSPs and

MDGs to the regional level. Improved data collection of regional statistic offices and capacity building in the field of the construction and interpretation of SAMs and SAM-based models can thus make a contribution towards a better understanding of structural causes of regional disparities and poverty.

Second, positive economy-wide and poverty reducing impacts of roads emphasise the importance of connecting disadvantaged regions to national and international markets. They have to play a vital part in national strategies that aim at reducing regional disparities and poverty. In the case of Vietnam, public investments in rural roads are crucial to prevent the further increase in regional disparities and to create opportunities for the rural poor to gain from growth in the national growth centers and the WTO accession of the country.

Third, the construction of large-scale dams has to be supplemented by comprehensive regional development plans. The Vietnamese Comprehensive Poverty Reduction and Growth Strategy includes a chapter on large-scale infrastructure, aimed at including large-scale infrastructure into growth and poverty planning. This is an important step and could serve other countries as a positive example. To effectively combine large-scale infrastructure and poverty reduction efforts in Vietnam, large-scale public investment projects should also be embedded in regional PRSPs, as they have the power to substantially contribute to regional socio-economic development.

Fourth, complimentary to infrastructure investments, the agricultural sector has the highest potential to contribute to poverty reduction in the mountainous regions of Vietnam. Agriculture should thus be a prime target of public investments. Area-specific potentials to increase agricultural productivity, such as irrigation, higher yielding crops, expansion of area etc. should be promoted to foster pro-poor growth.

Finally, the international donor community that has largely retreated from supporting large-scale infrastructure should re-engage in this sector. Infrastructures such as roads and power plants are directly or indirectly related to all MDGs and can therefore play an important role in achieving a world free of poverty and sound opportunities for all.

6.3 Directions for Further Research

Further research directions relate to possible improvements of the model presented in this dissertation and to further research needs in Vietnam. The above presented model is a step towards integrating different regions of a country into a CGE framework. The approach taken has been to link two independent regional models by creating a national commodity market. The assumption of one common commodity market can be criticised on the ground that there are regional markets and non-tradable goods. The current model takes this situation partly into account by including home-consumption of self-produced goods. Those goods do not enter markets and therefore cover a substantial part of the non-tradable sector.

The first improvement of the model thus could be to include interregional trade to account for price differences and the imperfect substitutability between regional exports and regional production and regional imports and regional production, respectively. The framework of LÖFGREN AND ROBINSON (1999) for including spatial networks into multi-region CGE models offers a potential starting point to perform this task.

A dynamic CGE model could shed light on the intertemporal impacts of infrastructure investments. This would be especially valuable for large-scale dam investments, where cost and benefits occur in distinctly different time periods. Dynamics occur on different levels, including changes in production technologies, savings-and investment decisions, population growth and changes in the macroeconomic environment. As an extension of the IFPRI standard model LÖFGREN et al. (2002, 2004) employ a recursive dynamic model for analysing the prospects for growth and poverty reduction in Zambia. This recursive dynamic model solves for one period at a time and allows for the separation of the within-period component and the between period component. The between period component accounts for the dynamics of the model and includes exogenously updated parameters such as demography and technology. Capital accumulation is determined endogenously. Investment of the previous period generates the respective new capital stock. Such kind of approach can be taken to incorporate dynamics into the model presented in this dissertation.

Regarding the scenario definition of large-scale infrastructure investments, improved data availability can further refine the results. In the case of the Son La dam, more data on affected households, regional electricity networks, resettlements, compensation payments etc. would be especially valuable to further disaggregate the model to assess the distributional and poverty effects in more detail. In this context, the comparison of an actual CBA for such a large-scale infrastructure project and the CGE results could further improve insights into the role of indirect effects and allow for a comprehensive assessment of impacts.

The application of the CGE models of the type presented in this dissertation could be further extended to public investments and foreign aid induced investments. As in the case of infrastructure investments, such kind of analysis can complement sector-specific approaches by incorporating intersectoral effects, trade and labour market transmission mechanisms. Especially MDG-relevant sectors such as health and education could be incorporated into CGE models to examine the level of investment needed to achieve certain targets. This could not only contribute to the better understanding of linkages between different MDG goals, but also inform governments and donors on how much the achievement of certain goals could cost and under which conditions they can be met. The applied model developed in this dissertation provides a promising basis to incorporate the further research directions mentioned above.

References

ADB. 2002. Indigenous People/Ethnic Minorities and Poverty Reduction in Vietnam. Manila, Philippines, Environment and Social Safeguard Division and Regional and Sustainable Development Department, Asian Development Bank (ADB).

Adelmann, I. and S. Robinson. 1978. Income Distribution Policy: A Computable General Equilibrium Model of South Korea. Stanford, USA, Stanford University Press.

Agénor, P.-R., D. H. C. Cheng, and M. Grimm. 2004. Linking Representative Household Models with Household Surveys for Poverty Analysis. A Comparison of Alternative Methodologies. World Bank Policy Research Working Paper, 3343. Washington D.C., USA, World Bank.

Agénor, P.-R., N. Bayraktar, and K. El Aynaoui. 2005. Roads out of Poverty? Assessing the Links between Aids, Public Investment, Growth, and Poverty Reduction. World Bank Policy Research Working Paper, 3490. Washington D.C., USA, World Bank.

Ahlfeld, S., H.-R. Hemmer, and A. Lorenz. 2005. The Economic Growth Debate - Geography versus Institutions. Is There Anything Really New? Discussion Papers in Development Economics, 35. Justus-Liebig-Universität Gießen. Germany.

Anderson, K. 2004. "Agriculture and Agricultural Policies in China and India post-Uruguay Round." In Agricultural Policy Reform and the WTO, eds. G. Anania, M. Bohman, C. Carter, and A. McCalla . Where are we heading? Edward Elgar Publishing Limited. Cheltenham, U.K. 98-128.

Armington, P. S. 1969. A Theory of Demand for Products Distinguishes by Place of Production. IMF Staff Papers, 16. Washington, D.C., USA, International Monetary Found (IMF).

Aschauer, D. A. 1989. "Public investment and productivity growth in the Group of Seven." *Economic Perspectives*. Vol. 9 17-25.

Baulch, B., Truong Thi Kim Chuyen, H. Dominique, and H. Jonathan. 2002. Ethnic Minority Development in Vietnam: A Socioeconomic Perspective. Washington D.C., USA, World Bank.

Bautista, R. M. 2000. Agriculture-based Development: A SAM Perspective on Central Vietnam. TMD Discussion Paper, 51. Washington D.C., USA, International Food Policy Research Institute (IFPRI), Trade and Macroeconomic Division (TMD).

Beausejour, L., G. Lenjosek, and M. Smart. 1995. "A CGE Approach to Modelling Carbon Dioxide Emissions Control in Canada and the United States." *World Economy*. Vol. 18 (3):457-488.

Berg, A., and A. Krüger. 2003. Trade, Growth and Poverty: A Selective Survey. International Monetary Found (IMF).

Bhatia, R., M. Scatasta, and R. Cestti. 2003. Multiplier effects and income distribution impacts of dams. Methodology issues and preliminary results. Paper prepared for the Third World Water Forum Kyoto, Japan, Washington D.C., USA.

Binswanger, H. P., S. R. Khandker, and M. R. Rosenzweig. 1993. "How infrastructure and financial institutions affect agricultural output and investment in India." *Journal of Development Economics*. Vol. 41 (2):337-366.

BMZ. 2005A. Kapitalverkehrsliberalisierung und Armutsreduktion. BMZ Spezial, 125. Bundesministerium für wirtschaftliche Zusammenarbeit und Entwicklung (BMZ).

BMZ. 2005B. Die Handelspolitik subsaharischer afrikanischer Länder - Status quo, Rahmenbedingungen und entwicklungspolitische Implikationen für Bekämpfung der Armut. BMZ Spezial, 133. Bundesministerium für wirtschaftliche Zusammenarbeit und Entwicklung (BMZ).

BMZ. 2006. Afrika-Rahmenpapier. Arbeitspapier des Wissenschaftlichen Beirates.

Bourguignon, F. 2002. The growth elasticity of poverty reduction: explaining heterogeneity across countries and time periods. Eicher, T., and Turnovsky, S. Growth and Inequality, MIT Press.

Bourguignon, F., A.-S. Robilliard, and S. Robinson. 2003. Representative versus real households in the macro-modeling of inequality. Working Paper, 05. Paris, France, Département et Laboratoire d'Economie théorique et appliquée (DELTA).

Bourguignon, F. 2004. The Poverty-Growth-Inequality Triangle. Paper presented at the Indian Council for Research on International Economic Relations, New Delhi, India, World Bank.

Bowen, H.-P., A. Hollander, and J.-M. Viaene. 1998. Applied Trade Analysis. London, U.K., Houndmills.

Breisinger, C. and F. Heidhues. 2004. Regional Development Perspectives in Vietnam -Insights from a 2002 Provincial Social Accounting Matrix (SAM). Discussion Paper, 02. Stuttgart, Germany, University of Hohenheim, Institute of Agricultural Economics and Social Sciences in the Tropics and Subtropics.

Breisinger, C. 2005. Do Ethnic Minorities care about Markets? Paper presented at the 8th Annual Conference on Global Economic Analysis, Lübeck, Germany,

Breisinger, C. and O. Ecker. 2006. "Agriculture-led Development in Northwest Vietnam. A SAM-based Multiplier Model." *Journal of International Agriculture*. Forthcoming .

Calderón, C. and A. Chong. 2004. "Volume and Quality of Infrastructure and the Distribution of Income: An Empirical Investigation." *Review of Income and Wealth*. Vol. 50 (1):87-106.

Chan, N., D. H. Dao, H. M. Hai, and N. T. Dung. 1998. Evaluating tax reform in Vietnam using general equilibrium methods. Paper presented at the Micro Impacts of Macroeconomic and Adjustment Policies (MIMAP) in Katmandu, Nepal. Hanoi, Vietnam, Center for System and Management Research Institute of Information Technology.

Chenery, H., M. S. Ahluwalia, C. L. G. Bell, J. H. Duloy, and R. Jolly. 1974. Redistribution with growth. Institute of Development Studies (University of Sussex), Oxford University Press.

Cogneau, D. and A.-S. Robilliard. 2000. Growth, Income Distribution and Poverty in Madagascar: Learning from Microsimulation Model in a General Equilibrium Framework. TMD Discussion Paper, 61. Washington D.C., USA, International Food Policy Research Institute (IFPRI), Trade and Macroeconomic Division.

Conrad, K. and S. Heng. 2000. Financing Road Infrastructure by Savings in Congestion Cost: A CGE Analysis. Working Paper, 579-00.

Coudouel, A., J. Hentschel, and Q. Wodon. 2002. Poverty Measurement and Analysis in Poverty Reduction Strategies. Washington D.C., USA, World Bank.

Cuong, T. H. 2005. The Impacts of Market Access, Marketing Development and Interregional Trade on Agricultural Productivity in Vietnam. Dissertation. Stuttgart, Germany, University of Hohenheim, Institute for Agricultural Economics and Social Sciences in the Tropics and Subtropics.

Dang N. A, Tacoli C, and Hoang X.T. 2003. Migration in Vietnam. A review of information on current trends and patterns, and their policy implications. Paper prepared for the Regional Conference on Migration, Development and Pro-Poor Policy Choices in Asia. Dhaka, Bangladesh.

Dapice, D. O. 2003. Vietnam's Economy: Success Story or Weird Dualism? A SWOT Analysis. Vietnam Program, Center for Business and Government, prepared for UNDP & Prime Minister's Research Commission.

Daude, S. 2005. "The Doha Development Round and its Poverty Implications for a WTO Accession Candidate: The Case of Vietnam." In Development Economics and Policy, eds. F. Heidhues and J. von Braun. Dissertation. Frankfurt a.M., Germany. Peter Lang - Europäischer Verlag der Wissenschaften.

Deichmann, U., M. Fay, J. Koo and S.V. Lall. 2000. Economic Structure, Productivity and Infrastructure Quality in Southern Mexico. World Bank Policy Research Working Paper, 2990. Washington D.C., USA, World Bank.

Deininger, K. and L. Squire. 1997. "Economic Growth and Income Inequality: Reexamining the Links." Finance and Development. Vol. 34 (1):38-41.

Deininger, K. and L. Squire. 1998. "New ways of looking at old issues - inequality and growth." Journal of Development Economics. Vol. 57 (2):259-287.

Demetriades, P. O. and T. P. Mamuneas. 2000. "Intertemporal Output and Employment Effects of Public Infrastructure Capital: Evidence from 12 OECD Economies." The Economic Journal. Vol. 110 (465):687-712.

Dervis, K., J. de Melo, and S. Robinson. 1982. Modeling distributional Mechanisms. General Equilibrium Models for Development Policy, Chapter 12. A World Bank Research Publication, World Bank.

Devarajan, S., L. Squire, and S. Suthiwart-Narueput. 1995. Reviving Project Appraisal at the World Bank. World Bank Policy Research Working Paper, 1496. Washington D.C., USA, World Bank.

DFID. 2002. Making Connections: Infrastructure for poverty reduction. U.K., Department for International Development (DFID). http://www.dfid.gov.uk/pubs/files/makingconnections.pdf (accessed 28/02/2006)

Diao, X., J. Rattso, and H. Ekroll Stokke. 2005. "International spillovers, productivity growth and openness in Thailand: An intertemporal general equilibrium analysis." *Journal of Development Economics*. Vol. 76 (2):429-450.

Dimarana, B., D. Le, and W. Martin. 2005. Potential Economic Impacts of Merchandise Trade Liberalization under Viet Nam's Accession to WTO. Paper presented at the 8th Annual Conference on Global Economic Analysis, Lübeck, Germany,

Doanh, L. D., V. T. Thanh, P. T. L. Huoan, D. H. Minh, and N. Q. Thang. 2002. Global Research Project: Explaining Growth in Vietnam (Final Draft). Global Development Network, East Asian Development Network. Hanoi, Vietnam, Central Institute for Economic Management (CIEM).

Dollar, D. and A. Kraay. 2002. "Growth Is Good for the Poor." *Journal of Economic Growth*. Vol. 7 (3):195-225.

Dollar, D. and A. Kraay. 2004. "Trade, Growth and Poverty." *The Economic Journal*. Vol. 114 (493):22-49.

Dumont, J.-C. and S. Mesplé-Somps. 2000. The Impact of Public Infrastructure on Competitiveness and Growth: A CGE Analysis Applied to Senegal. Centre de Recherche en Economie et Finance Apliquées (CRÉFA).

Eastwood, R. and M. Lipton. 2001. Pro-poor Growth and Pro-growth Poverty Reduction: What do they Mean? What does the Evidence Mean? What can Policymakers Do? Asia Development Bank (ADB).

EIU. 2004. Country Report Vietnam. Economist Intelligence Unit (EIU).

EVN. 1999. National Hydropower Plan Study, Vietnam, Inception (PhaseI) Report, Volume I: Main Report. Electricity of Vietnam (EVN).

EVN. 2001. National Hydropower Plan (NHP) Study Vietnam, Draft Final
    Report, Volume IV: Da River Basin. Electricity of Vietnam (EVN).

Fan, S. and P. Hazell. 1999. Are Returns to Public Investment Lower In Less-
    Favored rural Areas? An Empirical Analysis of India. EPTD Discussion
    Paper, 43. Washington D.C., USA, International Food Policy Research
    Institute (IFPRI), Environmental and Production Technology Division
    (EPTD).

Fan, S., X. Zhang, and Zhang L. 2002. Growth, Inequality and Poverty in rural
    China. Research Report, 125. Washington D.C., USA, International Food
    Policy Research Institute (IFPRI).

Fan, S. and N. Rao. 2003. Public Spending in Developing Countries: Trends
    Determination, and Impact. EPTD Discussion Paper, 99. Washington
    D.C., USA, International Food Policy Research Institute (IFPRI),
    Environmental and Production Technology Division (EPTD).

Fan, S. 2003. Public Investment and Poverty Reduction. What have we learned
    from India and China? Paper Prepared for the ADBI conference.
    International Food Policy Research Institute (IFPRI).

Fan, S., P. L. Huong, and T. Q. Long. 2004. Government Spending and Poverty
    Reduction in Vietnam. Prepared for the World Bank, Washington D.C.,
    USA, International Food Policy Research Institute (IFPRI), Central
    Institute for Economic Management (CIEM).

Fan, S. and C. Chang-Kang. 2005. Road Development, Economic Growth and
    Poverty Reduction in China. Research Report, 138. Washington D.C.,
    USA, International Food Policy Research Institute (IFPRI).

FitzGerald, E. V. K. 1978. Public Sector Investment Planning for Developing
    Countries. The Macmillan Press Ltd.

Foster, J., J. Greer, and E. Thorbecke. 1984. "A Class of Decomposable Poverty
    Measures." *Econometrica*. Vol. 52 (3):761-765.

Gaile, G. L. 1992. "Improving rural-urban linkages through small town market
    based development." *Third World Planning Review* . Vol. 14 (2):131-148.

Gittinger, J. 1982. Economic Analysis of the Agricultural projects. Baltimore
    and London, U.K., The Economic Development Institute of the World
    Bank. The John Hopkins University Press.

Glewwe, P., M. Gragnolati, and H. Zaman. 2002. "Who gained from Vietnam's boom in the 1990's. An Analysis of Poverty and Inequality Trends." *Economic Development and Cultural Change.* Vol. 50: 773-792.

GSO. 1998. Handbook for the Implementation of the System of National Accounts (SNA) in Vietnam. Hanoi, Vietnam, General Statistic Office (GSO).

GSO. 1998. Vietnam Living Standard Survey (VLSS). Hanoi, Vietnam, General Statistic Office (GSO).

GSO. 2003. Vietnam National Input-Output Table 2000. Hanoi, Vietnam, General Statistic Office (GSO).

GSO. 2004. Vietnam Household Living Standard Survey (VHLSS) 2002. Hanoi, Vietnam, General Statistic Office (GSO).

GSO SL. 2001. Agricultural Yearbook for the year 2000. Son La, Vietnam, General Statistic Office Son La (GSO SL).

GSO SL. 2003A. Statistical Yearbook 2002 for Son La Province. Son La, Vietnam, General Statistic Office Son La (GSO SL).

GSO SL. 2003B. Yearbook of Commercial Statistics. Son La, Vietnam, General Statistic Office Son La (GSO SL).

GSO SL. 2003C. Tableau of Gross Output, Intermediate Consumption, Value Added. Son La, Vietnam, General Statistic Office Son La (GSO SL).

GSO SL. 2003D. Preliminary Data Survey of the Vietnam Household Living Standard Survey (VHLSS) 2002 for the Son La Province. Son La, Vietnam, General Statistic Office Son La (GSO SL).

GSO SL. 2003E. National Accounts, Bank Finance and Enterprises. Son La, Vietnam, General Statistic Office Son La (GSO SL).

Haddad, E. and F. Perobelli. 2005. Trade Liberalization and Regional Inequality: Do Transportation Costs Impose a Spatial Poverty Trap? Conference Paper, 8th Annual Conference on Global Economic Analysis, Lübeck, Germany,

Häuser, I. 2005. Measuring Poverty in Vietnam: Strengths and Weaknesses of Different Indicators. Master Thesis." Stuttgart, Germany, University of Hohenheim, Institute for Agricultural Economics and Social Sciences in the Tropics and Subtropics.

Heidhues, F. and G. Schrieder. 1993. "The Role of the Infrastructure Components for Rural Households' Access to Financial Markets: A Case Study of Cameroon." In Regional Food Security and Rural Infrastructure (Volume II), eds. H.-U. Thimm, and H. Hahn. Münster, Germany, LIT Verlag. 191-211.

Hemmer, H.-R. 2002. Wirtschaftsprobleme der Entwicklungsländer. München, Germany, Vahlen.

Hertel, T. W. and L. A. Winters. 2005. "Estimating the Poverty Impacts of a Prospective Doha Development Agenda." The World Economy. Vol. 28 (8):1057-1071 (15).

Hertel, T. W. and J. J. Reimer. 2004. Predicting the Poverty Impacts of Trade Reform. World Bank Policy Research Working Paper, 3444. Washington D.C., USA, World Bank.

Ianchovichina, E. and W. Martin. 2004. "Impacts of China's Accession to the World Trade Organization." World Bank Economic Review. Vol. 18 (1):3-28.

IFPRI. 2003. Income Diversification and Poverty in The Northern Uplands of Vietnam. Report prepared for Social Development Division, Sector Strategy Development Department, Japan Bank for International Cooperation, Tokyo, Japan. Washington D.C., USA, International Food Policy Institute (IFPRI).

Isard, W., I. J. Azis, M. T. Drennan, R. E. Miller, S. Saltzman, and E. Thorbecke. 1998. Methods of interregional and regional analysis. Aldershot, U.K., Ashgate.

Jacoby, H. G. 2000. "Access to markets and the benefits of rural roads." The Economic Journal. Vol. 110 (7):713-737.

JBIC. 2003. Linking Economic Growth and Poverty Reduction. Large-Scale Infrastructure in the Context of Vietnam's CPRGS. Consultation Draft, Japan Bank for International Cooperation (JBIC).

Jensen Tarp, H. and F. Tarp. 2005. "Trade Liberalization and Spatial Inequality: A Methodological Innovation in a Vietnamese Perspective." Review of Development Economics. Vol. 9 (1):69-86.

Kanbur, R. and L. Squire. 2001. "The Evolution of Thinking about Poverty: Exploring the Interactions." In World Bank Publications, eds. J. E. Stiglitz and G. M. Meier, 183-226.

Kanbur, R., A. J. Venables, and G. Wan. 2005. "Introduction to the Special Issue: Spatial Inequality and Development in Asia." *Review of Development Economics*. Vol. 9 (1):1-4.

Kanbur, R. and A. J. Venables. 2005. Rising Spatial Disparities and Development. Policy Brief, 3. United Nations University.

Klasen, S. 2003. In Search of the Holy Grail: How to Achieve Pro-Poor Growth? Diskussionsbeiträge des Ibero-Amerika Institutes für Wirtschaftordnung (IAI), 96. Göttingen, Germany, Georg-August-Universität.

Klasen, S. 2005. Economic Growth and Poverty Reduction: Measurement and Policy Issues. OECD Development Center Working Paper, 246. Paris, France, Organisation for Economic Co-operation and Development (OECD).

Klump, R. and T. Bonschab. 2004. Operationalising Pro-Poor Growth- A Country Case Study on Vietnam. A joint initiative of AFD, BMZ (GTZ, KfW Development Bank), DFID, and the World Bank.

Kraay, A. 2004. When is growth pro-poor? Evidence from a panel of countries. Revised Draft Paper World Bank, Washington D.C., USA, World Bank.

Kuiper, M. H. 2005. Village Modeling: A Chinese recipe for blending general equilibrium and household modelling. Dissertation. Wageningen University.

Kuznets, S. 1968. Toward a theory of economic growth. New York, USA, Norton.

Larsen, T. I., H. L. Pham, and M. Rama. 2004. Vietnam's Public Investment Program and its Impact on Poverty Reduction. Conference. Singapur: "Scaling Up Poverty Reduction".

Limao, N. and A. J. Venables. 2001. "Infrastructure, Geographical Disadvantage, Transport Costs and Trade." *The World Bank Economic Review*. Vol. 15 (3):451-479.

Lipton, M., and M. Ravallion. 1995. "Poverty and Policy." In Handbook of Development Economics, eds. J. Behrmann and T. N. Srinivasan, Amsterdam, Netherlands.

Litchfield, J., and P. Justino. 2004. "Welfare in Vietnam During the 1990s." *Journal of the Asian Pacific Economy*. Vol. 9 (2):145-169.

Lopez, H. J. 2004. Pro-growth, pro-poor: Is there a trade-off? World Bank Policy Research Working Paper, 3378. Washington D.C., USA, World Bank.

Löfgren, H., and S. Robinson. 1999. Spatial Networks in Multi-Region Computable General Equilibrium Models. TMD Discussion Paper, 35. Washington D.C., USA, International Food Policy Institute (IFPRI), Trade and Macroeconomics Division (TMD).

Löfgren, H., R. L. Harris, S. Robinson, M. Thomas, and M. El-Said. 2002. A Standard Computable General Equilibrium (CGE) Model in GAMS. International Food Policy Research Institute (IFPRI).

Löfgren, H., J. Thurlow, and S. Robinson. 2004. Prospect for growth and poverty reduction in Zambia, 2001-2015. DSG Discussion Paper, 11. Washington D.C., USA, International Food Policy Institute (IFPRI).

Lysy, F., and L. Taylor. 1980. The General Equilibrium Income Distribution Model. Models of Growth and Distribution for Brazil, Oxford, U.K., Oxford University Press.

McCulloch, N., A. L. Winters, and X. Cirera. 2001. Trade Liberalization and Poverty: A Handbook. London, U.K., CEPR.

Mellor, J. W. 1999. Faster, More Equitable Growth - The Relation between Growth in Agriculture and Poverty Reduction. 4. Abt Associates Inc. Agricultural Policy Development Project.

Milanovic, B. 2002. "True world income distribution, 1988 and 1993: First calculation based on household surveys alone." *The Economic Journal*. Vol. 112 (476):51-92.

Minot, N. 2000. "Generating Disaggregated Poverty Maps: An Application to Vietnam." *World Development*. Vol. 28 (2):319-331.

Minten, B. and S. Kyle. 1999. "The effect of distance and road quality on food collection, marketing margins, and trader's wages: evidence from the former Zaire." *Journal of Development Economics*. Vol. 60: 467-495.

Nicita, A. 2004. Who Benefited from Trade Liberalization in Mexico? Measuring the Effects on Household Welfare. World Bank Policy Research Working Paper, 3265. Washington D.C., USA, World Bank.

OECD. 2005. Draft guiding principles on infrastructure for poverty reduction. DAC Network on Poverty Reduction, DCD/DAC/POVNET(2005)3. Organisation for Economic Co-operation and Development (OECD).

Pau, S. 2003. "Effects of Public Infrastructure on Cost Structure and Productivity in the Private Sector." *The Economic Record*. Vol. 79 (247):446.

Pritchett, L. 2000. "Understanding Patterns of Economic Growth: Searching for Hills among Plateaus, Mountains, and Plains." *World Bank Research Observer*. Vol. 14 (2):221-250.

Prud'homme, R. 2004. Infrastructure and Development. Annual Bank Conference on Development Economics.

Pyatt, G. F. and J. I. Round. 1977. "Social Accounting Matrices for Development Planning." *Review of Income and Wealth*. Vol. 23 (4):339-364.

Pyatt, G. F. and J. I. Round. 1985. "Accounting and Fixed-Price Multipliers in a Social Accounting Matrix Framework." A World Bank Symposium. Washington D.C., USA, World Bank. Chapter 9, Part III.

Ravallion, M. 1996. Issues in Measuring and Modeling Poverty. World Bank Policy Research Working Paper, 1615. Washington D.C., USA, World Bank.

Ravallion, M. and S. Chen. 1997. What can new survey data tell us about recent changes in distribution and poverty? World Bank Policy Research Working Paper, 1694. Washington D.C., USA, World Bank.

Ravallion, M. and G. Datt. 1999. When is Growth Pro-Poor? Evidence of the Diverse Experiences of India's States. World Bank Policy Research Working Paper, 2263. Washington D.C., USA, World Bank.

Ravallion, M. and S. Chen. 2001. Measuring Pro-Poor Growth. World Bank
    Policy Research Working Paper, 2666. Washington D.C., USA, World
    Bank.

Ravallion, M. 2004. Pro-Poor Growth: A Primer. World Bank Policy Research
    Working Paper, 3242. Washington D.C., USA, World Bank.

Reimer, J. J. 2002. Estimating the Poverty Impacts of Trade Liberalization.
    GTAP Working Paper, 1163. Purdue University, Indiana, USA, Center
    for Global Trade Analysis and Department of Agriculture Economics.

Reinert, K. A. and D. W. Roland-Holst. 1997. "Social Accounting Matrices." In
    Social Accounting Matrices: A Basis for Planning, eds. G. Pyatt and J.
    Round. World Bank. Washington D.C., USA.

Robinson, S., A. Cattaneo, and M. El-Said. 2001. "Updating and Estimating a
    Social Accounting Matrix Using Cross Entropy Methods." *Economic
    System Research*. Vol.13 (1):47-64.

Rodríguez, F. and D. Rodrik. 1999. Trade Policy and Economic Growth: A
    Sceptic's Guide to the Cross National Evidence. CEPR Discussion Paper,
    2143. London, U.K., Centre for Economic Policy Research (CEPR).

Round, J. I. 2005. "Social Accounting Matrices and SAM-based Multiplier
    Analysis." World Bank. Washington D.C., USA. Chapter 14.

Saith, A. 2005. "Poverty Lines versus the Poor. Method versus Meaning."
    Economic and Political Weekly. (Oct 22):4601-4610.

Schweickert, R., R. Thiele, and M. Wiebelt. 2005. Exchange Rate Policy in a
    Dollarized Economy: A CGE Analysis for Bolivia. Working Paper, 1255.
    Kiel, Germany, Institute for World Economics.

Scudder, T. 2005. The Future of Large Dams: Dealing with social,
    environmental, institutional and political costs. London, U.K.,
    James&James/Earthscan.

Sen, A. 1976. "Poverty: An Ordinal Approach to Measurement." *Econometrica*.
    Vol. 44 (2):219-231.

Seung, C. K., and D. S. Kraybill. 2001. "The Effects of Infrastructure
    Investment: A Two-Sector Dynamic Computable General Equilibrium
    Analysis for Ohio." *International Regional Science Review*. Vol. 24
    (2):261-281.

Sharma, R., and T. T. Poleman. 1993. The New Economics of India's Green Revolution: Income and Employment Diffusion in Uttar Pradesh. Ithaka, USA, Cornell University Press.

Shoven, J. B., and J. Whalley. 1984. "Applied General Equilibrium Models of Taxation and International Trade: an Introduction and Survey." *Journal of Economic Literature.* Vol. 22 (3):1007-1051.

Singer, H. W. 1997. "Editorial: The Golden Age of the Keynesian Consensus - The Pendulum Swings Back." *World Development.* Vol. 25 (3):293-295.

SRV. 2003. The Comprehensive Poverty Reduction And Growth Strategy (CPRGS). 2685/VPCP-QHQT. Socialist Republic of Vietnam (SRV).

Tacoli, C. 1998. "Rural-urban interactions: a guide to the literature." *Environment & Urbanization.* Vol. 10 (1):147-166.

Tacoli, C. 2003. "The links between urban and rural development." *Environment & Urbanization.* Vol. 15 (1):3-12.

Tarp, F., D. Roland-Holst, J. Rand, and H. Tarp Jensen. 2002. A Social Accounting Matrix for Vietnam for the Year 2000: Documentation. Hanoi, Vietnam, Central Institute for Economic Management (CIEM) and Nordic Institute of Asian Studies (NIAS).

The Economist. 1999. "Water power in Asia: The dry facts about dams." *The Economist.* Nov 18th.

The Economist. 2002. "Trucking in Cameroon: The road to hell is unpaved." *The Economist.* Dec 19th.

The Economist. 2006A. "Economic growth: The jobless boom." *The Economist.* Jan 12th 57-58.

The Economist. 2006B. "Vietnam: Trouble at the mill." *The Economist.* Jan 26th.

Thorbecke, E. 1985. The Social Accounting Matrix and Consistency-Type Planning Models. Social Accounting Matrices, a Basis for Planning. Chapter 10, Part III, World Bank.

Thorbecke, E. 1998. Social Accounting Matrices and Social Accounting Analysis. Isard, Walter, Saltzman Sidney, and Thorbecke, Erik. Methods of Interregional and Regional Analysis. Chapter 7Ashgate, Aldershot, Brookfield, USA.

Thu Houng Le, and P. Winters. 2001. "Aid Policies and Poverty Alleviation: The Case of Viet Nam." *Asia-Pacific Development Journal*. Vol. 8 (2):27-43.

Timmer, P. C. 1997. How Well do the Poor Connect to the Growth Process. CAER Discussion Paper, 178. Cambridge, USA, Harvard Institute for International Development (HIID).

Timmins, C. 2005. "Estimable equilibrium models of locational sorting and their role in development economics." *Journal of Economic Geography*. Vol. 5 (1):83-100.

UN. 2002. Millennium Development Goals: Bringing the MDGs Closer to the People. United Nations in Vietnam.

van de Walle, D., and D. Gunewardena. 2001. "Sources of the ethnic inequality in Viet Nam." *Journal of Development Economics*. Vol. 65 (1):177-207.

van de Walle, D. 2002. "Choosing Rural Road Investments to Help Reduce Poverty." *World Development*. Vol. 30 (4):575-589.

Venables, A. J. 2005. "Spatial disparities in developing countries: cities, regions and international trade." *Journal of Economic Geography*. Vol. 5 (1):3-21.

von Braun, J., A. Gulati, S. Fan, M. S. Ahluwalia, and J. Liu. 2005. IFPRI Annual Report 2004-2005: Lessons Learned from the Dragon (China) and the Elephant (India). International Food Policy Institute (IFPRI). Washington D.C., USA.

von Oppen, M., and D. M. Gabagambi. 2003. "Contribution of Markets to Agricultural Productivity: evidence from Developing Countries." *Quarterly Journal of international Agriculture*. Vol. 42 (1):49-61.

WCD. 2000. Dams and Development: A new Framework for Decision-Making. London, U.K., Earthscan Publication Ltd.

Winters, A. L. 2000. "Trade, Trade Policy and Poverty: What are the links?" *World Economy*. Vol. 25:1339-1367.

Winters, A. L. 2002. Trade Liberalisation and Poverty: Two Partial Empirical Studies. London, U.K., Centre for Economic Policy Research.

Winters, A. L., N. McCulloch, and A. McKay. 2004. "Trade Liberalization and Poverty: The Evidence So Far." *The Journal of Economic Literature*. Vol. 42 (2):72-115.

Wobst, P. 2001. Structural adjustment and intersectoral shifts in Tanzania - A computable general equilibrium analysis. IFPRI Research Report, 117. Washington D.C., USA, International Food Policy Research Institute (IFPRI).

World Bank. 1990. World Development Report: Poverty. PUB8507. Washington D.C., USA, World Bank.

World Bank. 1994. World Development Report 1994: Infrastructure for Development. 13184. Oxford University Press.

World Bank. 1999A. Vietnam Development Report 2000: Attacking Poverty. Country Economic Memorandum. 19914. Hanoi, Vietnam, World Bank.

World Bank. 1999B. Vietnam moving forward. Achievements and challenges in the transport sector. 18748-VN. World Bank. East Asia Transport Sector Unit, East Asia and Pacific Regional Office.

World Bank. 2000. World Development Report 1999/2000: Entering the 21st Century. Washington D.C., USA, Oxford University Press.

World Bank. 2005. World Development Report 2006: Equity and Development. 32204. Washington D.C., USA, World Bank and Oxford University Press.

World Bank et al. 2003. Vietnam Development Report 2004: Poverty. Joint Donor Report to the Vietnam Consultative Group Meeting. Hanoi, Vietnam, World Bank.

World Bank et al. 2004. Vietnam Development Report 2005: Governance, Rethinking the Role of Government in Vietnam. Hanoi, Vietnam, World Bank.

WTO. 2005. WTO - Accession Status: Vietnam. http://www.wto.org/english/thewto_e/acc_e/a1_vietnam_e.htm (accessed 28/02/2006)

Zeller, M. 2004. Review of Poverty Assessment Tools. Maryland, USA, Center for Institutional Reform and the Informal Sector (IRIS), United States Agency for International Development (USAID).

Appendices

Appendix 1: Mapping of Son La SAM activities to national I/O table

National I-O table Code	National SAM code	Commodities in National I-O	SAM Son La		
			Code SL	Commodities	Activities
1	C001	Paddy (all kinds)	CRice	1	Rice	1
2	C002	Raw rubber			Other Crops	
3	C003	Coffe beans	CCoffe	2	Coffee	3
4	C004	Sugarcane			Other Crops	
5	C005	Tea	CTea	3	Tea	5
6	C006	Other crops	COtCro	4	Other Crops	2, 4, 6
7	C007	Pig (All kinds)	CLifes	5	Lifestock	7, 8, 9, 10
8	C008	Cow (All kinds)			Lifestock	
9	C009	Poultry			Lifestock	
10	C010	Other Livestock			Lifestock	
11	C011	Irrigation service	CAgSer	6	Agricultural Services	11, 12
12	C012	Other Agricultural services			Agricultural Services	
13	C013	Forestry	CFores	7	Forestry	13
14	C014	Fishery	CFishe	8	Fishery	14, 15
15	C015	Fish - Farming			Fishery	
16	C016	Coal	CMinin	9	Mining	16, 17, 18, 19, 20
17	C017	Metallic ore			Mining	
18	C018	Stone			Mining	
19	C019	Sand, Gravel			Mining	
20	C020	Other none-metallic minerals			Mining	
21	C021	Crude oil, natural gas (except exploration)			Mining	

22	C022	Processed, preserved meat and by-products	CFoPro	10	Food & Beverage	22, 23, 24, 25, 26, 27, 28, 29, 30, 31, 32, 35, 36
23	C023	Processed vegetable, and amimals oils and fats			Food & Beverage	
24	C024	Milk, butter and other dairy products			Food & Beverage	
25	C025	Cakes, jams, candy, coca, chocolate products			Food & Beverage	
26	C026	Processed and preserved fuits and vegetables			Food & Beverage	
27	C027	Alcohol, beer and liquors			Food & Beverage	
28	C028	Beer and liquors			Food & Beverage	
29	C029	Non-alcohol water and soft drinks			Food & Beverage	
30	C030	Sugar, refined			Food & Beverage	
31	C031	Coffee, processed			Food & Beverage	
32	C032	Tea, processed			Food & Beverage	
33	C033	Cigarettes and other tobacco products			Food & Beverage	
34	C034	Processed seafood and by products			Food & Beverage	
35	C035	Rice, processed			Food & Beverage	
36	C036	Other food manufactures			Food & Beverage	

37	C037	Glass and glass products			Other goods	
38	C038	Ceramis and by products			Other goods	
39	C039	Bricks, tiles			Other Construction materials	
40	C040	Cement	CCemen	11	Cement	40, 41
41	C041	Concrete, mortar and other cement products			Cement	
42	C042	Other building materials	COtCoM	12	Other Construction materials	39, 42
43	C043	Paper pulp and paper products and by products	CForPr	13	Carpentry & Forestry Products	43, 44
44	C044	Processed wood and wood products			Carpentry & Forestry Products	
45	C045	Basic organix chemicals	CChemi	14	Chemical Products	
46	C046	Basic inorganix chemicals			Chemical Products	
47	C047	Chemical fertilizer			Chemical Products	
48	C048	Fertilizer			Chemical Products	
49	C049	Pesticides			Chemical Products	
50	C050	Veterinary			Chemical Products	
51	C051	Health medicine			Chemical Products	
52	C052	Processed rubber and by products			Chemical Products	
53	C053	Soap, detergents			Chemical Products	
54	C054	Perfumes and other toilet preparation			Chemical Products	

55	C055	Plastic (including semi-plastic products)			Chemical Products
56	C056	Other plastic products			Chemical Products
57	C057	Paint			Chemical Products
58	C058	Ink, varnish and other painting materials			Chemical Products
59	C059	Other chemical products			Chemical Products
60	C060	Health instrument and apparatus	CMachi	15	Machinery
61	C061	Precise and optics equipment, meter (all kinds)			Machinery
62	C062	Home appliances and its spare parts			Machinery
63	C063	Motor vehicles, motor bikes and spare parts			Machinery
64	C064	Bicycles and spare parts			Machinery
65	C065	General - purpose machinery			Machinery
66	C066	Other generel - purpose machinery			Machinery
67	C067	Other special - purpose machinery			Machinery
68	C068	Automobiles			Machinery
69	C069	Other transport mean			Machinery
70	C070	Electrical machinery			Machinery

71	C071	Other electrical machinery and equipment			Machinery	
72	C072	Machinery used for broadcasting, television and information activities			Machinery	
73	C073	Non-ferrous metals and products (except machinery equipment)	CMetal	16	Metal Products	73, 74
74	C074	Ferrous metals and products (except machinery equipment)			Metal Products	
75	C075	Weaving of cloths (all kinds)	CTexGa	17	Textiles, Carpets, Leather	75, 76, 77, 78, 79, 80, 81
76	C076	Fibers, thread (all kinds)			Textiles, Carpets, Leather	
77	C077	Ready -made clother, sheets (all kinds)			Textiles, Carpets, Leather	
78	C078	Carpets			Textiles, Carpets, Leather	
79	C079	Weaving and embroidery of textile -based goods (except carpets)			Textiles, Carpets, Leather	
80	C080	Products of leather tanneries			Textiles, Carpets, Leather	
81	C081	Leather goods			Textiles, Carpet, Leather	

82	C082	Animal feeds			Food processing	
83	C083	Products of printing activities	CPuPri	18	Publishing & Printing	83, 84
84	C084	Products of publising house			Publishing & Printing	
85	C085	Other physical goods	COthGo	19	Other Goods	
86	C086	Gasoline, lubricants (already refined)	CFueLu	20	Fuel	
87	C087	Electricity, gas	CElGaW	21	Electricity, Gas, Water	87, 88
88	C088	Water			Electricity, Gas, Water	
89	C089	Civil construction	CConst	22	Construction Services	89, 90
90	C090	Other construction			Construction Services	
91	C091	Trade	CTraRe	23	Trade & Repair	91, 92
92	C092	Repair of small transport means, motorbikes and personal household appliances			Trade & Repair	
93	C093	Hotels	CGastr	24	Restaurants & Hotels	93, 94
94	C094	Restaurants			Restaurants & Hotels	
95	C095	Transportation	CTrans	25	Transport	95
96	C096	Railway transport services			Transport	
97	C097	Water transport services			Transport	
98	C098	Air transport services			Transport	
99	C099	Communication services	CPosCo	26	Post and Communication	99

100	C100	Tourism			Other services	
101	C101	Banking, credit, treasury	CFiSer	27	Financial Services	101
102	C102	Lottery			Other services	
103	C103	Insurance			Other services	
104	C104	Science and technology	CScTec	28	Science & Technology	104
105	C105	Real estate			Other services	
106	C106	Real estate business and consultancy services			Other services	
107	C107	State management, defence and compulsory social security	CStMan	29	State Management	107
108	C108	Education and training	CEduTr	30	Education	108
109	C109	Health care, social relief	CHealt	31	Health	109
110	C110	Culture and sport			Other services	
111	C111	Association			Other services	
112	C112	Other services	COtSer	32	Other services	(100, 102, 103, 105,106,110, 111, 112)

Appendix 2: Multiplier Matrix Son La (2002)

		1	2	3	4	5	6	7	8
Paddy rice	1	1.190	0.255	0.252	0.284	0.251	0.295	0.182	0.027
Coffee	2	0.001	1.002	0.002	0.002	0.002	0.003	0.002	0.000
Tea	3	0.005	0.008	1.012	0.009	0.008	0.009	0.006	0.001
Other crops	4	0.062	0.095	0.093	1.147	0.283	0.109	0.068	0.011
Lifestock	5	0.064	0.098	0.097	0.109	1.246	0.113	0.070	0.013
Forestry	6	0.045	0.069	0.070	0.079	0.074	1.136	0.063	0.007
Fishery	7	0.021	0.032	0.032	0.036	0.032	0.038	1.102	0.004
Mining	8	0.002	0.003	0.003	0.003	0.003	0.004	0.003	1.015
Primary sector		1.391	1.562	1.561	1.669	1.899	1.707	1.496	1.080
Food, beverages	9	0.103	0.157	0.157	0.176	0.154	0.184	0.117	0.024
Textiles, garment	10	0.048	0.074	0.073	0.082	0.069	0.086	0.054	0.010
Forestry products	11	0.019	0.030	0.031	0.036	0.088	0.052	0.029	0.008
Publishing, printing	12	0.001	0.001	0.002	0.002	0.003	0.003	0.002	0.000
Other goods	13	0.015	0.023	0.024	0.026	0.024	0.028	0.024	0.006
Cement	14	0.002	0.002	0.003	0.003	0.003	0.005	0.005	0.019
Construction material	15	0.001	0.002	0.002	0.003	0.002	0.004	0.003	0.006
Metals	16	0.004	0.007	0.009	0.008	0.009	0.009	0.019	0.012
Chemicals	17	0.081	0.214	0.178	0.120	0.068	0.083	0.047	0.013
Machinery	18	0.039	0.062	0.063	0.068	0.057	0.080	0.065	0.019
Electricity, gas, water	19	0.012	0.019	0.037	0.027	0.026	0.026	0.013	0.007
Fuel, lubricants	20	0.014	0.030	0.041	0.026	0.086	0.031	0.037	0.022
Secondary sector		0.339	0.620	0.619	0.576	0.590	0.591	0.415	0.147
Agricultural service	21	0.051	0.021	0.028	0.022	0.014	0.018	0.013	0.001
Construction	22	0.003	0.004	0.004	0.005	0.004	0.005	0.003	0.001
Trade, repair	23	0.030	0.038	0.043	0.045	0.043	0.056	0.034	0.013
Restaurant, hotel	24	0.007	0.011	0.014	0.012	0.010	0.015	0.008	0.004
Transport	25	0.005	0.010	0.008	0.009	0.006	0.015	0.007	0.001
Post, communication	26	0.003	0.005	0.007	0.013	0.007	0.015	0.005	0.001
Financial service	27	0.002	0.002	0.003	0.003	0.003	0.004	0.005	0.001
Science, technology	28	0.003	0.003	0.004	0.004	0.003	0.005	0.013	0.001
State management	29	0.005	0.007	0.008	0.008	0.007	0.010	0.010	0.004
Education	30	0.017	0.027	0.026	0.029	0.024	0.031	0.018	0.005
Health	31	0.030	0.046	0.046	0.051	0.043	0.054	0.033	0.006
Other services	32	0.030	0.047	0.047	0.052	0.043	0.058	0.034	0.008
Tertiary sector		0.187	0.221	0.238	0.253	0.208	0.284	0.184	0.047
Gross output		1.916	2.403	2.418	2.498	2.698	2.581	2.095	1.274
Employed labour	33	0.037	0.063	0.066	0.073	0.062	0.100	0.061	0.046
Self-employed labour	34	0.024	0.032	0.036	0.037	0.035	0.046	0.028	0.113
Agricultural labour	35	0.682	1.044	1.027	1.159	0.969	1.194	0.737	0.036
Capital	36	0.065	0.099	0.100	0.114	0.083	0.072	0.060	0.023
Value added		0.808	1.238	1.229	1.383	1.149	1.412	0.886	0.219
Urban Kinh HH	37	0.026	0.040	0.041	0.045	0.039	0.054	0.033	0.050
Urban ethnic HH	38	0.027	0.042	0.042	0.047	0.039	0.052	0.033	0.024
Rural Kinh HH	39	0.085	0.130	0.129	0.145	0.122	0.153	0.094	0.028
Rural Thai HH	40	0.283	0.434	0.428	0.482	0.404	0.500	0.309	0.039
Rural Hmong HH	41	0.090	0.137	0.135	0.153	0.128	0.157	0.097	0.007
Other rural ethnic HH	42	0.221	0.339	0.334	0.376	0.315	0.388	0.240	0.017
Household income		0.733	1.122	1.110	1.249	1.047	1.304	0.806	0.166
TOTAL		3.456	4.763	4.758	5.130	4.894	5.298	3.787	1.659

	9	10	11	12	13	14	15	16	17	18	19
1	0.038	0.005	0.023	0.047	0.000	0.015	0.041	0.012	0.000	0.000	0.021
2	0.015	0.000	0.000	0.001	0.000	0.000	0.001	0.000	0.000	0.000	0.000
3	0.055	0.000	0.001	0.002	0.000	0.001	0.002	0.001	0.000	0.000	0.001
4	0.023	0.007	0.009	0.019	0.000	0.006	0.017	0.005	0.000	0.000	0.009
5	0.020	0.003	0.010	0.023	0.000	0.007	0.020	0.006	0.000	0.000	0.011
6	0.011	0.001	0.062	0.022	0.000	0.005	0.013	0.003	0.000	0.000	0.005
7	0.005	0.001	0.003	0.006	0.000	0.002	0.006	0.002	0.000	0.000	0.004
8	0.006	0.002	0.001	0.002	0.000	0.030	0.131	0.002	0.000	0.000	0.002
	0.172	0.019	0.108	0.123	0.000	0.066	0.229	0.031	0.000	0.000	0.053
9	1.064	0.004	0.016	0.042	0.000	0.013	0.036	0.011	0.000	0.000	0.019
10	0.012	1.043	0.007	0.017	0.000	0.005	0.015	0.004	0.000	0.000	0.008
11	0.010	0.002	1.012	0.187	0.000	0.019	0.020	0.003	0.000	0.000	0.005
12	0.001	0.000	0.000	1.137	0.000	0.000	0.002	0.000	0.000	0.000	0.001
13	0.012	0.003	0.004	0.205	1.000	0.007	0.025	0.009	0.000	0.000	0.004
14	0.001	0.005	0.002	0.005	0.000	1.136	0.070	0.003	0.000	0.000	0.001
15	0.001	0.002	0.001	0.003	0.000	0.009	1.070	0.002	0.000	0.000	0.000
16	0.008	0.005	0.002	0.012	0.000	0.007	0.008	1.072	0.000	0.000	0.004
17	0.023	0.006	0.013	0.050	0.000	0.044	0.044	0.004	1.000	0.000	0.006
18	0.014	0.003	0.011	0.043	0.000	0.018	0.029	0.016	0.000	1.000	0.026
19	0.010	0.004	0.006	0.016	0.000	0.022	0.029	0.011	0.000	0.000	1.010
20	0.010	0.003	0.008	0.012	0.000	0.069	0.069	0.006	0.000	0.000	0.004
	1.165	1.081	1.083	1.727	1.000	1.329	1.416	1.142	1.000	1.000	1.089
21	0.003	0.000	0.001	0.002	0.000	0.001	0.002	0.001	0.000	0.000	0.001
22	0.001	0.000	0.001	0.002	0.000	0.001	0.002	0.000	0.000	0.000	0.001
23	0.032	0.007	0.015	0.095	0.000	0.049	0.045	0.014	0.000	0.000	0.032
24	0.003	0.001	0.002	0.006	0.000	0.002	0.007	0.002	0.000	0.000	0.003
25	0.002	0.000	0.002	0.005	0.000	0.003	0.004	0.001	0.000	0.000	0.002
26	0.002	0.000	0.005	0.005	0.000	0.003	0.003	0.001	0.000	0.000	0.004
27	0.001	0.000	0.001	0.005	0.000	0.001	0.002	0.001	0.000	0.000	0.003
28	0.002	0.001	0.002	0.005	0.000	0.002	0.003	0.002	0.000	0.000	0.003
29	0.005	0.001	0.003	0.013	0.000	0.007	0.007	0.003	0.000	0.000	0.005
30	0.004	0.001	0.003	0.008	0.000	0.003	0.007	0.002	0.000	0.000	0.004
31	0.008	0.001	0.005	0.012	0.000	0.004	0.010	0.003	0.000	0.000	0.006
32	0.008	0.002	0.005	0.013	0.000	0.005	0.015	0.004	0.000	0.000	0.007
	0.070	0.015	0.044	0.172	0.000	0.081	0.107	0.033	0.000	0.000	0.072
	1.407	1.115	1.236	2.022	1.000	1.475	1.752	1.206	1.000	1.000	1.215
33	0.043	0.004	0.022	0.218	0.000	0.048	0.092	0.008	0.000	0.000	0.121
34	0.022	0.019	0.028	0.062	0.000	0.034	0.142	0.061	0.000	0.000	0.021
35	0.132	0.010	0.073	0.070	0.000	0.020	0.056	0.016	0.000	0.000	0.029
36	0.029	0.010	0.033	0.146	0.000	0.072	0.074	0.021	0.000	0.000	0.037
	0.226	0.043	0.155	0.497	0.000	0.174	0.364	0.106	0.000	0.000	0.208
37	0.018	0.008	0.015	0.066	0.000	0.022	0.070	0.024	0.000	0.000	0.032
38	0.015	0.004	0.011	0.056	0.000	0.017	0.039	0.010	0.000	0.000	0.027
39	0.023	0.005	0.015	0.037	0.000	0.012	0.039	0.013	0.000	0.000	0.017
40	0.063	0.008	0.037	0.072	0.000	0.022	0.060	0.018	0.000	0.000	0.032
41	0.018	0.002	0.010	0.014	0.000	0.004	0.011	0.003	0.000	0.000	0.006
42	0.045	0.004	0.025	0.032	0.000	0.009	0.026	0.008	0.000	0.000	0.014
	0.181	0.031	0.114	0.277	0.000	0.087	0.245	0.076	0.000	0.000	0.127
	1.814	1.189	1.505	2.796	1.000	1.737	2.361	1.388	1.000	1.000	1.550

	20	21	22	23	24	25	26	27	28	29	30	31
1	0.000	0.020	0.060	0.139	0.103	0.072	0.059	0.052	0.014	0.108	0.081	0.036
2	0.000	0.000	0.001	0.002	0.004	0.001	0.001	0.001	0.000	0.001	0.001	0.000
3	0.000	0.001	0.003	0.007	0.017	0.003	0.003	0.002	0.001	0.005	0.004	0.002
4	0.000	0.008	0.025	0.057	0.057	0.030	0.024	0.021	0.006	0.045	0.034	0.015
5	0.000	0.010	0.030	0.069	0.107	0.036	0.029	0.026	0.007	0.054	0.041	0.018
6	0.000	0.005	0.018	0.034	0.028	0.017	0.015	0.013	0.003	0.027	0.020	0.009
7	0.000	0.003	0.008	0.019	0.042	0.010	0.008	0.007	0.002	0.015	0.011	0.005
8	0.000	0.001	0.033	0.006	0.022	0.003	0.002	0.002	0.001	0.004	0.003	0.001
	0.000	0.048	0.177	0.333	0.381	0.173	0.139	0.124	0.033	0.259	0.194	0.085
9	0.000	0.018	0.054	0.126	0.322	0.065	0.051	0.046	0.012	0.098	0.073	0.032
10	0.000	0.007	0.040	0.049	0.057	0.026	0.021	0.019	0.005	0.038	0.028	0.014
11	0.000	0.005	0.045	0.035	0.053	0.018	0.020	0.022	0.004	0.031	0.019	0.009
12	0.000	0.001	0.001	0.004	0.016	0.001	0.002	0.025	0.001	0.012	0.002	0.002
13	0.000	0.003	0.018	0.021	0.028	0.011	0.014	0.022	0.002	0.021	0.012	0.007
14	0.000	0.000	0.147	0.004	0.015	0.002	0.004	0.002	0.000	0.003	0.002	0.001
15	0.000	0.000	0.086	0.003	0.033	0.001	0.002	0.001	0.000	0.005	0.001	0.001
16	0.000	0.001	0.130	0.007	0.008	0.008	0.005	0.004	0.001	0.005	0.003	0.002
17	0.000	0.005	0.113	0.039	0.055	0.030	0.016	0.014	0.004	0.031	0.020	0.044
18	0.000	0.013	0.135	0.116	0.092	0.057	0.071	0.029	0.009	0.077	0.046	0.035
19	0.000	0.003	0.017	0.027	0.026	0.015	0.019	0.014	0.003	0.023	0.013	0.009
20	1.000	0.004	0.046	0.034	0.041	0.269	0.017	0.016	0.005	0.054	0.014	0.009
	1.000	0.061	0.834	0.465	0.743	0.502	0.241	0.213	0.046	0.398	0.233	0.165
21	0.000	1.167	0.003	0.007	0.005	0.003	0.003	0.003	0.001	0.005	0.004	0.002
22	0.000	0.001	1.003	0.005	0.003	0.003	0.003	0.003	0.001	0.006	0.004	0.002
23	0.000	0.047	0.065	1.048	0.035	0.040	0.027	0.024	0.010	0.056	0.030	0.028
24	0.000	0.003	0.008	0.019	1.012	0.010	0.007	0.006	0.002	0.014	0.010	0.005
25	0.000	0.004	0.008	0.019	0.007	1.009	0.007	0.008	0.005	0.055	0.013	0.005
26	0.000	0.008	0.004	0.006	0.004	0.005	1.002	0.004	0.001	0.008	0.005	0.003
27	0.000	0.018	0.004	0.007	0.009	0.011	0.010	1.023	0.005	0.031	0.011	0.006
28	0.000	0.018	0.005	0.039	0.007	0.006	0.095	0.116	1.002	0.067	0.004	0.002
29	0.000	0.012	0.013	0.139	0.014	0.021	0.007	0.016	0.013	1.045	0.010	0.005
30	0.000	0.003	0.011	0.026	0.017	0.013	0.009	0.008	0.002	0.019	1.014	0.006
31	0.000	0.008	0.015	0.038	0.022	0.018	0.016	0.017	0.004	0.073	0.048	1.011
32	0.000	0.009	0.018	0.045	0.027	0.021	0.018	0.017	0.030	0.060	0.040	0.017
	0.000	1.299	1.156	1.398	1.163	1.160	1.206	1.245	1.076	1.438	1.194	1.092
	1.000	1.408	2.167	2.196	2.287	1.836	1.586	1.582	1.154	2.095	1.621	1.342
33	0.000	0.105	0.180	0.210	0.084	0.111	0.302	0.278	0.088	0.713	0.563	0.226
34	0.000	0.029	0.184	0.605	0.367	0.300	0.022	0.020	0.009	0.056	0.027	0.024
35	0.000	0.027	0.082	0.184	0.204	0.096	0.077	0.069	0.018	0.144	0.108	0.047
36	0.000	0.030	0.074	0.104	0.078	0.148	0.524	0.407	0.014	0.091	0.036	0.032
	0.000	0.190	0.521	1.103	0.734	0.654	0.925	0.774	0.129	1.004	0.734	0.329
37	0.000	0.031	0.103	0.262	0.152	0.131	0.068	0.062	0.021	0.161	0.121	0.053
38	0.000	0.025	0.061	0.123	0.069	0.067	0.086	0.075	0.018	0.144	0.110	0.047
39	0.000	0.017	0.056	0.143	0.094	0.072	0.038	0.035	0.011	0.085	0.063	0.028
40	0.000	0.030	0.088	0.200	0.153	0.105	0.092	0.082	0.021	0.165	0.125	0.054
41	0.000	0.005	0.016	0.038	0.035	0.020	0.018	0.016	0.003	0.027	0.020	0.009
42	0.000	0.013	0.039	0.087	0.081	0.045	0.038	0.034	0.009	0.070	0.053	0.023
	0.000	0.121	0.363	0.853	0.584	0.441	0.340	0.304	0.083	0.652	0.491	0.214
	1.000	1.720	3.051	4.152	3.605	2.931	2.851	2.660	1.367	3.751	2.847	1.886

	32	33	34	35	36	37	38	39	40	41	42
1	0.035	0.145	0.193	0.345	0.029	0.144	0.188	0.224	0.379	0.464	0.316
2	0.000	0.002	0.002	0.003	0.000	0.002	0.003	0.003	0.003	0.003	0.003
3	0.002	0.007	0.009	0.011	0.001	0.009	0.012	0.011	0.011	0.010	0.011
4	0.014	0.060	0.080	0.127	0.011	0.067	0.077	0.091	0.155	0.115	0.117
5	0.017	0.073	0.096	0.131	0.013	0.093	0.118	0.101	0.153	0.138	0.115
6	0.009	0.035	0.045	0.093	0.007	0.024	0.045	0.054	0.106	0.097	0.095
7	0.005	0.020	0.027	0.044	0.004	0.024	0.024	0.023	0.057	0.024	0.045
8	0.004	0.004	0.006	0.003	0.000	0.012	0.006	0.003	0.004	0.003	0.002
	0.087	0.347	0.459	0.757	0.066	0.375	0.474	0.509	0.868	0.853	0.704
9	0.031	0.129	0.173	0.211	0.022	0.177	0.224	0.207	0.217	0.196	0.211
10	0.013	0.050	0.067	0.098	0.009	0.071	0.069	0.062	0.108	0.103	0.101
11	0.013	0.032	0.041	0.038	0.006	0.047	0.069	0.036	0.048	0.026	0.028
12	0.005	0.001	0.002	0.001	0.000	0.002	0.002	0.002	0.002	0.001	0.001
13	0.007	0.018	0.026	0.030	0.003	0.031	0.026	0.030	0.031	0.034	0.027
14	0.003	0.002	0.003	0.003	0.000	0.002	0.006	0.003	0.003	0.002	0.002
15	0.005	0.002	0.002	0.002	0.000	0.003	0.005	0.002	0.002	0.002	0.002
16	0.005	0.005	0.006	0.009	0.001	0.005	0.011	0.006	0.009	0.008	0.010
17	0.011	0.033	0.045	0.059	0.006	0.049	0.049	0.043	0.067	0.057	0.056
18	0.026	0.075	0.101	0.077	0.011	0.147	0.133	0.070	0.105	0.038	0.055
19	0.013	0.021	0.028	0.022	0.003	0.039	0.042	0.021	0.022	0.018	0.022
20	0.015	0.017	0.024	0.026	0.003	0.032	0.026	0.020	0.028	0.019	0.027
	0.147	0.386	0.516	0.576	0.064	0.604	0.663	0.501	0.641	0.506	0.542
21	0.002	0.007	0.009	0.016	0.001	0.007	0.009	0.011	0.018	0.021	0.015
22	0.002	0.008	0.007	0.005	0.002	0.001	0.033	0.008	0.005	0.005	0.003
23	0.023	0.027	0.035	0.044	0.005	0.036	0.049	0.035	0.048	0.044	0.043
24	0.004	0.019	0.027	0.014	0.002	0.050	0.027	0.015	0.017	0.012	0.010
25	0.008	0.004	0.006	0.008	0.001	0.006	0.006	0.008	0.008	0.008	0.009
26	0.005	0.004	0.005	0.005	0.000	0.006	0.005	0.009	0.005	0.004	0.004
27	0.019	0.002	0.003	0.003	0.000	0.003	0.003	0.003	0.003	0.003	0.003
28	0.007	0.002	0.003	0.003	0.000	0.003	0.003	0.003	0.004	0.003	0.003
29	0.024	0.005	0.007	0.008	0.001	0.007	0.009	0.007	0.009	0.008	0.008
30	0.006	0.025	0.037	0.034	0.003	0.047	0.032	0.049	0.036	0.019	0.032
31	0.012	0.035	0.042	0.061	0.007	0.035	0.080	0.035	0.063	0.070	0.065
32	1.014	0.040	0.055	0.062	0.007	0.056	0.064	0.074	0.072	0.048	0.050
	1.126	0.178	0.236	0.265	0.030	0.258	0.320	0.257	0.289	0.244	0.245
	1.361	0.911	1.211	1.598	0.160	1.237	1.457	1.266	1.798	1.603	1.491
33	0.133	1.043	0.057	0.065	0.007	0.062	0.073	0.066	0.070	0.056	0.062
34	0.052	0.027	1.036	0.038	0.004	0.045	0.048	0.033	0.042	0.036	0.035
35	0.047	0.193	0.254	1.425	0.037	0.202	0.262	0.287	0.489	0.467	0.399
36	0.297	0.033	0.044	0.057	1.006	0.043	0.052	0.053	0.065	0.055	0.051
	0.528	1.295	1.392	1.585	1.054	0.353	0.435	0.438	0.665	0.614	0.547
37	0.045	0.215	0.389	0.048	0.004	1.031	0.036	0.029	0.036	0.031	0.031
38	0.047	0.199	0.148	0.048	0.054	0.023	1.027	0.025	0.031	0.027	0.026
39	0.026	0.112	0.214	0.175	0.008	0.036	0.044	1.044	0.069	0.064	0.057
40	0.055	0.223	0.273	0.586	0.049	0.098	0.124	0.130	1.213	0.202	0.175
41	0.011	0.035	0.053	0.186	0.015	0.028	0.036	0.039	0.065	1.062	0.053
42	0.023	0.094	0.120	0.461	0.018	0.069	0.088	0.095	0.161	0.153	1.131
	0.206	0.878	1.196	1.505	0.147	1.285	1.356	1.362	1.576	1.539	1.473
	2.095	3.084	3.799	4.688	1.362	2.875	3.248	3.067	4.039	3.757	3.511

Appendix 3: Annual expenditures of urban households Son La (in 1000 VND)

HH number	HH member	Educa-tion t16*	Health t17*	Food t26*	Non-food t27*	Other exp t28*	Fixed assets t31*	Dura-bles t32*	Housing t34*	Annual Exp. per capita	Poor=1 Non-poor=0 Poverty line 2006
1	5	1902	3700	12942	6256	1075	0	0	924	5360	0
2	4	3460	330	12999	5854	788	0	0	572	6001	0
3	3	3600	320	10500	6751	1655	0	0	756	7861	0
4	2	0	515	5164	2864	1530	0	0	984	5528	0
5	5	1020	500	9421	5355	500	0	0	492	3458	0
6	3	480	196	8542	7144	965	0	0	540	5956	0
7	5	1200	291	11580	7421	1485	0	488	876	4668	0
8	4	4500	368	15615	6602	1213	976	4394	1020	8672	0
9	4	730	261	10182	5451	585	0	0	780	4497	0
10	4	1020	255	7469	3355	906	0	0	1020	3506	0
11	4	185	186	5197	2794	654	0	0	910	2482	0
12	4	530	222	6858	3947	2795	0	1595	60520	19117	0
13	3	0	1725	4369	2190	674	0	325	10600	6628	0
14	4	421	242	4640	2432	527	0	0	465	2182	0
15	5	509	2348	6258	3777	482	0	1383	460	3043	0
16	6	630	335	9461	2206	655	0	0	465	2292	0
17	4	0	185	6621	4552	967	0	0	690	3254	0
18	6	866	231	8382	2808	473	0	0	467	2205	0
19	4	452	181	6261	2526	750	0	0	685	2714	0
20	4	430	182	7486	2322	508	0	0	395	2831	0
21	4	450	193	5112	2187	330	0	0	545	2204	0
22	4	746	165	7009	1912	510	0	0	480	2706	0
23	4	428	247	5110	2920	671	0	0	510	2472	0
24	3	645	359	7277	2265	2160	0	0	500	4402	0
25	5	263	575	5923	2372	430	0	0	643	2041	0
26	3	0	415	4640	1103	463	0	0	375	2332	0
27	4	410	223	6341	2931	490	0	0	591	2747	0
28	5	1565	162	7064	2232	1514	0	0	575	2622	0
29	5	1458	278	8207	2286	644	0	0	420	2659	0
30	5	870	370	11409	1835	200	0	0	435	3024	0
31	5	0	238	7120	2285	365	0	0	640	2130	0
32	6	396	165	8560	2769	720	0	0	687	2216	0
33	4	563	165	11225	4124	870	0	407	675	4507	0
34	7	690	408	11749	4908	840	0	0	735	2761	0
35	4	492	395	7760	2131	391	0	0	351	2880	0

HH number	HH member	Educa-tion t16*	Health t17*	Food t26*	Non-food t27*	Other exp t28*	Fixed assets t31*	Dura-bles t32*	Housing t34*	Annual Exp. per capita	Poor=1 Non-poor=0 Poverty line 2006
36	4	0	220	9422	4143	1166	0	0	2113	4266	0
37	4	0	427	8639	2193	410	0	0	687	3089	0
38	5	0	245	9268	2917	395	0		95	2584	0
39	4	490	84	8149	2986	1280	0	0	495	3371	0
40	3	0	410	3506	1302	100	0	0	364	1894	1
41	3	435	20020	5668	3095	1080	0	1790	10600	14229	0
42	4	1325	620	11598	5797	1131	0	2311	225	5752	0
43	4	850	300	9415	5532	1950	423	195	960	4906	0
44	2	0	400	7683	5568	11680	0	0	600	12966	0
45	4	1025	200	9960	3153	666	81	0	336	3855	0
Average	4.2	779	886	8172	3590	1103	33	286	2406	4464	0.02

* code in VHLSS

Appendix 4: Annual expenditures of rural households Son La (in 1000 VND)

HH number	HH member	Educa-tion t16*	Health t17*	Food t26*	Non-food t27*	Other exp t28*	Fixed assets t31*	Dura-bles t32*	Housing t34*	Annual Exp. per capita	Poor=1 Non-poor=0 Poverty line 1957
1	5	1902	3700	12942	6256	1075	0	0	924	5360	0
2	6	65	350	4559	2538	236	0	342	380	1412	1
3	5	1010	1000	5571	2327	76	0	0	3360	2669	0
4	4	215	750	3884	3638	80	0	0	445	2253	0
5	4	350	450	5161	2636	112	0	0	180	2222	0
6	6	178	350	4874	2144	230	0	0	336	1352	1
7	6	90	800	6135	1392	78	0	0	340	1473	1
8	4	35	350	4868	1030	60	0	0	510	1713	1
9	3	45	390	4376	2544	390	0	130	300	2725	0
10	5	930	1200	4121	2165	125	0	0	180	1744	1
11	4	322	70	3848	1942	571	0	0	1960	2178	0
12	7	383	370	6136	2221	460	456	0	0	1432	1
13	6	0	150	6443	3702	284	0	0	590	1862	1
14	5	147	86	6504	2228	183	0	130	480	1952	1
15	5	439	450	5071	2840	600	0	212	0	1922	1
16	5	491	180	3891	1392	389	0	0	422	1353	1
17	8	454	156	7555	2423	233	0	0	336	1395	1
18	9	245	400	7668	2086	679	0	0	596	1297	1
19	5	0	450	4845	2058	545	0	57	0	1591	1
20	10	456	700	10035	5526	929	0	0	820	1847	1
21	11	280	300	9532	3932	842	0	179	0	1369	1
22	9	577	120	8238	2720	3601	0	0	270	1725	1
23	5	451	750	3700	2501	300	0	0	0	1541	1
24	6	622	350	4323	1924	385	895	0	0	1417	1
25	5	195	217	4626	2154	195	0	0	73	1492	1
26	6	254	246	7687	3544	301	0	0	234	2044	0
27	6	413	1100	4871	1823	405	0	0	300	1485	1
28	8	763	990	8805	4353	4385	407	0	2818	2815	0
29	6	0	50	7469	2014	1606	0	0	400	1923	1
30	9	0	141	6646	2291	211	0	0	250	1060	1
31	4	437	125	3560	2062	465	0	464	26	1785	1
32	7	593	1700	5705	1638	4230	0	508	12	2055	0
33	5	314	211	7974	3408	987	0	0	402	2659	0
34	6	294	426	6551	4622	261	0	244	2919	2553	0
35	10	424	1500	6297	2697	515	0	0	500	1193	1
36	10	0	115	12243	3384	180	0	684	480	1709	1
37	5	50	200	5774	1798	0	0	0	0	1564	1

HH number	HH member	Education t16*	Health t17*	Food t26*	Non-food t27*	Other exp t28*	Fixed assets t31*	Dura-bles t32*	Housing t34*	Annual Exp. per capita	Poor=1 Non-poor=0 Poverty line 1957
38	9	0	93	8430	2696	85	0	0	600	1323	1
39	5	0	150	5660	1980	50	0	0	0	1568	1
40	6	30	110	4796	1892	110	0	0	200	1190	1
41	5	480	134	5780	2225	85	0	2929	840	2495	0
42	4	340	88	6366	1829	130	0	0	200	2238	0
46	5	0	40	5071	1428	56	309	0	200	1421	1
47	5	50	70	5780	1754	66	0	0	200	1584	1
48	6	135	50	5925	1948	85	0	0	200	1391	1
49	6	0	60	6244	2420	110	0	0	200	1506	1
50	5	120	40	5579	1880	75	814	0	200	1742	1
51	6	0	415	3818	1151	80	0	0	0	911	1
52	8	0	100	6465	2006	2040	0	0	0	1326	1
53	7	30	30	5885	1078	65	0	0	0	1013	1
54	12	0	450	8102	2330	160	667	0	0	976	1
55	5	100	450	4715	1390	140	0	0	0	1359	1
56	4	272	1353	4739	1581	100	0	0	0	2011	0
57	10	689	100	8664	4075	300	0	0	0	1383	1
58	6	230	626	5881	3345	474	0	0	0	1759	1
59	4	302	770	5475	1062	105	0	0	0	1928	1
60	6	150	100	3522	1954	210	0	0	0	989	1
61	6	352	40	5559	1538	210	0	0	600	1383	1
62	7	0	1430	4439	1461	1772	0	0	0	1300	1
63	7	185	480	4422	927	245	0	0	0	894	1
64	5	290	350	5356	2240	186	814	73	0	1862	1
65	6	133	30	5014	1045	106	0	0	0	1055	1
66	8	360	360	6572	2769	294	0	0	0	1294	1
67	7	292	60	6622	2810	620	0	0	0	1486	1
68	7	115	50	5783	1265	128	0	0	0	1049	1
69	10	205	340	6050	1773	220	0	0	0	859	1
70	4	103	40	3692	1422	154	0	0	0	1353	1
71	7	200	650	5662	1745	447	0	0	0	1243	1
72	6	0	430	3625	989	112	0	0	0	859	1
73	5	230	70	4057	1351	330	0	0	0	1208	1
74	8	286	80	5384	2284	158	0	0	3000	1399	1
75	8	522	100	6231	2137	188	0	0	0	1147	1
76	6	170	4100	3824	954	195	0	0	0	1540	1
77	3	0	150	2774	590	78	0	0	0	1197	1
78	4	65	50	3506	968	108	0	0	0	1174	1
79	9	270	1000	3921	1101	695	0	0	0	776	1
80	9	230	130	4589	1752	210	0	1139	0	894	1

HH number	HH member	Educa-tion t16*	Health t17*	Food t26*	Non-food t27*	Other exp t28*	Fixed assets t31*	Dura-bles t32*	Housing t34*	Annual Exp. per capita	Poor=1 Non-poor=0 Poverty line 1957
81	5	60	85	3642	995	108	0	0	0	978	1
82	5	125	20	4045	777	89	0	0	0	1011	1
83	4	0	50	2502	780	140	0	0	0	868	1
84	8	170	50	4560	1074	165	81	0	0	763	1
85	6	195	50	4705	950	88	0	0	0	998	1
86	4	215	100	3955	1058	334	0	0	130	1448	1
87	4	0	180	4606	1458	392	0	0	180	1704	1
88	7	260	900	7262	2467	462	0	0	205	1651	1
89	9	0	200	7108	2866	482	0	0	240	1211	1
90	5	0	100	5399	1754	432	0	0	145	1566	1
91	6	125	40	4553	1776	180	0	0	3024	1616	1
92	9	365	150	5486	2750	290	0	0	48	1010	1
93	7	120	130	5539	2460	300	0	0	40	1227	1
94	10	230	80	6319	2276	380	0	0	120	940	1
95	12	226	2100	8558	2864	180	325	732	200	1265	1
96	9	50	120	8069	3242	560	0	334	0	1375	1
97	6	0	590	6707	1892	200	0	0	3000	2065	0
98	18	690	590	14811	4466	450	0	122	4000	1396	1
99	5	75	6640	4327	714	40	0	0	0	2359	0
100	7	30	20	5670	823	50	0	0	0	942	1
101	12	640	180	10118	2434	160	0	0	0	1128	1
102	8	0	1050	5015	2588	90	33	0	0	1097	1
103	6	0	100	3217	1996	60	33	0	0	901	1
104	12	0	960	8158	2824	190	114	0	0	1021	1
105	2	0	30	2353	408	50	0	0	0	1420	1
106	15	40	80	9624	2435	260	0	277	0	848	1
107	6	0	30	4113	2110	120	33	0	0	1068	1
108	6	15	300	4211	2253	110	0	0	0	1148	1
109	12	40	50	10080	948	140	0	0	0	938	1
110	6	20	20	4347	815	60	0	0	0	877	1
111	6	0	820	5965	1011	120	0	0	0	1319	1
112	7	25	1000	5024	2342	290	16	0	2500	1600	1
113	14	0	300	9314	2541	270	325	0	0	911	1
114	11	0	210	7472	2682	180	49	0	0	963	1
115	10	0	40	6482	2546	180	41	0	0	929	1
116	11	40	50	7550	1553	200	0	114	0	864	1
117	6	0	1520	4279	1835	150	814	0	0	1433	1
118	9	0	50	17920	2575	3730	16	0	2600	2988	0
119	9	40	500	30616	1891	160	0	0	0	3690	0
120	12	20	1620	32146	2211	150	0	0	0	3012	0

HH number	HH member	Educa-tion t16*	Health t17*	Food t26*	Non-food t27*	Other exp t28*	Fixed assets t31*	Dura-bles t32*	Housing t34*	Annual Exp. per capita	Poor=1 Non-poor=0 Poverty line 1957
121	9	26	1050	6367	2058	160	57	0	0	1080	1
122	7	75	110	21117	2031	70	0	0	0	3343	0
123	6	70	210	4840	2142	60	0	0	0	1220	1
124	5	0	50	3630	1854	90	0	0	0	1125	1
125	11	50	60	10246	2520	220	0	0	0	1191	1
126	4	390	220	3331	1548	200	0	0	135	1456	1
127	7	190	80	4842	2504	395	0	60	144	1174	1
128	5	220	100	3582	1271	415	0	0	48	1127	1
129	6	320	400	6355	2645	260	0	0	120	1683	1
130	4	202	50	3171	1791	332	0	0	180	1431	1
131	5	660	900	10082	3024	785	1383	0	244	3416	0
132	5	283	100	8123	3702	1245	0	1465	240	3032	0
133	3	0	200	5023	1424	173	0	0	72	2297	0
134	5	0	100	3779	1922	205	0	0	1672	1536	1
135	2	0	120	2713	1209	80	0	0	60	2091	0
136	5	164	2324	6258	2495	179	0	0	144	2313	0
137	9	685	1705	11189	4336	610	0	0	6180	2745	0
138	5	60	350	6128	2509	300	0	0	216	1913	1
139	3	0	120	3044	1612	345	0	0	100	1740	1
140	5	145	60	3185	2745	166	0	0	84	1277	1
141	6	125	330	11950	6190	815	0	1302	216	3488	0
142	3	0	150	4966	2314	320	0	52	1500	3101	0
143	4	0	1440	4617	2022	340	0	0	192	2153	0
144	6	475	300	11091	4562	745	1139	244	216	3129	0
145	4	600	270	7068	3050	645	1302	0	216	3288	0
146	3	0	170	6772	4076	715	0	0	216	3983	0
147	6	462	1600	9238	2393	440	260	0	192	2431	0
148	7	140	430	11436	5692	955	0	0	216	2696	0
149	5	715	700	5105	2356	545	1790	130	192	2307	0
150	3	0	200	3985	1586	255	814	0	192	2344	0
151	4	0	3500	3847	4082	279	0	0	192	2975	0
152	7	575	4557	9233	5128	1087	98	0	404	3012	0
153	6	1075	2100	8006	4567	1249	0	98	192	2881	0
154	9	863	2889	11666	4204	710	0	0	192	2280	0
155	3	0	400	5282	1661	310	976	0	12	2881	0
156	6	334	703	8716	3353	454	0	0	192	2292	0
157	6	1935	1920	6874	4143	200	0	0	192	2544	0
158	4	295	350	8677	4411	600	0	0	192	3631	0
159	4	310	225	4511	1791	100	0	0	192	1782	1
160	5	0	2250	6795	2114	320	0	0	192	2334	0

HH number	HH member	Educa-tion t16*	Health t17*	Food t26*	Non-food t27*	Other exp t28*	Fixed assets t31*	Dura-bles t32*	Housing t34*	Annual Exp. per capita	Poor=1 Non-poor=0 Poverty line 1957
161	4	0	500	6311	5556	281	0	0	3192	3960	0
162	5	275	430	5171	2308	205	0	317	192	1780	1
163	4	290	318	4806	1997	350	195	0	192	2037	0
164	4	110	590	4999	1661	210	0	0	192	1941	1
165	6	187	250	6416	2403	230	1562	195	192	1906	1
166	5	0	730	6325	1946	160	0	0	175	1867	1
167	5	260	555	4723	1768	284	0	0	150	1548	1
168	6	715	270	7480	2468	193	0	1644	250	2170	0
169	2	0	105	3126	1043	198	0	0	150	2311	0
170	3	221	1028	3923	1120	338	0	0	200	2277	0
171	5	200	845	3697	938	180	0	0	320	1236	1
172	8	192	700	7850	2574	11300	0	0	500	2889	0
173	4	493	280	3929	1754	275	0	2929	0	2415	0
174	7	482	1250	6878	2178	319	0	0	360	1638	1
175	6	410	2300	6189	1921	355	0	1969	0	2191	0
176	6	312	40	4819	1454	230	0	1383	0	1373	1
177	6	142	30	4353	1245	160	0	0	0	988	1
178	3	0	45	4186	1202	157	0	0	0	1863	1
179	3	0	50	3832	1290	210	0	0	0	1794	1
180	4	350	50	4409	1184	145	0	1383	0	1880	1
181	5	200	150	4380	1352	85	0	0	0	1233	1
182	8	782	275	12711	5648	250	586	0	100	2544	0
183	12	450	1550	13472	5243	250	228	7	0	1767	1
184	8	778	180	9497	2512	145	0	0	0	1639	1
185	4	70	315	4240	954	105	0	0	0	1421	1
186	4	169	104	4437	1249	50	0	0	0	1502	1
187	8	485	250	13181	4325	150	0	0	300	2336	0
188	4	0	30	3992	275	60	0	0	0	1089	1
189	4	100	40	3527	830	90	0	0	0	1147	1
190	7	405	400	8801	2521	73	0	0	220	1774	1
191	7	505	170	7098	2083	400	0	0	3200	1922	1
192	5	1585	80	6031	1544	205	0	0	0	1889	1
193	7	413	325	8357	3648	498	0	0	0	1892	1
194	3	0	165	3709	1306	105	0	0	0	1762	1
195	6	848	302	7310	2893	710	0	0	0	2010	0
196	5	75	213	7414	1996	135	0	0	0	1967	0
197	3	0	105	4825	2292	300	0	0	0	2507	0
198	2	0	158	3188	1382	360	0	0	0	2544	0
199	5	3190	239	7754	2546	445	0	0	0	2835	0
200	5	730	140	6116	1947	355	0	0	0	1858	1

HH number	HH member	Educa-tion t16*	Health t17*	Food t26*	Non-food t27*	Other exp t28*	Fixed assets t31*	Dura-bles t32*	Housing t34*	Annual Exp. per capita	Poor=1 Non-poor=0 Poverty line 1957
201	5	1516	221	6464	1494	175	0	0	0	1974	0
202	6	365	197	10909	2129	685	0	0	20000	5714	0
203	6	506	155	7451	1853	265	0	0	0	1705	1
204	4	1470	295	6768	2287	105	0	0	0	2731	0
205	5	365	205	7694	2064	218	0	0	820	2273	0
206	6	1490	215	7494	1890	75	0	0	0	1861	1
207	4	485	366	7391	2906	305	0	0	0	2863	0
208	3	0	118	4741	1254	135	0	0	0	2083	0
209	4	570	345	7628	2283	150	0	0	0	2744	0
210	6	475	185	7506	1755	155	0	0	0	1679	1
211	3	0	113	4728	1294	105	0	0	0	2080	0
212	4	190	133	5955	1460	125	0	0	0	1966	0
213	3	0	96	4183	1114	115	0	0	0	1836	1
214	3	0	80	4852	1490	125	0	0	0	2182	0
215	4	0	345	7403	1738	125	0	0	0	2403	0
216	8	340	125	8797	1814	172	0	0	0	1406	1
217	6	110	155	6414	1883	250	0	0	0	1469	1
218	5	0	195	6364	1628	160	0	0	0	1669	1
219	8	175	250	7837	2083	250	0	0	0	1324	1
220	3	0	105	4104	1016	130	0	0	0	1785	1
221	3	0	216	3343	1238	160	0	0	4000	2986	0
222	5	576	148	6711	2305	273	0	0	0	2003	0
223	5	479	220	6375	2364	188	0	0	0	1925	1
224	4	0	164	5338	1428	372	0	0	0	1825	1
225	4	0	148	4740	1879	240	0	0	0	1752	1
226	6	0	570	6201	3693	495	0	488	72	1920	1
227	5	0	400	8151	3450	255	0	0	600	2571	0
228	3	0	220	4738	1483	70	0	0	36	2182	0
229	4	0	230	6075	1846	5640	0	0	120	3478	0
230	4	0	190	5293	2080	55	0	0	72	1922	1
231	9	478	402	11640	3967	375	0	0	0	1874	1
232	5	148	355	6331	2063	336	651	0	0	1977	0
233	4	256	125	6483	1262	42	0	0	0	2042	0
234	5	0	420	5219	1008	136	456	0	0	1448	1
235	6	316	280	7854	3186	312	651	0	0	2100	0
236	3	204	340	3649	883	246	0	0	0	1774	1
237	5	187	435	7779	2661	357	0	814	0	2447	0
238	3	137	220	4178	1724	132	0	0	0	2130	0
239	3	0	120	4516	1037	165	20	0	0	1953	1
240	4	74	160	4903	1607	138	0	0	0	1720	1

HH number	HH member	Educa-tion t16*	Health t17*	Food t26*	Non-food t27*	Other exp t28*	Fixed assets t31*	Dura-bles t32*	Housing t34*	Annual Exp. per capita	Poor=1 Non-poor=0 Poverty line 1957
241	5	281	145	5530	2586	212	0	0	0	1751	1
242	10	281	291	12014	3131	197	0	0	0	1591	1
243	3	92	260	3924	1476	112	0	0	0	1955	1
244	5	219	125	5816	1216	92	0	0	0	1494	1
245	7	261	302	8732	2421	72	0	0	0	1684	1
246	7	428	210	6872	2587	132	0	0	0	1461	1
247	7	475	325	7809	1951	382	0	0	0	1563	1
248	7	421	210	4608	1495	100	0	0	0	976	1
249	5	286	352	6932	2467	3077	0	0	0	2623	0
250	6	237	178	7214	2975	102	0	0	0	1784	1
251	9	421	1238	12020	4113	758	439	0	2500	2388	0
252	4	229	85	3755	1353	118	0	0	0	1385	1
253	5	239	95	5627	2107	92	0	0	0	1632	1
254	4	157	145	6112	2377	188	0	488	0	2367	0
255	4	229	260	5823	1293	62	0	0	0	1917	1
256	5	266	300	3673	2366	280	0	0	0	1377	1
257	4	98	100	2838	1256	235	0	0	0	1132	1
258	2	0	500	2380	1463	120	0	0	0	2232	0
259	5	276	200	2623	1317	232	0	0	0	929	1
260	4	0	250	3761	1154	240	0	0	0	1351	1
261	4	1454	1776	8411	7879	1650	570	1505	3540	6696	0
262	5	2244	2230	11288	5429	5994	0	0	1116	5660	0
263	6	4417	449	11582	4967	18942	0	0	840	6866	0
264	4	1804	722	7837	3444	910	0	0	720	3859	0
265	3	1047	100	7229	1807	905	0	0	264	3784	0
266	3	210	400	2593	975	331	0	0	3012	2507	0
267	4	386	30	3294	1183	395	0	0	20	1327	1
268	3	390	0	1757	1069	236	0	0	10	1154	1
269	4	0	485	3048	1359	308	0	65	10	1319	1
270	4	0	525	3903	655	245	0	0	10	1335	1
271	4	52	50	3866	1197	198	0	0	0	1341	1
272	6	233	230	5838	1019	111	0	0	0	1239	1
273	3	32	45	3016	760	120	325	0	2250	2183	0
274	3	130	1500	3342	1092	118	0	81	0	2088	0
275	5	381	120	4243	1696	118	0	260	0	1364	1
276	5	0	360	7147	2261	168	0	456	0	2078	0
277	5	205	385	9606	3144	425	0	2295	0	3212	0
278	4	88	1127	6444	1391	228	0	2604	0	2971	0
279	4	0	68	4354	930	128	0	0	0	1370	1
280	5	300	345	7247	1210	65	0	0	0	1833	1

HH number	HH member	Educa-tion t16*	Health t17*	Food t26*	Non-food t27*	Other exp t28*	Fixed assets t31*	Dura-bles t32*	Housing t34*	Annual Exp. per capita	Poor=1 Non-poor=0 Poverty line 1957
281	7	275	215	8798	2332	173	0	0	6400	2599	0
282	6	425	70	6475	1249	122	0	0	0	1390	1
283	2	0	229	3600	598	22	0	0	0	2225	0
284	4	178	212	6295	1910	128	0	0	0	2181	0
285	6	165	263	8085	1483	193	0	0	0	1698	1
286	5	117	381	4696	696	204	0	0	0	1219	1
287	7	90	118	4522	857	100	0	0	0	812	1
288	7	56	100	10628	3062	266	1383	24	0	2217	0
289	7	182	100	11837	2694	259	0	57	0	2161	0
290	5	0	392	5981	1414	130	0	0	0	1583	1
291	4	197	600	6022	1544	122	0	0	0	2121	0
292	10	0	266	2383	558	0	0	0	0	321	1
293	4	0	1300	5205	975	105	0	0	0	1896	1
294	4	369	395	7137	1707	153	0	1269	0	2758	0
295	10	168	100	16472	3432	400	0	1872	0	2244	0
296	6	509	850	9709	2914	242	0	7	0	2372	0
297	5	169	107	7893	2804	238	260	0	0	2294	0
298	8	0	250	14521	3270	237	0	0	0	2285	0
299	7	455	100	9695	2472	2214	651	1221	0	2401	0
300	2	440	50	3609	2416	820	0	0	0	3667	0
301	4	177	300	6069	1944	257	0	114	0	2215	0
302	4	339	182	9305	1894	254	0	1676	0	3413	0
303	5	0	42	5678	1018	394	0	0	0	1426	1
304	4	190	800	6484	1095	105	0	0	0	2169	0
305	4	28	18	4567	994	165	81	0	0	1463	1
Average 6		275	445	6408	2153	479	73	130	380	1884	0.63

* code in
VHLSS

Band 42   Roukayatou Zimmermann: Biotechnology and Value-added Traits in Food Crops: Relevance for Developing Countries and Economic Analyses. 2004.

Band 43   F. Markus Kaiser: Incentives in Community-based Health Insurance Schemes. 2004.

Band 44   Thomas Herzfeld: *Corruption begets Corruption*. Zur Dynamik und Persistenz der Korruption. 2004.

Band 45   Edilegnaw Wale Zegeye: The Economics of On-Farm Conservation of Crop Diversity in Ethiopia: Incentives, Attribute Preferences and Opportunity Costs of Maintaining Local Varieties of Crops. 2004.

Band 46   Adama Konseiga: Regional Integration Beyond the Traditional Trade Benefits: Labor Mobility contribution. The Case of Burkina Faso and Côte d'Ivoire. 2005.

Band 47   Beyene Tadesse Ferenji: The Impact of Policy Reform and Institutional Transformation on Agricultural Performance. An Economic Study of Ethiopian Agriculture. 2005.

Band 48   Sabine Daude: Agricultural Trade Liberalization in the WTO and Its Poverty Implications. A Study of Rural Households in Northern Vietnam. 2005.

Band 49   Kadir Osman Gyasi: Determinants of Success of Collective Action on Local Commons. An Empirical Analysis of Community-Based Irrigation Management in Northern Ghana. 2005.

Band 50   Borbala E. Balint: Determinants of Commercial Orientation and Sustainability of Agricultural Production of the Individual Farms in Romania. 2006.

Band 51   Pamela Marinda: Effects of Gender Inequality in Resource Ownership and Access on Household Welfare and Food Security in Kenya. A Case Study of West Pokot District. 2006.

Band 52   Charles Palmer: The Outcomes and their Determinants from Community-Company Contracting over Forest Use in Post-Decentralization Indonesia. 2006.

Band 53   Hardwick Tchale: Agricultural Policy and Soil Fertility Management in the Maize-based Smallholder Farming System in Malawi. 2006.

Band 54   John Kedi Mduma: Rural Off-Farm Employment and its Effects on Adoption of Labor Intensive Soil Conserving Measures in Tanzania. 2006.

Band 55   Mareike Meyn: The Impact of EU Free Trade Agreements on Economic Development and Regional Integration in Southern Africa. The Example of EU-SACU Trade Relations. 2006.

Band 56   Clemens Breisinger: Modelling Infrastructure Investments, Growth and Poverty Impact. A Two-Region Computable General Equilibrium Perspective on Vietnam. 2006.

www.peterlang.de

Beyene Tadesse Ferenji

The Impact of Policy Reform and Institutional Transformation on Agricultural Performance

An Economic Study of Ethiopian Agriculture

Frankfurt am Main, Berlin, Bern, Bruxelles, New York, Oxford, Wien, 2005.
XXIII, 216 pp., num. tab. and graf.
Development Economics and Policy.
Edited by Franz Heidhues and Joachim von Braun. Vol. 47
ISBN 3-631-53577-5 / US-ISBN 0-8204-7691-9 · pb. € 42.50*

Inspired by the World Bank and the International Monetary Fund, many less developed countries have carried out economic policy reforms and institutional changes. However, it has become increasingly clear that due to lags in institutional and infrastructure development results of policy reforms are unsatisfactory. This study focuses on assessing the impact of policy reform on agricultural production in Ethiopia. It investigates components of output growth, input use, technical efficiency and technological progress by applying a Stochastic Production Frontier model on a detailed rural household database. It also examines the degree of product price instability and its impacts on modern input use and food supply using a Vector Error Correction model on time series data. The study concludes by pointing out the prospects and constraints of agricultural transformation in Ethiopia.

Contents: Synopsis of Development Theories: The Significance of Agricultural Transformation and Its Roles in the Dynamics of Economic Growth · Review of Ethiopian Development Policies, the Position of Agriculture in the Economy and the Challenges · Analysis of Dynamics in Sources of Agricultural Output Growth at Farm Household Level · Constraints to Technical Efficiency Improvement in Maize Producing Farmers · Market Liberalization, Price Instability and Its Impacts on Modern Input Use and Food Production

Frankfurt am Main · Berlin · Bern · Bruxelles · New York · Oxford · Wien
Distribution: Verlag Peter Lang AG
Moosstr. 1, CH-2542 Pieterlen
Telefax 00 41 (0) 32 / 376 17 27

*The €-price includes German tax rate
Prices are subject to change without notice
Homepage http://www.peterlang.de